The World's
GREATEST
MYSTERIES

The World's GREATEST MYSTERIES

Nigel Blundell

OCTOPUS BOOKS

Acknowledgements

For a book such as this, covering as it does an extremely wide variety of true stories, the author must draw much of his information from earlier works. I wish to acknowledge in particular the following:

John Barnes: *Evita, A Biography* (W. H. Allen, 1978); Charles Berlitz: *The Bermuda Triangle* (Souvenir Press, 1974); Len Deighton and Arnold Schwartzman: *Airshipwreck* (Jonathan Cape, 1978); Editors of Reader's Digest Inc: *The World's Last Mysteries*: Rupert Furneaux: *The World's Most Intriguing Mysteries, The World's Strangest Mysteries* and *The Money Pit Mystery* (Odhams): A. G. Galanopoulos and Edward Bacon: *Atlantis, The Truth Behind The Legend* (Nelson, 1969): Justine Glass: *The Story of Fulfilled Prophecy* (Cassell, 1969); Peter Haining: *Ancient Mysteries* (Sidgwick and Jackson, 1977); W. A. Harbinson: *Evita, A Legend For The Seventies* (Star Books, 1978); Francis Hitching: *World Atlas Of Mystery* (Collins, 1978); Rodney Hoare: *The Testimony Of The Shroud* (Quartet Books, 1978); Fred Hoyle and Chandra Wickramasinghe: *Lifecloud, The Origin Of Life In the Universe* (Dent, 1978); Vince Kelly: *The Shark In The Arm Case* (Angus and Robertson, 1963); Lawrence Kusche: *The Bermuda Triangle Mystery Solved* (New English Library, 1975); Roy P. Mackal: *The Monsters Of Loch Ness* (Swallow Press, 1976); John Michell and J. M. Rickard: *Phenomena, A Book Of Wonders* (Thames and Hudson, 1977); Colin Simpson: *Lusitania* (Longman, 1972).

Acknowledgements
The publishers would like to thank the following organizations and individuals for their kind permission to reproduce the photographs in this book:

Mary Evans Picture Library 29, 125; Keystone Press Agency 6 above left, 10, 66, 97, 165, 168, 202; Mansell Collection 23, 26, 34, 41, 51, 54, 57, 63, 88, 102, 109; N.A.S.A. 99; National Army Museum 167; National Portrait Gallery, London 115; News of the World 77, 83; Popperfoto 6, 13, 35, 74, 91, 105, 108, 113, 119, 129, 135; 141, 142, 154, 157, 159, 161, 173, 189, 193, 205, 207, 209, 212, 213, 215, 217, (Donald McLeish Collection) 147; Radio Times, Hulton Picture Library 71.

**First published in hardback in 1980
by Octopus Books Limited
59 Grosvenor Street
London W1**

Paperback edition first published in 1984

© Octopus Books Limited

ISBN 0 7064 2143 4

Second impression, reprinted 1984, 1985, 1987

Printed in Great Britain
at the Bath Press

Contents

Introduction

The sum of man's knowledge increases daily. Yet, seemingly, for every mystery that is solved, a new one emerges. Science never ceases to push back the frontiers of knowledge, yet so many questions still remain unanswered.

It is with these questions, both old and new, that this book is concerned: the lost world of Atlantis, the legendary monster of Loch Ness and the fearsome mountain creature known as Bigfoot, the spontaneous combustion of human beings, UFOs . . .

These and many, many more enigmas have been gathered together in this volume to puzzle, challenge, intrigue and enthral the reader.

Chapter
One

Mysteries of Crime and Intrigue

As Agatha Christie discovered, criminal mysteries never fail to fascinate. Crime has led men and women to perform amazing feats of duplicity and to create puzzles that defy solution. Who, for example, spirited away Eva Peron's body for 16 years? Who was the killer they called Jack the Ripper? And did the outlaw known as Robin Hood really exist?

Evita and the body-snatchers

The embalmed body of Eva Peron was missing for 16 years

Eva Peron died in 1952. Yet her hair is still blonde and beautiful, her face doll-like and delicate. She represents the perfection of the embalmer's art as she lies 15 feet underground in an armoured family vault in a Buenos Aires cemetery.

Eva, the most vibrant life-force South America has ever known, is resting at last. She was finally buried in her homeland after her frail body, was returned from 16 years of secret, mysterious exile, 16 years during which the paint was never allowed to fade from the slogans that plastered the walls of Buenos Aires, the capital that adored her: 'Give back the body of Evita.'

Evita – 'little Eva' – was the pet name given to their heroine by the *descamisados*, the 'shirtless ones', the poor of Argentina. Their adulation made Eva Peron, for a while, the most powerful woman in the world.

Eva was born, the illegitimate child of a poor provincial woman, in 1919 – though she always claimed, with beguiling femininity, that the year of her birth was 1922. By the time she was 15 she had moved to Buenos Aires with her first lover and was trying to get jobs as an actress.

She was 24 when she met Colonel Juan Peron, who was twice her age. She was then a radio starlet earning $10 a week as a disc jockey and as heroine of the station's soap operas. Peron and the other leaders of Argentina's right-wing military junta arrived at the radio station to appeal for funds for the victims of an earthquake. The colonel – a young 48, straight-backed and athletic – was captivated by Eva's deep, seductive voice.

From that moment on, it was Eva who appealed for money on behalf of Peron's social services ministry. In doing so, she became his spokeswoman.

'He doesn't care a button for the glittering uniforms and the frock coats,' she purred. 'His only friends are you, the *descamisados*.'

When the too-powerful Peron was ousted by the rest of the junta in 1945, it was Eva who single-handedly organized the support of the young officers and the workers to reinstate him. Two months later, she married him. And the following year, with Eva at his side, Peron was swept into the presidential palace on the shoulders of the *descamisados* and with the backing of the powerful unions.

As the wife of the president, Eva was a woman of dramatic contrasts. She dripped with diamonds and wrapped herself in mink yet launched a social aid fund and organized the delivery of second-hand clothes to farms and shanty towns. With jewelled hands she threw the crowds toys for their children. The people were mesmerized. They worshipped her.

Then Eva fell ill with incurable cancer. She grew thin and shrunken. At the few political functions she attended she had to be physically supported by her husband. She complained: 'I am too little for so much pain.'

On 26 July 1952, at 8.25 pm, Eva died. She was 33. She had scarcely breathed her last when her body was rushed away to be embalmed by an eminent Spanish pathologist, Dr Pedro Ara, who had been standing by for weeks. He operated on her emaciated body, replacing her blood with alcohol, then glycerine, which kept the organs intact and made the skin almost translucent. The entire process of embalming took almost a year, and Dr Ara was paid $100,000 for his work.

All this time, the nation had been in mourning for Santa Evita – as she was now known – and when her body lay in state two million people filed past the coffin. Seven were killed in the crush.

Plans were made to build memorials to Eva throughout Argentina, but most of them got no further than the drawing board – for in July 1955 roaring inflation led to Peron's overthrow. The former president went into exile in Spain, from where he demanded that his successor, General Eduardo Lonardi, send him his wife's body. Lonardi refused, and instead he set about discrediting the Perons. He opened the former president's homes to the public and put on display Peron's 15 custom-built sports cars, 250 motor-scooters and safes containing $10,000,000 in 'ready cash'. Also revealed were his secret Buenos Aires love-nests – apartments lined with furs and mirrors where Peron had satisfied his appetite for teenaged girls, including his regular mistress, 16-year-old Nelly Rivas.

The new military rulers also displayed Eva's fabulous jewels. But this had no effect on her glittering reputation, for she had never hidden her personal wealth from the people. In fact, during the months following Peron's overthrow the Eva death cult grew. General Lonardi tried to summon up the courage to destroy the unflawed body, which still lay in Room 63 of the Confederation of Labour building in Buenos Aires. But before he could act, he himself was ousted from power, in November 1955, by General Pedro Aramburu. The new leader realized the danger of leaving Eva's body readily accessible in the capital – a rallying point for any future Peronist revival – and ordered it to be removed, secretly.

In December, Eva's corpse vanished. It was to remain missing for 16 years.

On the night that the body was stolen, Dr Ara was visiting Room 63 to make one of his regular inspections of the corpse. He heard the sound of heavy boots clumping up the main stairway. The door burst open and Colonel Carlos Mori-Koenig, head of the army's intelligence service, strode into the room, a platoon of soldiers at his heels.

'I have come for the body,' he said. And, ignoring Dr Ara's protests, he ordered his men to lift Eva from her flag-draped bier, place her in a plain wooden coffin and carry her out to a waiting army truck. The only explanation Dr Ara was given was that the body was to get 'a decent burial'. The truck started up and vanished into the night.

News of the body-snatching soon leaked out and the outlawed Peronists ran riot. Pictures of Eva and slogans demanding the return of the body appeared across the country. But General Aramburu remained silent. Rumours were spread that Juan Peron had arranged for the body to be stolen. But however much the military leaders of Argentina tried to repress the Peronists, their outcry over the missing Santa Evita grew even stronger.

To the *descamisados*, the theft was the crime of the century – a crime that could never be forgiven. It remained a source of grievance throughout the next 16 years, during which the body's whereabouts remained a mystery to the people of Argentina, and to Peron.

Much of the story is still a mystery today. What is known is that, after the army truck drove off from the Confederation of Labour building that night in December 1955, General Aramburu, concerned about public reaction, abandoned his plans to have the corpse destroyed.

Colonel Mori-Koenig ordered the truck to be driven to a quiet corner of a military barracks, where it remained throughout the rest of the night while he awaited further instructions. The colonel would have been happy to dispose of the body in any way his leaders demanded, for he had good reason to hate the Perons – as president, Peron had once demoted him after an argument. However, the order to destroy the body was never given. The colonel was simply told to hide it.

Eva's body was sealed in a packing case and moved to a warehouse close to military intelligence headquarters. It remained there for a month until, in January 1956, the crate was shuttled between half a dozen warehouses and

The remains of Evá Peron drawn through the streets on a gun carriage.

offices around Buenos Aires. It ended up at the smart apartment of Mori-Koenig's deputy, Major Antonio Arandia.

At this time, Peronist agents were still scouring the capital for Eva. Afraid that the trail might lead to him, Arandia took to sleeping with his revolver under his pillow.

One morning, just before dawn, Arandia awoke in a sweat. He listened terrified as footsteps approached his bedroom door. When it opened, he whipped his revolver from beneath the pillow and fired twice at the shadow framed in the doorway. His pregnant wife, who had just visited the bathroom, fell dead on the carpet.

Eva's body was then moved to the fourth floor of Mori-Koenig's intelligence headquarters. Her packing case was stamped 'radio sets' and stacked along with several others – all identical.

A few months later, the colonel was replaced as intelligence chief by the president's own head of secret service, Colonel Hector Cabanillas, who was horrified to discover the body still hidden in the HQ. He ordered it to be removed.

No one knows who personally organized the next moves in the macabre itinerary. But several identical coffins were made and weighted with ballast. The coffins, plus the packing case containing Eva, were transported to various parts of South America and further afield.

The coffins were all immediately buried, but Eva's packing case was shipped to Brussels, then taken by train to Bonn. There, unknown to the Argentinian Ambassador, it was stored in a cellar with his old files.

During September or October of 1956 the body was placed in a coffin and moved again, first to Rome and then to Milan. For the last stage of the journey it was accompanied by a lay sister of the Society of St Paul. She had been told that the body was that of an Italian widow, Maria Maggi de Magistris, who had died in Rosario, Argentina.

It was under this name that Eva was buried in Lot 86 of the Mussocco Cemetery, Milan. There she remained, her whereabouts known to only a handful of people, for 15 years.

During those years, a succession of military juntas in Argentina stumbled from one economic crisis to another. Eventually, the head of one junta, Lieutenant-General Alexjandro Lanusse, decided to invite the aging Juan Peron back to his homeland, despite the fact that Peron had personally ordered him sentenced to life imprisonment 20 years earlier. But first Lanusse arranged to return to Peron the body of his wife.

On 2 September 1971, a man who claimed to be Carlos Maggi watched as the coffin of his 'sister' was exhumed from its Milan grave and loaded on to a hearse for a 500-mile journey to Madrid. Carlos was in fact Hector Cabanillas, the now-retired intelligence chief.

The hearse spent one night in a garage at Perpignan, France, and arrived at Peron's home in Madrid the following day. Waiting there were Peron, now 74, his new 39-year-old wife, Isabel, whom he had met in a Panamanian night-club, and Dr Ara. The coffin of Eva was set down in the lounge and the lid prised open by Cabanillas.

Peron burst into tears as he saw the face of his long-dead wife, her blonde hair in disarray but otherwise seemingly as tranquil and beautiful as he remembered her two decades earlier. 'She is not dead,' he said. 'She is only sleeping.'

In 1972, Peron's long exile came to an end. He was allowed back home to Argentina. But he chose to leave the body of Eva behind in Madrid. The following year he was again elected president, with Isabel as vice-president. But his rule was short. On 1 July 1974, he died.

Isabel became president and ordered Eva's body to be flown home from Spain. Thousands of weeping Argentinians lined the route from the airport to throw flowers at the hearse containing their beloved Santa Evita. Her body was again laid in state, this time beside the coffin of Juan Peron, at the presidential palace at Olivos. Isabel mourned for both of them, trying to turn the reflected glory of Eva on to herself.

Isabel clung to power for two years before being ousted by yet another military junta. And the new leaders tried to erase the name of Peron from the history books.

Though Peron had been buried soon after his lying in state, Eva's body had been placed in storage again. The nation's leaders had been unable to agree on a final resting place for her. It was not until October 1976 that the new junta decided on a permanent burial place: Eva's still-beautiful body was placed in a tomb 15 feet underground in a private section of Recoleta Cemetery, Buenos Aires.

The tomb was built stronger than a bank vault – to discourage anyone from ever again trying to remove the body of Eva Peron.

Riddle of the arm that a shark spat out

The Shark Arm Case, one of the most bizarre mysteries in criminal history, has been described as too fantastic for fiction. The story hit the headlines in Australia on 25 April 1935 – Anzac Day. But it really began a few days earlier off the beach of a Sydney suburb.

Bert Hobson went out in his small boat to examine lines that he had baited with mackerel about a mile off Coogee Beach. On one of the lines was a small shark which was in the process of being eaten by a larger tiger shark. By the time Hobson had hauled in the line, he found that attached to the hook was the larger shark, a 14-ft giant.

The fisherman towed it to shore and presented it live to his brother, Charles, who ran an aquarium at Coogee. The tiger shark swam around the aquarium for a few days, providing a popular spectacle for the paying customers. Then, on 25 April, it went into convulsions.

The shark surged around in the water, disgorging the contents of its stomach: rats, birds, parts of the smaller shark – and a human arm.

The sight sickened the several patrons who were watching at the time. But Charles Hobson acted swiftly. He fished out the arm and telephoned the police. They found the grisly specimen to be the left arm of a man, with a tattoo on the forearm of two boxers. There was also a piece of rope attached to the wrist.

The police put the case down as a shark attack on a lone swimmer or yachtsman, until, over the days, their suspicions became aroused. No one had been reported missing off a Sydney beach. And a police surgeon who examined the arm claimed that it had not been bitten off by a shark, but cleanly amputated with a sharp knife.

Fingerprints were taken of the hand and, although they were blurred, experts were able to match the prints of the thumb and ring finger with those of a man in police files. They belonged to James Smith, who ran a billiard room grandly titled the Rozelle Sports Club, and who had once been arrested for illegal bookmaking.

Smith had been missing from his home for 18 days. His brother, Edward, positively identified the arm but was unable to give any hint as to Smith's movements. And all that the victim's wife, Gladys, knew was that her husband had left home saying that he was taking a party on a paid fishing trip.

The police next sought out John Brady, a friend of the dead man. It was no easy task tracking him down, for Brady was wanted by Tasmanian police on a forgery charge. But he was eventually run to ground on 16 May, living with his wife in a small flat in north Sydney. Under interrogation, Brady admitted having stayed with Smith in a cottage at Cronulla, on the same stretch of coastline as the shark had been caught. But he denied knowing anything about his friend's death.

The investigation went on for seven months. Divers and specially chartered aircraft searched the waters of Gunnamatta Bay, near Cronulla, hoping to find further clues, but to no avail.

Police suspected that Smith and Brady had been plotting an insurance fraud over a yacht that had seemingly disappeared. They interviewed the yacht's former owner, whom they regarded as a key witness. But the day before an inquest was due to be held into Smith's death, the witness was found shot dead in his car beneath the approaches to Sydney's famous Harbour Bridge.

The following day, detectives received another blow. The coroner who was to have held the inquest ruled that he could not do so without a complete body. Nevertheless, Brady was charged with murder and sent for trial.

The trial lasted only two days. The judge refused to admit as evidence signed statements that had been taken from the witness before he was found shot dead. Without this evidence, the jury was directed to acquit Brady. Two men were later charged with murdering the witness, but they too were acquitted.

Brady continued his career of crime. In all, he spent more than 20 years of his life in jail. He died of a heart attack at the age of 71 in a prison repatriation hostel. And with him died any hope of solving the Shark Arm Case mystery.

Police, however, have always held their own theory about the death of James Smith. And it is indeed stranger than fiction. They believe that Smith went to stay with Brady at Cronulla to plan their latest fraud, but that the two men fell out over the sharing of the loot.

Brady, it is believed, killed his accomplice and hacked up the body. He placed the remains in a metal trunk – but could not fit in the arm. So he roped it to the outside of the trunk and dumped the terrible evidence into the sea. A small shark, attracted by the blood, attacked the trunk, severing the rope with its razor-sharp teeth. As the arm floated free, the shark swallowed it whole.

The shark's next meal was a mackerel from the line of fisherman Hobson. And that was when the shark became a meal itself – for the 14-ft giant attraction of Coogee Aquarium.

Murder on Aconcagua

John Cooper and Jeanette Johnson tried to do the impossible – climb South America's highest mountain during the worst month of the year. But they never made it to the top of Mount Aconcagua, Argentina. Their adventure was cut short by murder, a brutal and vicious crime that has baffled authorities for almost ten years.

The macabre mystery began in the summer of 1972. It was then that eight climbers first got together to discuss scaling the 22,840-foot mountain. There was lawyer Carnie DeFoe, the group leader; John Shelton, a doctor; James Petroske, a psychologist; William Eubank, a geologist; William Zeller, a policeman; Arnold McMillen, a farmer; Jeanette Johnson, a teacher, and John Cooper, an engineer. They chose January 1973 as their starting date.

When the group arrived in the tiny town of Mendoza in the Andes, local experts and other mountaineers warned that January was a bad time of year to consider climbing Aconcagua. The expedition brushed their fears aside. But they agreed to hire local climber Miguel Angel Alfonso as a guide. Miguel told them to wait for better weather, but they were determined to begin as soon as possible, and on a freezing morning the party set out.

At first the climbing was easy but as the going became harder several of the group found they were not equal to the challenge. The first to drop out of the running were DeFoe and Shelton. They found that the combination of icy conditions coupled with a driving wind was too much. They urged the others to give up but to no avail.

Soon Eubank succumbed to the strain and dropped out. Alfonso takes up the story . . .

'From 5,700 metres there were only six of us left. By 6,300 metres Petroske was showing signs of mountain sickness. He was looking very weak and seemed to have lost control of his limbs. Whatever we did he did not seem to improve, and after a discussion, we agreed that he should be taken back to our base camp, several hundred metres below. They asked me to accompany him and in the end I agreed.'

Preparations were made and the guide left for the base camp – leaving behind Zeller, McMillen, Cooper and Johnson.

'That was the last time I saw Jeanette and Cooper alive,' Alfonso said. 'I went back to the camp with Petroske. The others told me they were going to carry on.

'Three days later I was in base camp, with a terrible storm blowing. I looked out of my cabin window and saw figures in the distance.

'I left the cabin intending to help the others. But the weather forced me back. The next day I went out again and managed to reach them. I was staggered to find only Zeller and McMillen. I had assumed the party had turned back and Johnson and Cooper should have been with them.

'Both men were in an awful state. Zeller had become blind because of frostbite, and McMillen was bleeding heavily around his face, also because of frostbite.

'Both were totally disoriented and incoherent. They were muttering and shouting: 'Cooper is sitting where the paved road gets near the trees.' 'Jeanette has been taken away by those women who came on mules'.

'I took them back to the camp, where Petroske questioned them in his tent. I don't know what was said. None of them would tell me.'

Later that year an Argentine expedition recovered the grisly remains of John Cooper. His face was pitted and scarred from the ravages of frostbite. His body was taken back to Mendoza and there doctors found a curious wound, probably caused by an ice pick, in his stomach. But they also found multiple fractures of the skull and it was those fractures that caused his death. An inquest called it murder.

Two years later another party of climbers came across Jeanette's corpse perfectly preserved by the ice. She had been brutally battered. Once again, the police decided it was murder.

No one has since been able to find the reason for the deaths. It seems the secret of the cruel killings will be kept by the massive mountain forever.

Who was Jack the Ripper? The elusive outlaw

A question that still baffles criminologists

In the late 19th century Britain was the greatest, most prosperous nation in the world, and London the greatest city. But one part of the capital lay like a festering sore on the face of the British Empire. The jumble of ill-lit, foul-smelling little streets known as the East End offered its inhabitants only degradation and poverty.

More than half the children born there died before the age of five. Women were old by the time they were 40. Men turned to drink, and often crime, as their only escape. Many women would sell their worn, raddled bodies for a few pennies. And it was these 'fallen' women – the 'unfortunates', as they were euphemistically known to more genteel society – who became the prey of the world's most infamous murderer. Even today, nearly a century later, the very name Jack the Ripper induces a feeling of horror in London's East End.

The Ripper's reign of terror was short. He first struck on a warm night in August 1888. And on a chill, foggy evening three months later he claimed his last victim. It is known for certain that he slaughtered at least five women, and some criminologists have credited him with 11 murders.

Why does this man who killed only a handful of people during such a short span of time continue to exert such a frightful fascination? Why is he still held in awe around the world long after he has joined his pathetic victims in death?

Is it because of the unknown? Because he came from the darkness and struck in the most brutal, bloody and bestial way? Because he stalked the grim, dark alleys and yards at the dead of night? Because he eluded one of the most efficient and sophisticated police forces of the day? Because he left a frightened city whispering his gruesome name and then disappeared forever, back into the darkness?

All that is known for certain about Jack the Ripper is that he was left-handed – this was deduced by the police surgeons who examined the grisly remains of his victims – and that he had at least some medical knowledge. He was probably a tall, slim, pale man with a black moustache. This was the description given by witnesses who saw someone scurrying away from the vicinity of several of the crimes. Each time, the man wore a cap and a long coat, and he walked with the vigorous stride of a youth.

THE WORLD'S GREATEST MYSTERIES

Writers, scientists, psychologists, detectives of every nation have sought to discover the identity of this most ghastly of killers. But none has done so. And it is unlikely that anyone ever will. Even when the secret Scotland Yard files on the case are finally made public in 1992, they are expected to cast little new light on the riddle.

The story of London's most mysterious and ferocious mass-murderer began shortly after 5 am on the morning of 7 August 1888. A man, desperately hoping for a job of which he had heard, hurried down the stairs of the Whitechapel hovel in which he had a room. He was determined to be first in the queue but was halted in his progress by a bundle lying on the first-floor landing. He went to push the bundle out of his way, and then recoiled with horror when he realized that what lay at his feet were the bloody remains of a woman.

He forgot about the job and rushed off to alert the police. The woman was identified as Martha Turner, a 'lady of easy virtue'. Her throat had been slit, she had been stabbed several times and bestial mutilations had been carried out on her body.

There is some doubt whether this woman was, in fact, a Ripper victim. And, as the murder of prostitutes was no rare thing in those days, the case was soon shelved. But when a second, similar murder happened 24 days later, fear and panic began to sweep the mean streets of the East End.

On the night of 30 August, Mary Ann Nicholls, known as Pretty Polly in the sleazy pubs of Whitechapel, was desperate for the money for a doss-house bed. So, when a client approached her, she leapt at the chance of making a few coppers, which would perhaps leave her with something over for a couple of tots of gin.

The man drew her into the shadows. If she finally realized there was anything wrong, it was too late. Her end was swift. The Ripper put a hand over her mouth and dextrously slit her throat. Then the killer set about his savage butchery.

Some time later, a police constable passing the tiny, unlit courtyard thought he heard a scuffling sound. He paused uncertainly, his eyes trying to pierce the gloom. As he moved forward, his foot slipped on something wet. It was blood, and the gory trail led him to the mutilated body of Mary Nicholls.

Had the constable disturbed the Ripper? If so, it was the nearest the police ever came to him at work.

A white-faced detective, sickened after examining the body, told a newspaper reporter: 'Only a madman could have done this.' And pathologist Dr Ralph Llewellyn told the coroner: 'I have never seen so horrible a case. She was ripped about in a manner that only a person skilled in the use of a knife could have achieved.'

The Ripper waited just a week before he struck again. His prey was 'Dark Annie' Chapman, who was dying of tuberculosis when she was hacked down. When she was found in Hanbury Street by a porter from nearby Spitalfields Market, her pitifully few possessions had been neatly laid out below her disembowelled corpse.

Rumours swept Whitechapel. One was that the Ripper carried his instruments of death in a little black bag – and so any innocent passer-by seen carrying such a bag was immediately chased by the crowd. Another rumour was that the Ripper was a foreign seaman. So any stranger with a foreign accent in Whitechapel had to be careful of what he said. Some had it that the killer was a Jewish butcher – and latent anti-Semitism, already simmering because of the influx of Jewish immigrants fleeing the Russian and Polish massacres, began bubbling to the surface.

An even wilder theory, popular in the most squalid areas, where there was no love lost between the inhabitants and the police, was that the killer was a policeman. How else, it was asked, would he be able to safely prowl the streets at night without creating suspicion?

The growing fear developed into irrational anger. And the spark needed to set the flames of panic coursing through Whitechapel came on the morning of Sunday, 30 September. As church bells chimed at eight o'clock, a constable on his way home spotted a white-stockinged leg projecting from a factory gateway. He had found the body of Elizabeth 'Long Liz' Stride.

It seems that the killer had been disturbed in his work – for the body of Long Liz was not mutilated – and that, to satisfy his frustrated bloodlust, the Ripper had struck again that same night. It was during this killing that he left what may be the only positive clue in his reign of terror. Just 15 minutes' walk from where the body of Long Liz was discovered lay the bloody remains of Catherine Eddowes. From her body, the most terribly mutilated so far, a trail of blood led to a message scrawled in chalk on a wall: 'The Jews are not men to be blamed for nothing.'

Did this mean that the Ripper was a Jew who, driven beyond endurance by persecution, had struck back at the only victims he could find? The message, a vital piece of evidence, was never studied properly. Sir Charles Warren, head of the Metropolitan Police, perhaps fearing a violent backlash of hatred against the Jews, ordered the chalked message to be rubbed out and kept a secret.

Two days earlier, a letter had been sent to the Central News Agency in Fleet Street. It read:

Dear Boss, I keep on hearing that the police have caught me. But they won't fix me yet ... I am down on certain types of women and I won't stop ripping them until I do get buckled.

Grand job, that last job was. I gave the lady no time to squeal. I love my work and want to start again. You will soon hear from me, with my funny little game. I saved some of the proper red stuff in a ginger beer bottle after my last job to write with, but it went thick like glue and I can't use it. Red ink is fit enough, I hope. Ha, Ha!

Next time I shall clip the ears off and send them to the police just for jolly.

The letter was signed Jack the Ripper, the first time the name had been used. And the killer of Catherine Eddowes had indeed attempted to cut off her ears . . .

The rumours continued to spread. The killer was a mad doctor. He was a homicidal Russian sent by the Czar's secret police to discredit the London police, because they were not taking enough action against emigré anarchists. He was a puritan, obsessed with cleansing the East End of vice. He was a crazed midwife with a murderous hatred of prostitutes.

But still nobody was any nearer to naming the Ripper. And, on 9 November, he struck again. Mary Kelly was unlike any of the other victims. She was younger – only 25, whereas the others had been in their 40s – blonde and attractive. The last person to see her alive was George Hutchinson, whom she had asked for money to pay her rent. When he said he could not help, she approached a slim, well-dressed man with a trim moustache and a deer-stalker hat. . . .

Early next morning, a man named Henry Bowers knocked impatiently at Mary's door for her unpaid rent. Finally he went to the window of her room and pushed aside the sacking curtains. The sickening sight within made him forget all about the rent and sent him running for the landlord. Later, he was to say: 'I shall be haunted by this for the rest of my life.'

With Mary Kelly's death, the Ripper's reign ended as suddenly and mysteriously as it began.

Today we are no nearer than ever to discovering his identity. If the style and spelling of his messages were genuine and he was a poor, badly educated man, where did he obtain his medical expertise? If he was wealthy, how did he know the back streets and slums of Whitechapel so well that he could melt into the shadows as expertly as a native?

Two convicted murderers claimed to be the Ripper. One, who poisoned his mistress, said when arrested: 'You've got Jack the Ripper at last.' But there is little evidence to suggest that he was telling the truth. The second cried out, as the trap door of the gallows opened: 'I am Jack the . . .' But it was later proved that he was in America when the Ripper crimes were committed.

Some members of the police force were sure they knew the identity of the Ripper. In 1908, the assistant commissioner of police said flatly: 'In stating that he was a Polish Jew, I am merely stating a definitely established fact.'

But Inspector Robert Sager, who played a leading part in the Ripper investigations and who died in 1924, said in his memoirs: 'We had good reason to suspect a man who lived in Butcher's Row, Aldgate. We watched him carefully. There was no doubt that this man was insane, and, after a time, his friends thought it advisable to have him removed to a private asylum. After he was removed, there were no more Ripper atrocities.'

Even Queen Victoria's eldest grandson has been named as a suspect. He was Prince Albert Victor, Duke of Clarence, who, if he had lived, would have become King when his father, Edward VII, died.

A contemporary print of 'vigilantes' watching for Jack the Ripper suspects.

Perhaps the two most intriguing solutions are the two most recent. Author and broadcaster Daniel Farson points his finger at Montagu John Druitt, a failed barrister who had medical connections and a history of mental instability in his family. Farson bases his accusation on the notes of Sir Melville Macnaghten, who joined Scotland Yard in 1889 and became head of the Criminal Investigation Department in 1903. Macnaghten names three main Ripper suspects – a Polish tradesman who probably hated women, a homicidal Russian doctor, and Druitt. Finally, police decided that Druitt was the murderer. A few weeks after Mary Kelly's death, his body was found floating in the River Thames.

Writer Stephen Knight proposes the fascinating theory that three men were responsible for the Ripper murders. He says that a royal physician, a coachman and an artist committed the crimes. Their motive was to silence a gang of prostitutes who had concocted a plan to blackmail the royal family about the secret marriage of the Duke of Clarence. The resulting scandal, it was feared, might lead to possible revolution. So a tortuous plot to murder the prostitutes was worked out by members of the royal family, Prime Minister Lord Salisbury, police chiefs and freemasons.

The East End of London is changing now. High-rise blocks replace the mean little houses. The streets are well lit, the public houses respectable. The people are relatively prosperous. But however much the East End changes, the ghost of Jack the Ripper will haunt its streets until the end of time.

Did Robin Hood really exist?

Deep in the heart of Sherwood Forest in the early 14th century roamed an outlaw whose escapades have established him as the most enduring folk hero of his time. His name is known today throughout the world – Robin Hood. Stories of his heroic deeds are legion. But are they true? And did Robin even exist?

Some historians believe that the stories of the sprite-like hero may be connected with a mythological pagan woodland spirit. Robin was a name often given to fairies, and green, which the outlaw was supposed to have worn, is the traditional colour of wood spirits. There is also a theory that

Robin Hood was simply one of the characters in the ancient May Day ceremonies who over the years became changed in legend into a historical character. Maid Marion may also have been Queen of the May in the same
celebrations.

However, records do show that in the 13th and 14th centuries a man
named Robin Hood lived in Wakefield, Yorkshire, and may have been the
outlaw of romantic legend. Robin (christened Robert) Hood was born in
about 1290. His father, Adam Hood, was a forester in the service of John,
Earl Warenne, lord of the manor of Wakefield. The surname in old court
documents is variously spelt Hod, Hode and Hood.

On 25 January 1316, Robin Hood's 'handmaid' is recorded as having been
brought before a court for taking dry wood and vert from the 'old oak'.
(Vert is the old English term for trees which provide shelter and food for
deer.) She was fined twopence. Other court records for the year 1316 show
that Robin Hood and his wife Matilda paid two shillings 'for leave to take
one piece of land of the lord's waste' to build a five-roomed house.

In 1322, Robin's landlord – at this time, Thomas, Earl of Lancaster –
called his tenants to arms in rebellion against King Edward II. A tenant had
no choice but to obey his lord implicitly, and Robin Hood followed the earl
into battle as an archer. The revolt was crushed. Lancaster was captured,
tried for treason, and beheaded. His estates were forfeited to the king and
his followers were outlawed.

Robin Hood fled into Barnsdale Forest, which at that time covered about
30 square miles of Yorkshire and was linked to Nottinghamshire's Sherwood
Forest, which covered 25 square miles. The forests were traversed by the
Roman-built Great North Road, which yielded rich pickings for robbers.
Here the legend of Robin Hood was born.

One of Robin's supposed escapades along the Great North Road concerned
the haughty Bishop of Hereford, who was travelling to York when he came
across the outlaw leader and some of his companions roasting venison. Taking
them for peasants, and infuriated by their flagrant breach of forest laws, the
bishop demanded an explanation. The outlaws calmly told him that they
were about to dine. The bishop ordered his attendants to seize them.

The outlaws prayed for mercy but the bishop swore that he would show
them none. So Robin blew on his horn, and the unhappy bishop found himself surrounded by archers in Lincoln green. They took him prisoner, with
all his company, and demanded a ransom. While the bishop was held captive,
he was made to dance a jig around a large oak tree. The tree is no longer
there, but the ground on which it stood is known as Bishop's Tree Root.

Several other oak trees in Barnsdale and Sherwood are associated with
Robin Hood and his band. Centre Tree, halfway between Thoresby and

Welbeck, is said to be the marker from which Robin Hood's network of secret routes stretched through the forest. But the most famous tree is Major Oak, at Birkland. It is reputedly 1,000 years old – predating the Norman Conquest of Britain – and has a girth of about 29 ft. Alfred, Lord Tennyson visited this oak in the last century and, in his poem 'The Foresters', has Little John referring to it as '. . . that oak where twelve men can stand inside nor touch each other'.

Among the stories passed down the centuries about Robin Hood's prowess is that of a visit he made with his closest friend, Little John, to Whitby Abbey. The abbot asked them to demonstrate their skill with the bow by shooting from the monastery roof. Both did so, and the arrows fell on either side of a lane at Whitby Lathes – more than a mile away. The abbot had two stone pillars erected on the spots where the arrows fell. The pillars survived until the end of the 18th century. The fields on either side were also named after the event: Robin Hood's Close and Little John's Close.

Little John, who was Robin's second-in-command, got his nickname because of his height. He was said to have died at Hathersage, in Derbyshire, and in 1784 his grave there was reopened. In it were found the bones of an exceptionally tall man.

Robin and his men have certainly been credited with far-flung activities. Robin Hood's Bay, many miles away on the Yorkshire coast, was named after the outlaw because it was here that he and his band were reputed to own several boats, for fishing and possible escape from the authorities.

On one of his journeys, Robin Hood visited St Mary's Church, Nottingham, where a monk in the congregation recognized him and alerted the sheriff. Robin drew his sword and slew 12 soldiers before being captured. But before he could be brought to trial, Little John led a band of the outlaws into Nottingham and rescued him. They also sought out the monk and murdered him.

But it was Robin Hood's championing of the underdog that made him a folk hero. His robbing of the rich to give to the poor, and his flouting of unpopular authority, became an inspiration to the oppressed peasantry.

One of the most famous stories to emanate from the oaks of Sherwood Forest is the tale of the meeting between Robin Hood and King Edward II. The story goes that the king, hearing that the royal deer in Sherwood were diminishing because of the appetites of Robin Hood and his band, determined to rid the forest of the outlaws. So he and his knights disguised themselves as monks and rode into the forest.

They were met by Robin Hood and some of his band, who demanded money. The king gave them £40, saying that was all he had. Robin took £20 for his men and gave the rest back to the king. Edward then produced the royal seal and told the outlaw leader that the king wished to see him in Nottingham. Robin summoned all his men to kneel before the seal and swear their love for the king. They then invited the 'monks' to eat with them – and fed them on the king's venison. Later Edward revealed his identity and pardoned all the outlaws – on condition that they would come to his court and serve him.

The story is told in *A Lytell Geste of Robyn Hood*, published in 1459. It may not be all fiction – the king was certainly in Nottingham in November 1323 and the story of his action fits what is known of his character. And a few months later, in 1324, the name of Robin Hood appears in the household accounts of Edward II. There is a record of wages paid to him until November of the same year. After that date, he vanishes into folklore again. Perhaps after enjoying the free life of an outlaw, he was unable to settle in service, even for his king.

Robin Hood's adventures in the forests continued until about 1346, when he is reputed to have died at Kirklees Priory. The prioress there is said to have hastened his death when he begged her help to relieve his pain during an illness. She is said to have bled him until he was too weak to recover.

Robin Hood, the story ends, managed to blow his famous hunting horn, which summoned his faithful companion Little John to his side. Robin then shot an arrow from the window of his room and asked to be buried wherever it might fall. The spot claimed to be his grave can still be seen to this day.

It is a romantic, ever-popular story which has been told and retold for 600 years. But whether it is myth or history, fiction or fact, remains a mystery.

Mystery of the masked prisoner

On a freezing night in November 1703 a masked prisoner in the Bastille returned to his cell after attending Mass, complained of feeling unwell, took to his bed and died. It was all over so quickly he did not even have time to receive the sacrement.

Within hours, the most extraordinary steps had been taken to ensure that his identity, which had been kept secret from all but a handful of men for 30 years, should never be revealed. All the furniture and equipment he had used was burned or melted down. The walls of his cell were scraped and whitewashed. Every surface was scoured in case he had tried to leave a message for posterity. Even floor tiles were taken up and replaced and his clothes and personal possessions flung into a furnace.

By order of Louis XIV, the prisoner's face had been covered by a mask throughout his entire incarceration. He had been threatened with instant death should he try to remove it, to reveal anything about himself or to escape.

Legends about him spread all over France, then around the world. The solitary prisoner caught the public imagination. As one of the most enigmatic figures in history, he became known as 'The Man in the Iron Mask'.

Because so little was known of him or why he had been incarcerated in the top security prisons of France for so long, rumours spread like wildfire. Some claimed to have discovered that he was an illegitimate son of the Royal House, so closely resembling Louis that his face must never be seen. One astounding theory put forward was that Louis XIV himself was illegitimate and the prisoner was the rightful King. Other rumours named him as the twin brother of Louis, shut away to preserve the Sun King's glory.

Certainly, remarkable precautions were taken to ensure that no one ever saw the face behind the mask. He was always under the care of the same governor, M. de Saint Mars, who moved with him from prison to prison. He was forbidden to mix with other prisoners and his jailer had orders to kill him instantly if he tried to talk about anything other than his immediate neccessities. His name did not appear on the prison records and was never used in either direct address or correspondence. He was usually referred to as 'the prisoner you sent me' or in later days 'the ancient prisoner'.

Despite these harsh terms, he was treated in all other respects as an important person. The King and his ministers constantly inquired after his health and welfare. His food, clothes and furniture were of good quality, he

was allowed his rights as a devout Catholic and was always treated and referred to with courtesy.

The doctor who was allowed to treat him, but who had to examine his tongue and his body without removing the mask, said: 'He was admirably made. His skin was dark, his voice interesting.'

The only other reference to his physical appearance came at a time when the governor, M. de Saint Mars, was ordered to take the man from the island of St Marguerite, where he had been imprisoned, to the Bastille. On the way to Paris, the governor made a stop at his own chateau near Villeneuve, and local people caught glimpses of the masked prisoner. He was said to be tall, well made and white haired. When he dined with St Mars, servants noticed that the governor sat directly opposite his prisoner with two pistols by the side of his plate.

It is said that Louis XIV's great-grandson and successor, Louis XV, on being told the truth about the prisoner, exclaimed: 'If he were still alive I would give him his freedom.' But the secret was obviously not passed on. Louis XVI, in order to satisfy the curiosity of his wife Marie Antoinette, searched the royal archives in vain.

The first written references to the prisoner were available in 1761 when the journals of Etienne du Jonca, the King's Lieutenant in the Bastille, were published. He recorded for the year 1698: 'Thursday, 18 September at three o'clock in the afternoon, M. de Saint Mars, Governor of the Chateau of the Bastille, made his first appearance coming from his command of the Iles Sainte Marguerite, bringing with him in his litter a prisoner he had formerly at Pignerol, whom he caused to be always masked, whose name is not mentioned. . .'

Five years later du Jonca recorded the prisoner's death, stating that he was buried the following Tuesday, November 20 in the graveyard of St Paul under the false name of Marchioly.

It was du Jonca who referred to the fact that the prisoner was 'always masked, with a mask of black velvet'. Other sources described the mask as having been made of iron reinforced with steel, fitted with a chin piece of steel springs to allow the prisoner to eat. It was on the latter description that Alexandre Dumas based his novel *The Man in the Iron Mask* but du Jonca was the only eye witness.

Until the French Revolution, little more was known about the mysterious prisoner. It was at one point widely believed that he was a man named Mattioli, an envoy of the Duke of Mantua who had double-crossed King Louis XIV and been imprisoned under the care of St Mars. The theory was given some credence as it was thought the name Marchioly was a French version of Mattioli. But this was later disproved.

With the Revolution came the first clues. When the archives of the Ministry of War came to be classified they were found to be in chaos. But many years of patient cataloguing and research produced a mass of letters which had passed between the Minister of War, the Marquis de Louvois and M. de Saint Mars.

Towards the end of July 1669, the year in which it is known the masked man was first imprisoned, St Mars received this message from Louvois: 'The King has commanded that I am to have the man named Eustache Dauger sent to Pignerol. It is of the utmost importance to his service that he should be most securely guarded and that he should in no way give information about himself nor send letters to anyone at all. You will yourself once a day have to take enough food for the day to this wretch and you must on no account listen for any reason to all to what he may want to say to you, always threatening to kill him if he opens his mouth to speak of anything but his neccessities.'

Letters from the King himself saying that he was dissatisfied with the behaviour of a man named Eustache Dauger were also found. The King wanted him kept 'in good and safe custody, preventing him communicating with anyone at all by word of mouth or writ of hand'.

Further letters giving details of his imprisonment as the years passed correspond exactly with what is known of the imprisonment of the masked man.

Who was Eustache Dauger? For a long time no trace of him could be found.

At last someone noticed that a lieutenant in the King's Guards had borne that name. It had been overlooked because his family was more commonly called Cavoye after a property they owned in Picardy. A record of his birth exists, but not of his death and references to him disappear after 1668. He was one of six brothers, four of whom were killed in battle. His fifth brother, Louis, became a close friend of the King and was eventually created a marquis. But Eustache was always in trouble and seems to have drifted towards the intriguers of the Court, even possibly being involved in the devil worship and Black Masses encouraged by the king's mistress, Madame de Montespan. But we can only guess.

No more is known and the mystery of the king's masked prisoner remains a mystery.

Exploits of Spring-heeled Jack

He had hands of ice, breath of fire and bounded on to rooftops

He came bounding out of the night, his eyes glowing like balls of fire, his hands icy claws and his mouth spitting flames. For more than 60 years this terrifying figure, reputedly able to leap over high walls or on to roofs with superhuman ease, held England in a grip of fear.

At first, in the 1830s, tales of a frightening devil-like figure bounding through the air were treated as hysterical nonsense. But reports, mainly from people crossing Barnes Common in south-west London, continued.

In January 1838, this strange creature received official recognition. At London's Mansion House the Lord Mayor, Sir John Cowan, read out a letter from a terrified citizen of Peckham. It described the phenomenal jumping feats of a demoniacal figure. There was an immediate uproar.

Other complaints flooded in from people who until then had been too afraid of ridicule to report their encounters with the creature who had become known as Spring-heeled Jack.

Polly Adams, a pretty farmer's daughter from Kent, who worked in South London pub, had been savagely attacked several months earlier while walking across Blackheath. The attacker fled, leaping great distances into the air.

A servant girl, Mary Stevens, was terrorized on Barnes Common. And by

Clapham churchyard a woman on her way home from a visit to friends was confronted by the same mysterious creature.

Across the Thames, 18-year-old Lucy Scales and her sister, daughters of a London butcher, were on their way home from a visit to a brother's house when they were attacked in Green Dragon Alley, Limehouse. A cloaked figure sprang from the darkness, spat flames at Lucy, temporarily blinding her, and then soared away.

The next victim was Jane Alsop, who shared a house in Bearhind Lane, Bow, with her two sisters and their father. One night in February there came a loud knocking on the front door. Jane hurried to answer it, and found a dark figure swathed in a long cloak standing in the shadows.

He swung round and said, 'I am a policeman. For God's sake bring me a light. We have caught Spring-heeled Jack here in the lane!'

Jane's heart skipped a beat. The news stunned and excited her. So the stories of the strange bogyman were true after all, she thought. She hurried back into the house to get a candle and handed it to the man. But, instead of hurrying away, the 'policeman' shrugged off the cloak – to reveal a terrifying figure clad in a horned, close-fitting helmet and a tight, white costume.

He grabbed hold of her by the neck, pinning her head under his arm. But, as he ripped at her dress and pawed her body, she tore herself away with a terrified scream. He gave chase and caught her again by her long hair, but Jane's sister, hearing her cries, raised the alarm. Help arrived, but before any of the startled rescuers could grab him, the figure bounded away into the darkness.

Jane later described her attacker to the authorities: 'His face was hideous, his eyes like balls of fire. His hands had icy-cold great claws, and he vomited blue and white flames.'

Her colourful description was to be echoed repeatedly by other terrified – and presumably hysterical – victims. But it was a description that could hardly have helped the police in their search for the fantastic attacker. After all, where were they to start looking for such a creature?

Posses of vigilantes were organized, rewards were offered, the police strived in vain to track down the attacker. Even the Duke of Wellington, although nearly 60, armed himself and went out on horseback to hunt down the monster.

During the next few years, Spring-heeled Jack roamed the country. Sightings ranged from the back streets of London to remote villages.

In February 1855 the mystery spread to the West Country, where the folk of five South Devon towns awoke to find that there had been a heavy snowfall – and that mysterious footprints had appeared overnight. The footsteps ran along the tops of walls, over rooftops, and across enclosed courtyards. The frightened inhabitants labelled them the Devil's Footprints. Some attributed them to a ghostly animal (see p. 179) and others blamed Spring-heeled Jack.

Spring-heeled Jack was still bounding around the country in 1870. The army certainly took him seriously and organized a plan to trap him. The move was forced upon the authorities after sentries, many of them hardened veterans of the Crimean War, had been terrorized at their posts by a weird figure who sprang from the shadows to land on the roofs of their sentry boxes or to slap their faces with icy hands.

In Lincoln the townsfolk, wild with fear and anger, tried to hunt him down with guns. As always, he disappeared into the night with a maniacal laugh.

Jack's fiendish face was last seen in 1904 in Liverpool. He panicked people in the Everton area by leaping up and down the streets, 'bounding from pavement to rooftop and back again.' When a few bold souls tried to corner him, he melted back into the darkness.

Victorian Britain abounded in rich eccentrics, one of whom may have found it amusing to spend time and money in spreading terror through the country. Some people blamed the 'Mad Marquis' of Waterford. But, while he was wild and irresponsible, he was never vicious.

The mystery of Spring-heeled Jack remains unsolved. After his appearance in Liverpool, he disappeared – apparently for good.

I was Napoleon's general . . .

On his death bed in Florence, South Carolina, in 1846, an obscure but popular French teacher weakly declared: 'I am France's Marshal Ney.' The final words of a frail old man might have been taken as the product of a wandering mind – except for some remarkable evidence that he was perhaps telling the truth.

Marshal Michel Ney was one of Napoleon Bonaparte's most able generals. But after his army was defeated at Waterloo, Napoleon was exiled to St Helena, and Ney, less lucky than his leader, was sentenced to death by firing squad.

Shortly after 9 o'clock on the morning of 7 December 1815, Ney was led by a contingent of the troops he had once commanded into the Luxembourg Gardens in Paris. He was placed against a wall where he addressed his men in the most emotional terms.

A British diplomat witnessed the execution. He said that Ney shouted to the firing squad: 'Comrades, when I place my hand upon my breast, fire at

A contemporary print of Marshal Ney giving the word of command for his own death.

my heart.' The soldiers levelled their rifles, Ney put his hand to his chest, a volley rang out and Ney fell, his coat stained with blood.

According to the observer, the body was then whisked away with suspicious haste. It lay in a hospital overnight and was buried in the cemetery of Pierre la Chaise early the following day. Madame Ney did not attend the funeral. Only one distant relative was there to see the famous general laid to rest.

Three years later in Florence, South Carolina, a middle-aged French teacher using the name of Peter Stuart Ney claimed that he and Marshal Ney were the same person. He said he had been saved from execution by a plot hatched by his old soldiers, with the aid of his former enemy, the Duke of Wellington, who had been horrified at the ignoble fate proposed for his fellow general.

The teacher explained that the Paris firing squad had aimed above his head. He said that he had held in his hand a container of blood, which he had released when he struck his chest. He had then been smuggled by ship to America.

No one believed Ney until a doctor examined him and agreed that scars on his body conformed to Marshal Ney's battle scars. The teacher also claimed that during the passage to America he had been recognized by a fellow passenger – a soldier who had once been in his command. The man was later traced and confirmed the story. The French teacher also boasted a remarkably inti-mate knowledge of Marshal Ney and his family and of military tactics.

The renowned New York handwriting expert, David Carvalho, examined letters written by the teacher and by the general. He had no hesitation in stating that they were produced by the same person.

Six years after the Paris 'execution', one of Ney's pupils brought him a newspaper reporting the death of Napoleon on St Helena. The teacher fainted before his class and was carried home. Later that day he tried to cut his throat, but the knife broke in the wound.

Peter Ney – or Marshal Michel Ney, if that is indeed who he was – died peacefully in 1846, maintaining to the last the strange story that no one has ever been able to prove or disprove.

The queen of crime's lost 11 days

The riddle of Agatha Christie's disappearance remains unsolved

Agatha Christie was the most successful crime writer of all time. Her tales of Hercule Poirot and Miss Marple have de-lighted millions for more than 50 years', and some of her intricate plots have puzzled even the most sharp-witted of fans. Yet, on her death in January 1976, she left behind her a real-life mystery as baffling as any she concocted herself.

In December 1926, when she was already celebrated as a mystery writer, Agatha Christie disappeared for nearly two weeks. The newspaper headlines screamed sensational theories to a breathless public. Suicide. Abduction. Murder. The police searched for some clue as to why she had disappeared – but in vain.

Agatha Christie was born in September 1890, the youngest daughter of a wealthy American who lived with his English wife in Torquay, Devon. The family lived a life of luxurious ease and Agatha received little formal education. But the house was full of books and her mother encouraged her to read.

In 1914 she married Colonel Archibald Christie, and while her husband was abroad with the army she served as a nurse. She qualified as a dispenser and it was during this time that she gained the detailed knowledge of medicine, drugs and poisons that were to stand her in such good stead as a mystery writer.

She wrote her first detective story while recovering from an illness, and by 1926 she was a literary success. Perhaps this irritated her husband – who turned to another woman and confessed the love affair to his wife.

This news, following on the death of her mother, drove her to despair. And on the bitterly cold night of Friday, 3 December, she dressed in a green knitted skirt, a grey cardigan and a velours hat, stuffed a few pounds into her purse, climbed into her two-seater Morris car and drove off into the night.

Early the following morning, the car was found empty at the bottom of a slope near Newlands Corner, barely half a mile from her 12-bedroomed Berkshire home. Its front wheels hung over the edge of a 120-ft chalk pit in a narrow, rutted lane. The brakes were off, the gear lever was in neutral and the ignition switched on. In the car was some clothing, including a fur coat.

The following Monday, the police released the news of her disappearance, and the newspapers headlined it. Hundreds of policemen and thousands of volunteers scoured the countryside. Deep-sea divers searched the Silent Pool, a so-called bottomless lake in the area.

The favourite theory was that the famous authoress had committed suicide. But where was the body?

While the hue and cry grew, an attractive redhead in her mid-thirties was making herself popular with her fellow guests at The Hydro Hotel, some 250 miles away at Harrogate, Yorkshire. Her name, she said, was Theresa Neele – the same surname as that of Colonel Christie's new love – and she was from South Africa. But the hotel's head waiter, who had been closely following the story of Agatha Christie's disappearance in the newspapers, thought the sociable guest looked suspiciously like the missing writer, and he contacted the police.

Eleven days after her disappearance, 'Mrs Neele' finished a game of billiards and went to change for dinner. When she approached the dining room, Colonel Christie lowered the newspaper he had been hiding behind and walked over to her.

The press immediately suspected an elaborate publicity stunt – even though Colonel Christie's claim that his wife had been suffering from loss of memory was confirmed by a doctor. The papers led a public outcry, demanding that the £3,000 that the search had cost the taxpayer should be repaid. But gradually the ill-feeling vanished and Mrs Christie regained her popularity. Two years later she and Colonel Christie were divorced, and he was free to marry Miss Neele.

In 1930, Agatha married archaeologist Sir Max Mallowan and travelled widely with him, using the exotic places she visited as settings for some of her novels.

With the passage of years, the memories of the novelist's disappearance faded. She would agree to interviews only on the understanding that the matter was not mentioned. Even her autobiography passes over the episode quickly; she merely hints at a nervous breakdown. But is this the real explanation of what happened all those years ago? If she had lost her memory, where did the clothes she wore at The Hydro and the money she spent there come from?

Did she, on that cold December night, intend to kill herself – and then, when fate took a hand and her car failed to plunge into the chalk pit, decide to get away for a rest while she thought things over? If so, why did she not let the police know the truth?

Was the episode a plot to gain the sympathy of her errant husband and win him back? Was it an involved way of bringing her husband's affair out into the open? Or perhaps, more sinisterly, was it all a scheme to punish her husband's infidelity? Suppose a suicide attempt had succeeded. The police would have investigated and discovered in Colonel Christie's affair with Miss Neele a likely motive for him to get rid of his wife. Far-fetched perhaps, but no more so than some of Mrs Christie's mystery plots.

Most of the people who could help reveal the truth of the matter are now dead. Miss Neele died in 1958 and Colonel Christie in 1962.

Agatha Christie's second husband, Sir Max, once admitted that *Unfinished Portrait*, a romantic novel which she wrote in 1934 under the name Mary Westmacott, was a thinly disguised autobiography. In it, the heroine is shattered when her husband tells her he is in love with another woman. She tries to commit suicide, but fails.

Over the years, Agatha Christie wrote more than 80 novels, was more widely translated than William Shakespeare and achieved sales of 300 million books. But despite this popularity, she remained a private, enigmatic person. And, right up to her death, she refused to provide the solution to her greatest mystery story – that of her own disappearance half a century before.

Chapter Two

Mysteries of The Deep

The sea has always been a challenge, an inspiration –
and a mystery. Although man has plumbed the ocean
depths, there are still almost as many questions as
answers about the seas that cover two-thirds of our
globe. What was the dread secret of the *Mary Celeste*?
What is the true story behind the sinking of the
Lusitania? Does the Loch Ness Monster really exist?
Where is the lost world of Atlantis? The mysteries of
the deep are many and baffling.

The ghost ship 'Mary Celeste'

What caused her crew to vanish without trace?

There was a certain strangeness about the two-masted sailing ship that lurched through the Atlantic swell. Something was amiss, but it was not easy at first to discern what it was. The crew on the deck of the brigantine *Dei Gratia* had watched the erratic journey of the mysterious ship ever since it had emerged as a speck on the grey horizon. The *Dei Gratia* had gained steadily on it until, in the early afternoon, Captain David Morehouse took up a parallel course and began to study the ship's odd configuration through his telescope.

The strange ship was a square-rigged brigantine like his own, but it had only two sails set. The others were either furled or hanging in tatters. The ship veered to left and right in the lightly gusting wind as if the helmsman were drunk. But Captain Morehouse soon realized why the ship was not sailing straight and smooth. For as the *Dei Gratia* drew closer, he saw that there was no one at the wheel . . . no one on deck . . . in fact, no sign of life at all. . . .

Morehouse had a signal run up, but there was no answer from the ghostly stranger. He ordered a longboat to be lowered, and three men rowed across to the ship. As they approached, they shouted: 'Brig ahoy, brig ahoy.' There was no reply. They swung their boat around the stern of the ship and peered up at the name painted there: *Mary Celeste*, New York.

The last time anyone had seen the *Mary Celeste* had been a month earlier when, on 4 November 1872, it had sailed from New York bound for Genoa, carrying a cargo of 1,700 casks of crude alcohol. Aboard were the 37-year-old American master, Captain Benjamin Spooner Briggs, and his first mate, Albert Richardson, leading a crew of seven. Also on board were the captain's wife, Sarah, and their two-year-old daughter, Sophia. Briggs, an upright, God-fearing, bearded man, was making his first voyage in the *Mary Celeste*. His previous commands had been of a schooner and a barque, but he had leaped at the chance of commanding the *Mary Celeste* when the consortium that owned it offered him a third share in the ship. It had originally been called *The Amazon*, but the owners gave the ship a new name, along with a badly needed refit, before sending it off across the winter Atlantic.

The *Mary Celeste* sailed out of New York's East River and pointed its bow towards the Azores, which were sighted, according to the log, on 24 November.

The *Mary Celeste*.

The weather until then had been good, and Mrs Briggs had spent much of her days on deck. In the evenings she worked at her sewing machine or played on the melodeon which she had persuaded her husband to allow her to bring on the voyage.

However, once past the Azores, the weather changed for the worse. A moderate gale blew. It was hardly serious enough to worry an experienced captain, and Briggs ordered some of the sails to be furled. There was no panic and the ship's log recorded only the barest facts. The following day was 25 November, and that morning the ship's bearings were noted in the log.

It was the last entry ever made.

Ten days later the longboat from the *Dei Gratia* came alongside the *Mary Celeste*. First Mate Oliver Deveau and Second Mate John Wright clambered aboard, leaving the third man below to secure the boat. Deveau and Wright searched the ship, and what they saw deepened the mystery.

The rigging flapped loosely in the wind. The wheel swung noiselessly, water slurped in and out of the open galley door, a compass lay smashed on the deck, the ship's boat was missing. But below decks, things were very different. Everything seemed orderly . . . except that there was no one to be seen.

In the captain's cabin was Mrs Briggs' rosewood melodeon with a sheet of music still on it. The sewing machine was on a table. Little Sophia's toys were neatly stowed away. In the crew's quarters, the scene was equally ordered. Washing hung on a line. Clothing lay on bunks, dry and undisturbed. In the galley, preparations seemed to have been made for breakfast, although only half of it appeared to have been served.

Deveau and Wright clambered back into the longboat and reported their discoveries to Morehouse. He suggested that the *Mary Celeste* must have been abandoned in a storm. But why then, asked Deveau, was there an open and unspilled bottle of cough medicine along with the unbroken plates and ornaments in the captain's cabin? A mutiny, suggested Morehouse. But there was no sign of a struggle – and why should mutineers abandon ship along with their victims? Perhaps the ship had been taking water. Deveau confirmed that there was three feet of water in the hold and that a sounding rod had been found on deck, but three feet would be a normal intake over ten days for an old timber-hulled ship and could easily have been pumped out.

Morehouse decided to put the unanswered questions aside and concentrate for the moment on more important matters – salvage money, for instance. He sent some of his crew back across to the meandering *Mary Celeste* and within hours the hold was pumped dry. By the following day, the rigging was repaired.

The captain could spare only three of his seven-man crew to sail the *Mary Celeste*. He chose Deveau and seamen Augustus Anderson and Charles Lund. In an amazing feat of seamanship, the three sailed the *Mary Celeste* 600 miles to what was to have been her first port of call, Gibraltar, where the *Dei Gratia* was awaiting them.

The British authorities in Gibraltar impounded the *Mary Celeste* and ordered a public inquiry. Morehouse, Deveau and his men were closely questioned. A bloodstained sword was said to have been found under Captain Briggs' bunk – was this not proof of foul play? The sword was examined and the stains proved not to be blood. Nine casks of alcohol were found to be dry and a further cask had been breached – could not the crew have gone on a drunken rampage? Deveau patiently explained to the inquiry that below decks the ship had been in perfect order. Could Briggs have panicked during a storm and ordered the ship's boat to be launched? Little sign of this either – in the captain's cabin, everything had been as orderly as it should have been at a gentleman's breakfast table. The captain had even neatly cut the top off his boiled egg, which remained uneaten on his plate.

But the question the investigators found most baffling was: how was the *Mary Celeste* able to remain on course without a crew for ten days and 500 miles? When the *Dei Gratia* caught up with the mystery ship, Morehouse was sailing on a port tack. The *Mary Celeste* was on a starboard tack. It was inconceivable, the inquiry was told, that the *Mary Celeste* could have travelled the course it did with sails set that way. Someone must have been aboard for several days after the last log entry. . . .

The authorities in Gibraltar were certain that the *Mary Celeste*'s missing longboat and the crew would soon turn up to explain the unanswered questions. But they never did, and, on 10 March 1873, the court of inquiry awarded an ungenerous £1,700 salvage money to Morehouse and his men. It was about 15 per cent of the value of the 200-ton ship and its cargo.

The inquiry closed but the arguments raged on. The occupants of the *Mary Celeste* had all been captured by pirates, they had been seized by a giant squid, they had stepped off on to an iceberg, they had died from yellow fever, the captain had gone mad. But the most extraordinary explanation of all was suggested 40 years later, in 1913.

Howard Linford, headmaster of a school in Hampstead, London, claimed to have discovered a revealing manuscript among the property bequeathed to him by an old school servant as he lay on his deathbed. The servant, a much-travelled man named Abel Fosdyk, had written an account of how he had been an unrecorded passenger on the *Mary Celeste* – and the only survivor of the tragedy that befell her.

Fosdyk wrote that during the voyage Captain Briggs found his daughter playing precariously on the bowsprit – the spar that juts from the front of a sailing ship. He ordered the ship's carpenter to use an upturned table to make a safe platform for her to play there. In doing so, the carpenter cut deep notches in the woodwork on either side of the bow – mysterious marks that were indeed found on the *Mary Celeste*. One calm day, Briggs had an argument with his first mate over a man's ability to swim with his clothes on, and the eccentric captain leaped over the side to prove his point. All the occupants of the ship rushed to the makeshift platform to get a better view, and the woodwork collapsed, flinging everyone into the sea. Sharks soon appeared and polished off all but Fosdyk, who clung to the remains of the platform until he was washed up on the African coast.

The story captured the imagination of readers around the world, but has been rejected as being far-fetched.

So the mystery of what happened to the crew of the *Mary Celeste* remains to this day. But what of the ship itself?

When the *Mary Celeste* was released by the Gibraltar court of inquiry, sailors refused to serve on the ship. They believed it was cursed. The ship changed hands 17 times in the next 11 years until it was bought by a group of Boston businessmen in 1884. They over-insured the ship and sent it off to Haiti. There, on a clear day and in a calm sea, the captain ran on to a coral reef. The attempted fraud was detected, and master and owners were all brought to court. Meanwhile, the old wooden hulk of the *Mary Celeste* rotted away unseen on the remote Caribbean reef.

The civilization that sank beneath the sea

Still the search goes on for the lost kingdom of Atlantis

It was a rich land, blessed with lush vegetation and mines of valuable minerals, including silver and gold. Its people were cultured and scientifically advanced. At the centre of the island kingdom, on top of a small hill, was a palace and a temple, the hub of a vast city, 12 miles from end to end. Around the hill was a moat – indeed, more a canal – packed with sailing ships. Around that, in concentric circles, were more canals. These waterways were linked by yet further canals to the open sea via an extensive system of docks and harbours by which the nation's valuable produce was exported to the rest of the known world. It was a prosperous kingdom and a famous one. For, although it vanished from the face of the earth many centuries before Christ, its name is today still better known than those of many of the surviving nations of the globe. The name of that fabled kingdom and its great city . . . Atlantis.

The only description left to us of Atlantis was written by the Greek philosopher Plato in about 347 BC. And even he was not speaking of it first-hand. He was repeating stories written down by the Athenian traveller Solon who, in turn, had heard them from Egyptian priests. The story Plato passed on was that Atlantis was a great nation in decline. Its people had fallen into corrupt ways – and they earned a dreadful punishment. 'In one day and one night' the entire island, 350 miles across, was overtaken by a catastrophe of unsurpassed magnitude. Atlantis was rent by a volcanic explosion, followed by a tidal wave, and within 24 hours had vanished beneath the sea.

Plato puts the tragic fate of Atlantis at a period we would now date as 9600 BC. And the place? 'Beyond the Pillars of Hercules' – what we now call the Straits of Gibraltar. That puts Atlantis somewhere in the Atlantic Ocean, a theory which, as geologists tell us, cannot be correct. For there is no major subterranean land mass on the bed of the Atlantic to justify Plato's story. So, did the celebrated philosopher get his facts wrong? Or did he simply make up the whole story as a cautionary tale? The answer, in all likelihood, is that Plato's epic tale is based firmly on fact – although both his date and his geography are badly out. The result has been a riddle that has puzzled man for centuries. These are some of the areas suggested over the years as the site of the lost civilization.

Mid-Atlantic. A vast ridge runs in the shape of the letter S along the seabed the entire length of the North and South Atlantic, from Iceland to Tristan da Cunha. It has been suggested that the highest region of this mountain range, around the area of the Azores, was once all above sea level, forming the land of Atlantis. Until the present century, this was the most popular theory. But it has now been debunked by scientists who point out that the Atlantic Ridge is – and has been for thousands of years – slowly rising from the depths, not sinking.

North America. As soon as Christopher Columbus returned to Europe with his tales of lands across the ocean, interest in the lost kingdom of Atlantis was revived. English philosopher Sir Francis Bacon firmly linked legend and fact in his work *The New Atlantis.* And historian John Swain wrote: 'It may be supposed that America was one time part of that great land which Plato calleth the Atlantick Island, and that the kings of that island had some intercourse between the people of Europe and Africa.' Such a theory must be discounted, however. The North American races never achieved a level of civilization equal even to that which existed in Plato's time.

The Land Bridge. Various theories have been put forward about land bridges which may at one time have linked Africa with South America, or have joined Europe – via Britain, Iceland and Greenland – to North America. But geologists now know that no such bridge could have existed within the last 50 millions years.

The Sargasso Sea. Sargasso is the Portuguese word for floating seaweed, and the Sargasso Sea is just that. It is a $1\frac{1}{2}$-million-square-mile mass of weed that drifts off the Florida coast. Mariners once thought that it covered vast shallows beneath which may have been a sunken Atlantis. In fact, the sea is up to 1,500 ft deep.

The Scilly Isles. Phoenician, Greek and Roman historians all referred to the 'tin islands' off the British coast. These islands off Cornwall, Britain's only tin-mining region, do not fit, however, Plato's lush description.

Bimini. Between 1923 and his death in 1945, an American commercial photographer named Edgar Cayce made a name for himself as a faith healer and visionary. Although he had never read Plato's works, he claimed to have looked back in time and mentally visited Atlantis, and he described it in much the same way as the Greek philosopher had done 2,300 years before. Cayce added that Atlantis had been destroyed by an atomic explosion (the inhabitants having mastered the science of nuclear fission) around the year 10,000 BC – close to the date set by Plato. And he gave the site of Atlantis as North Bimini,

---

PLATO'S ATLANTIS

At the centre of the island (of Atlantis) was a plain, said to be the most beautiful and fertile of all plains, and near the middle of this plain was a hill of no great size. Around the hill were two rings of land and three of sea, like cartwheels. In the centre of the hill was a shrine sacred to Poseidon and Cleito, surrounded by a golden wall through which entry was forbidden. There was also a temple to Poseidon, which was covered all over in silver, except for the statues, which were of gold. Two springs, hot and cold, provided limitless water supplies, and there were indoor heated baths for kings and commoners, for women and for horses. On the outer rings of land there were dockyards and harbours, surrounded by a wall which was densely built up with houses. From this crowded area rose a constant din of shouting and noise throughout the day and night. Beyond were the plains, which brought to perfection all those sweet-scented stuffs which the earth produces now, whether made of roots or herbs or trees or flowers or fruits. All these, that hallowed island, as it lay then beneath the sun, produced in marvellous beauty and endless abundance.

– *Critias and Timaeus*, by Plato.

a small island in the Bahamas, forecasting that 'a portion of the temples may yet be discovered' in 1968 or 1969.

It was a preposterous story. And yet, in 1968, veteran American zoologist and deep-sea diver Dr J. Manson Valentine discovered some strange structures beneath the sea off the coast of North Bimini. They could be made out clearly only from the air, but when he dived to investigate he found that they were the walls of what seemed to be an enormous harbour, enclosing quays and jetties. The walls, about one-third of a mile long, were of massive stone blocks more than 16 ft square.

Subsequent expeditions – and there have been many – have alternately supported and debunked Dr Valentine's assertion that the formation amounts to a man-made harbour. In 1970, Dr John Hall, professor of archaeology at Miami University, led a survey of the site and reported: 'These stones constitute a natural phenomenon called Pleistocene beachrock erosion. We found no evidence whatever of any work of human hand. Therefore, alas for those who believe in the old legend, another Atlantis is dismissed.'

But two later American expeditions to Bimini, in 1975 and 1977, came up with very different findings. The expeditions' leader, Dr David Zink, of California, brought to the surface a block of stone with a tongue-and-groove worked edge. The conclusion: 'On balance, we believe that the structure at Bimini is archaeological rather than geological in origin – but its purpose must remain a matter for speculation.'

So the Bimini mystery is yet to be solved. The possibility that it is the site of a lost city has not been disproved. Yet the most likely site of Atlantis so far suggested is nowhere near the Caribbean. It is not even in the Atlantic. For most archaeologists now believe that Plato made two remarkable mistakes when he wrote about his lost island.

Firstly, it is most likely that Atlantis, if it existed at all, was not 'beyond the Pillars of Hercules', but in the Mediterranean itself. Secondly, when Plato recorded the disaster as having happened 9,000 years before the Egyptian priests' account, he may have written 9,000 in error for 900. If so, that would put the date of the demise of Atlantis at approximately 1500 BC instead of 9600 BC. And in 1500 BC, there did occur one of the most appalling cataclysms of ancient times . . .

Archaeologists now know that the civilization of Atlantis described by Plato was very much like the highly developed Bronze Age Minoan culture which flourished on the islands of the Aegean Sea until the 15th century BC. It ended abruptly in about 1470 BC – and until recent years no one has understood why.

It is now known, however, that around that time a volcanic explosion, unimaginably destructive, tore out the entire centre of the Minoan island of

Kalliste – now known as Santorini – which lies midway between Crete and the Greek mainland. Sea rushed in to fill the crater that was left.

Archaeologists are now excavating the 100-ft-deep deposits of volcanic ash that cover what may once have been Plato's fabulous island. What they have so far uncovered has enabled them to build up a frightening picture of the events that occurred there almost 3,500 years ago.

Because of the scarcity of human remains, it is assumed that the inhabitants of the island had some warning of the impending disaster through earth tremors and a series of minor volcanic eruptions. What probably happened next was this. The citizens took to their boats and headed for Crete, some 70 miles south. But before they had a chance to reach their goal, Kalliste exploded in a holocaust of fiery lava.

Molten rock spewed into the air, and ash and pumice stone rained down on the overcrowded boats. Soon the sea was an unnavigable mass of floating pumice. The people in the boats, unable to flee, died a slow and hideous death as the torrent of burning, choking ash became ever thicker. For some, the agony was ended by a tidal wave, perhaps 200 ft high, which swept out from the island, smashing the boats to matchwood. The giant wave, travelling at more than 150 miles an hour, soon reached Crete, heart of the Minoan empire. It swept away all the towns and villages along the northern coastline and obliterated the harbour serving the capital, Knossos.

The wave travelled on to the North African coast, where its effects may have been responsible for the Old Testament story of Moses' parting of the Red Sea. It has also been suggested that the rain of ash, which covered more than 100,000 square miles, may have been the origin of the story of the Egyptian plagues.

Some idea of what must have been the scale of the devastation can be gained from the example of the explosion of the volcanic Indonesian island Krakatoa in 1883. About 300 towns on the neighbouring islands of Java and Sumatra were wrecked, and 36,000 people died. The blast was heard 3,500 miles away in Australia, shock waves went round the world three times, volcanic dust reached Africa and even Europe, and tidal waves crossed the Pacific Ocean and damaged boats on the coast of South America.

Such must have been the fate of Kalliste. Today, as Santorini, it stands fragmented and desolate under its barren covering of ash. It is made up of two main islands, Thera and Therasia, whose sheer 1,000-ft cliffs curve round a seven-mile-wide expanse of water, in parts 1,000 ft deep. This water covers the caldera, the dead heart of the volcano, formed when the cauldron of molten rock burned out and collapsed in upon itself.

In the centre of the great sea-covered crater – at the spot where the palace and temple of Atlantis may once have stood – are two islets which arose from the depths long after the original catastrophe. They are rocks of black lava. Sometimes smoke rises from them in lazy wisps – a faint but threatening reminder of the cataclysm that may have destroyed the legendary kingdom of Atlantis.

LOST GARDEN OF EDEN

Atlantis is not the only legendary land lost beneath the waves. Two entire continents are reputed to have vanished without trace - each vastly larger than Atlantis and each, in its time, described as the cradle of mankind.

The names of these two lost Gardens of Eden were Mu and Lemuria. Mu was supposedly situated in the Pacific Ocean and was twice the size of Australia. Lemuria, according to legend, filled up most of the Indian Ocean and linked Africa with Malaysia.

The Mu theory was raised in 1870 by Colonel James Churchward, who claimed that, while serving with the Bengal Lancers in British colonial India, he was told the secrets of the lost land by Hindu priests. He was shown some tablets, since lost, and was taught a forgotten language called Naacal. Churchward also said that he had found identical stone tablets in Mexico. According to the tablets, Mu sank into the ocean in a great natural catastrophe 12,000 years ago, wiping out its 64 million people. Remarkably, the story of Mu was taken seriously at the time.

A somewhat better-argued tale was told about the lost continent of Lemuria. The name was coined by the 19th-century British zoologist Professor Philip Sclater, who named his nation after the lemur. It was fossils of this and of other animals, found in both Africa and Malaysia, that led Sclater to support legendary tales of a lost continent in the Indian Ocean. The many supporters of his theory included eminent biologist Ernst Haekel and evolutionist Thomas Huxley.

Less fanciful evidence is used to support the legend of Lyonesse - a land off the south-west English coast, said to have been visited by King Arthur and his knights. The 15th-century chronicler William of Worcester quoted monastery scrolls which referred to '140 parochial churches, all since submerged, lying between Cornwall and the Isles of Scilly'.

The land is said to have sunk into the sea in a single day. This extravagant punishment, so folklore has it, was meted out by the magician Merlin to drown King Arthur's treacherous knight Mordred and his rebel followers.

MIRACLE OF SURTSEY

Sunken cities? Lost continents? The world was inclined to treat such legends lightly - until the remarkable events of November 1963. It was then that the forces which obliterated Atlantis were seen at work, but in reverse.

The skipper of a fishing boat off the south coast of Iceland radioed his base to report a vast cloud of black smoke rising from the sea. He and his crew watched in awe as explosion after explosion burst from the depths. Rocks were hurled 500 ft into the air and the smoke billowed to more than 10,000 ft.

Then the fishermen noticed waves lapping over a vast black form which was slowly emerging from the ocean. It was the summit of a volcanic mountain rising from the depths.

Within 24 hours, the island was higher than a housetop. Within the week, its peak was 200 ft above sea level. And by the time that volcanic activity ceased two years later, the island was more than 500 ft high and over a mile long.

The Icelanders named their new-born island Surtsey, after Surtur, the god of fire in Norse mythology. Today, colonized by birds, insects and plants, it still stands as proof that new land can emerge from the depths as quickly as an old one can sink into legend.

Sinking of the 'Lusitania'

'War plot' theory of torpedoed luxury liner

'Torpedo . . . torpedo on starboard side.' That was the startled cry from the look-out on the foc'sle of the British liner *Lusitania* as it sped through the waters off the south coast of Ireland on 7 May 1915. There was no time to take evasive action, and the underwater missile found its mark.

Eleven miles away on the Old Head of Kinsale, south of Cork, people on shore were admiring the passage of the giant Cunard liner. Those with binoculars were puzzled to see a faint plume of smoke rise over the ship. One man checked his watch – the time was 2.11 pm. Eighteen minutes later the *Lusitania* had sunk beneath the waves, taking with it 1,198 people, 124 of them Americans.

It was that last figure that changed the course of history. For the death of the Americans precipitated the entry of the United States into World War One – and ultimately ensured victory for the Allies.

But the sinking of the *Lusitania* was not only a momentous event in the course of the bloodiest war the world had ever known. It also presented historians with a mystery that has not been solved to this day. That mystery is – was the *Lusitania* a passenger ship or a warship? Was the liner carrying arms? And was it knowingly sacrificed to bring America into the war?

The *Lusitania* was designed to wrest the Blue Riband, awarded for the fastest Atlantic crossing, from the two German lines that had held it since 1897. The liner was subsidized by the Admiralty under secret agreements that have never been released. It was 670 feet long, could carry 2,300 passengers in extreme luxury, had a crew of 900, travelled at 25 knots – and was to be able to mount twelve 6-in guns.

THE WORLD'S GREATEST MYSTERIES

The liner's final voyage, from New York to Liverpool, began on 1 May 1915. The Germans had warned passengers intending to travel on the *Lusitania* not to book aboard the ship, and made clear that every enemy passenger ship in war-zone waters was liable to be attacked, and that neutral governments 'should not entrust their crews, passengers or merchandise to such vessels'.

The German Embassy in Washington went so far as to place advertisements in American newspapers warning: 'Travellers planning to embark on the Atlantic voyage are reminded that a state of war exists between Germany and Great Britain and that vessels flying the British flag are liable to destruction. Travellers sailing in the war zone on ships of Great Britain or her allies do so at their own risk.'

Nevertheless, 188 Americans booked as passengers aboard the *Lusitania*, and more than 4,000 cases of ammunition for the war effort were added to the officially 'innocent' cargo manifest.

As the liner left New York, several people on the other side of the Atlantic had its future in mind. Winston Churchill, who was then first lord of the admiralty, met the first sea lord, Lord Fisher, along with naval intelligence experts who had earlier been asked to prepare a report on the effect of a liner being sunk with American passengers aboard. Coincidentally, the US ambassador in London, in a letter to his son, wrote: 'What will Uncle Sam do if a British liner full of American passengers is blown up?' And King George V granted an audience to President Woodrow Wilson's special envoy, Colonel Edward House, at which the King is reported to have inquired: 'What will America do if Germany sinks the *Lusitania*?'

The scene was set for disaster. The vessel approached the Irish coast on 7 May. The master, Captain William 'Bowler Bill' Turner, had received only one warning of the peril ahead. It was a radio message from Vice-Admiral Sir Henry Coke, whose headquarters were at Queenstown, Cork, and it read: 'Submarines active off the south coast of Ireland.'

One of those submarines was the U20, under the command of Kapitan-Leutnant Walter Schwieger. The U20 had been at sea since 30 April and was on its way back to base at Wilhelmshaven when the *Lusitania* was spotted on the horizon. Schwieger at first did not recognize the liner and could only describe it as 'a forest of masts and stacks' – in those days the *Lusitania* was the tallest ship in the world.

As it approached Kinsale Head, the liner changed course. 'She was now coming directly at us,' said Schwieger. 'She could not have chosen a more perfect course if she had deliberately tried to give us a dead shot.'

At a range of a mere 400 yards, Schwieger ordered the torpedo to be fired. It hit the *Lusitania* on the starboard side below the bridge. Water poured in at a pressure too strong to be contained by the 119 supposedly watertight compartments. The bow dipped beneath the calm sea, and at the same time, the liner began to list to starboard.

The bow hit the sea-bed 315 ft below, but the stern still hung in the air, the enormous propellors pointing skywards. Then the vast bulk of the liner slid, steaming and bubbling, to the bottom.

The sea was dotted with frantic figures. The *Lusitania* was well equipped with lifeboats, but there had been no time to launch them all. Of the 1,198 people who perished, 785 were passengers. They included 125 children. One expectant mother gave birth in the water, and she and her baby died.

Argument has raged ever since over whether the Germans were right to view the *Lusitania* as a legitimate target of war, over whether the liner was armed and carrying a military cargo, and over the biggest question of all – did the British government send the *Lusitania* on a suicide course through U-boat infested waters in order to force America into the war?

The mysteries surrounding the sinking of the *Lusitania* have been exhaustively argued by historians and authors, most notably by writer Colin Simpson, whose book on the subject* propounded several controversial theories about the tragedy – not least that the vessel was armed with twelve 6-in. guns and was carrying a large cargo of munitions and explosives. Simpson claimed that the *Lusitania* underwent modifications in a Liverpool dry dock in 1913, enabling the liner to take heavy guns if required and, in effect, turning it into an auxiliary cruiser. One of the boilers, it was claimed, had been converted into a magazine, and lifts had been installed to hoist the shells up to the decks.

More controversial is Simpson's allegation that the British admiralty – and that means Churchill – called off the *Lusitania*'s destroyer escort even though U-boats were known to be in its path. Captain Turner was never told that the warships which he had assumed were still in the vicinity had been diverted elsewhere. And Turner himself, who survived the sinking, claimed throughout his life that a message in naval code had directed him to change course towards the point where the U-boat was waiting.

During his years of researches, Simpson turned up hitherto-unpublished documents from Washington's national archives and from Cunard and the admiralty. They led him to believe, as many historians do, that a massive Anglo-American cover-up took place after the disaster. The cargo manifest was said to have been falsified, and both Sir Henry Coke's signal log and the official admiralty signal register had their entries removed for 7 May – the only pages missing for the entire period of the war.

The other main mystery that has intrigued researchers is why the *Lusitania* sank so swiftly. The German G-type torpedo which was fired from the U20

* *Lusitania* by Colin Simpson (Longman, 1972).

was neither powerful nor deeply penetrating. Yet it sank a mighty ocean liner in just 18 minutes. How?

It has been claimed that the liner had a dangerous design fault built into it. The engines and machinery took up too much space, so some of the coal carried had to be stored in compartments not intended for that purpose. The engineers chose for their coal stores the special buoyancy compartments that were a safety feature of the liner. The empty air traps that should have kept the ship afloat were, on that fateful voyage, loaded full of coal.

But a more sinister reason has been suggested for the swift demise of the *Lusitania*. Divers who have been down to the wreck report that the side and bottom of the ship were blown outwards by an internal explosion far more severe than could have been caused by a torpedo. What could have caused such a blast?

Could it have been that deep in the holds of the *Lusitania* were stacked more than butter, cheese, bully beef and brass rods, as the cargo manifest showed? More even than the 4,000 cases of ammunition that were later admitted to have been stowed aboard? Was the *Lusitania* in fact a virtual munitions ship hiding its identity behind 1,198 innocent, doomed people?

Creatures of the deep

Serpents - or just fanciful seadogs' tales

For as long as mariners have sailed the oceans, they have returned with tales of sea monsters and devils of the deep. Most reports are befogged by time, faulty memory – and sometimes alcohol. But there are some that cannot be ignored. . . .

Long before the film *Jaws* made holidaymakers afraid to bathe along North America's Atlantic shoreline, there was a strange series of sensational sightings of terrifying monsters. As early as 1638 there was discussion in the Boston press about sea serpents living off Cape Ann. But it was in 1817 that the New England sea monster mania really got under way. In that year, several people reported sightings off the Massachusetts coast.

The monster was first seen on 6 August, and its activities appeared to be centred on the fishing port of Gloucester. An official inquiry was set up and no fewer than 11 eyewitnesses gave sworn testimony. The descriptions of the monster are therefore well documented. The creature, it appears, was 70 ft long, dark brown and snake-like. A sailor called Amos Story claimed to have seen the monster twice. He said: 'Its head was shaped like a turtle's and was certainly larger than the head of any dog I ever saw. It carried it 10 or 12 inches above the water, and it moved through the water very rapidly.'

The local fisherfolk made a strong net to try to catch the beast, without success. Some formed armed search parties, but only one man got a shot at the creature. He was Matthew Gaffney, a ship's carpenter, who fired twice as the serpent circled his boat. The monster disappeared beneath the surface and, a few days later, left the vicinity altogether. It was last spotted heading north-east off Cape Ann.

Perhaps the creature later changed its mind and headed south again, because, in 1819, there was a report of a giant sea serpent attacking the schooner *Sally* off Long Island. That same year, a second attack was reported on the coast – a small sailing ship was sunk and the survivors blamed a sea monster.

First-hand documentation to substantiate such reports is rare and rightly regarded as suspect by scientifically-minded men. One sighting that was taken seriously, however, occurred on 6 August 1848. The master and several of the crew of the British warship *Daedalus* saw a dark brown head, with a shaggy mane down its neck, peering at them from the waters off the West African coast. Back in his home port, Captain Peter McQuhae reported to his lords commissioners of the Admiralty:

It was an enormous serpent, with head and shoulders kept about four feet constantly above the surface of the sea and, as nearly as we could approximate, there was at the very least 60 feet of the animal. It passed rapidly, but so close under our lee quarters that, had it been a man of my acquaintance, I should easily have recognized his features with the naked eye. The diameter of the serpent was about 15 or 16 inches behind the head, which was, without doubt, that of a snake. It was never, during the 20 minutes that it continued in sight of our glasses, once below the surface. It had no fins, but something like the mane of a horse, or rather a bunch of seaweed, washed about its back. It was seen by the quartermaster, the boatswain's mate and the man at the wheel, in addition to myself.

A similarly described serpent was seen in the same vicinity later that year by an American brig, the *Mary Ann*. Its crew described the creature in much the same terms as Captain McQuhae had done.

Why should an experienced captain of the Royal Navy lie and risk ridicule by reporting the fictitious sighting of a sea monster? There would seem to be even less reason why two respected members of the Royal Zoological Society should do so. In 1905 the two men, Meade Waldo and Michael Nicholl, were on the deck of the steamship *Valhalla* off the coast of Brazil when a mysterious creature surfaced alongside them. It was seen not only by them but by three members of the ship's crew. Waldo recorded the event later:

I saw a large fin or frill sticking out of the water, dark seaweed brown in colour, somewhat crinkled at the edge. I could see under the water the shape of a considerable body. A great head and neck rose out of the water ahead of the frill. The neck was about the thickness of a man's body: the head had a turtle-like appearance, as had also the eye. It moved its neck from side to side in a peculiar manner. We were sailing pretty fast and soon drew away from the object.

New England, West Africa, Brazil – three sightings of similar sea creatures. Could there really be such relics of another age lurking in the depths of the oceans?

Many hundreds of people must believe so, for they claim to have seen them. And not just at sea, but in lakes.

COLL, North-west Scotland: In 1808, a clergyman fishing off the isle of Coll encountered what he described as a hideous, long-necked sea monster. Thirteen local fishermen backed his claim and said that the creature was between 70 and 80 feet long.

PORT Fairy, Victoria: Australian settlers reported capturing a strange creature in a lake in 1848. It had a head like a kangaroo but with a long neck and shaggy mane. It was assumed to be a 'bunyip', a mysterious animal that was once believed to inhabit remote lakes and rivers in many parts of Australia. Its name is an aboriginal word meaning water devil.

GALAPAGOS ISLANDS, Pacific: Two American whalers from New Bedford were sailing alongside each other about 250 miles north-west of the Galapagos Islands in 1852. The captain of one of the ships, the *Monongahela*, sent three boats to tackle what he thought was a basking whale. The men harpooned and killed it – but not before it had sunk two of the boats. The crew of the second ship, the *Rebecca Sims*, watched the struggling creature and later described it as a grey-brown reptile about 150 ft long with gnashing jaws. The *Monongahela*'s captain had the monster's head cut off and preserved in a vat of alcohol on deck. Then he set sail for home with his prize. Neither his ship nor the crew were seen again.

ISLE OF LEWIS, Scotland: The *Times* of 22 March 1856 reported a sighting, in a loch on the Isle of Lewis, of a water creature that 'looked like a huge peat stack or a six-oared boat'. It swallowed a blanket left on the shore by a girl herding cattle, then vanished into the loch.

A gigantic squid found in 1861, 120 miles north-east of Teneriffe.

THE WORLD'S GREATEST MYSTERIES

SOUND OF SLEAT, North-west Scotland: In 1872, two clergymen claimed to have encountered a sea serpent with seven humps or coils stretching 100 ft.

NORTH SEA: In 1881, a Scottish fishing boat, the *Bertie*, was attacked by a fierce, humped monster that almost capsized it. One crewman fired a rifle at the creature but it continued to dive round the boat for several hours before finally disappearing at dusk.

LLANDUDNO, North Wales: A solicitor and a justice of the peace saw 'a dark, undulating creature as big as a large steamer' crossing the bay in 1882. Pressed for a more precise estimate of size, they guessed at 200 ft.

CAPE TOWN, South Africa: The crew of the steamship *Umfuli* saw a sea creature off the Cape in 1893. They described it as a 'giant eel, 80 ft long, with 7-ft jaws'.

ORKNEYS, Scotland: A father and son out sailing encountered a creature 'with giraffe-like neck which rose 18 ft out of the water'.

SANTA CRUZ, California: An enormous carcass was washed up on the beach in 1925. A zoologist who examined it described it as '37 ft long, with a long, thin neck, distended head and a mouth like the bill of a duck'. He expressed himself totally baffled.

PRAH SANDS, Cornwall: A headless corpse was washed up in 1928. It was 30 ft long, with four small flippers and a tapering tail. Species unknown.

CADBURY BAY, Chatham Islands, British Columbia: Canada's best-known sea serpent, nick-named Caddy, was seen by an archivist on holiday in 1932. He said 'fold after fold of its body came to the surface', and he reckoned its total length to be 80 ft. More than 100 other people claimed to have seen Caddy in the same area.

LAKE OKANAGAN, British Columbia: Since the 1950s, there have been frequent sightings in the lake of a huge creature, 70 ft long, with four or more humps. The serpent has been nicknamed the Ogopogo. Its original title was Naitaka ('monster spirit of the lake'), the local Indians' name for it long ago. The most dramatic claim about the Ogopogo is that in 1854 it ate a team of horses belonging to a settler that were swimming across the lake.

GORVAN, Ayrshire, Scotland: A 35-ft-long creature, again described as having a giraffe-like neck, was washed up on the beach in 1953. Locals burnt the carcass.

FLORIDA COAST: Five miles offshore, five US Air Force divers floated on a raft in a thick fog late in 1962. Suddenly they detected a sickening smell and, moments afterwards, 'an enormous head and neck' towered over them. The divers fell into the sea in panic. Only one survived to tell this tale. According to him, the other four were dragged under, screaming in terror.

SIBERIA: A Moscow University team reported seeing an animal looking like a dinosaur in remote Lake Khaiyr in 1964.

GREAT BARRIER REEF, Australia: Diver Robert Le Serer found on the sandy sea bed 'a gigantic beast, 70 ft long, with jaws 4 ft wide'.

CONNEMARA, Ireland: An amateur zoologist set off an explosion in Lough Fadda in 1965 after studying reports of monster sightings there. He was rewarded with the sight of a huge creature threshing around 50 yards offshore.

NORTH ATLANTIC: Captain John Ridgway and Sergeant Chay Blyth were rowing across the Atlantic in their tiny craft in 1966. On one particularly calm night, Ridgway was suddenly awakened by the sound of a mysterious creature 'writhing and twisting' through the ocean. He estimated it as being between 30 and 40 ft long and said it gave off a phosphorescent glow.

LOCH MORAR, West Scotland: In 1969, two fishermen reported seeing a basking monster with a gaping mouth and ribbed back.

Since then, there have been several other reports of monsters in lochs and bays along Scotland's rugged west coast. All, however, pale into insignificance beside the most mysterious monster that ever surfaced from the deep – the creature whose exploits are told in the following story.

The world's best-loved monster

Does a shy but friendly freak called Nessie lurk deep in a Scottish Loch?

More than 10,000 years ago, the last of the Ice Age glaciers gouged out a vast crevice in the Highlands of Scotland. As the ice receded, the 24-mile-long crack that remained filled with water – and provided a home for one of the most mysterious yet best-loved creatures of all time, the Loch Ness Monster.

The legend of the monster – 'Nessie', as she has affectionately come to be known – has haunted Loch Ness ever since she made her first recorded public appearance in 565 AD. In that year, St Columba was travelling to Inverness on a mission to bring Christianity to the Picts. He ordered one of his followers to swim out into the loch and bring back a small boat which had drifted from the shore. As the man started out, 'a strange beast rose from the water', only a few yards from him. St Columba, the story goes, faced the creature and shouted: 'Go thou no further, nor touch that man.' The monster fled.

THE WORLD'S GREATEST MYSTERIES

Ever since, the people of the Great Glen of Loch Ness have recognized Nessie and her forebears as shy, retiring and harmless creatures who rarely visit the surface of their mountain home. Although the locals have known about the inhabitants of their loch for centuries, it is only within the last 50 years that Nessie's fame has spread round the world.

On 14 April 1933, John Mackay and his wife were driving along a newly built road beside Loch Ness. The surface of the water, glass-smooth, mirrored the surrounding peaks. Suddenly Mrs Mackay clutched her husband's arm. 'John,' she gasped, 'what's that . . . out there?'

The sunlit water of the loch was foaming and bubbling as though a volcano had erupted beneath the surface. John Mackay, a local hotel owner, braked sharply. Then he and his wife watched with fear-tinged fascination as a gigantic creature emerged . . . a creature, with at least two humps or coils and a snake-like neck. The monster threshed the surface of the loch until the water was white with foam. Then it dived out of sight.

Since that day in 1933, Nessie has played a tantalizing game of hide-and-seek with scientists, naturalists and thousands of other monster-hunters. There have been more than 3,000 claimed sightings of the elusive creature.

The Mackays' remarkable experience was followed by a similar encounter in November of the same year. This sighting gave the impetus for the Nessie cult to start up in earnest – for it provided the first photograph of the monster. The photograph was taken by engineer Hugh Gray as he walked near his home in the village of Foyers after church one Sunday. The loch was like a millpond but, about 100 yards offshore, he noticed a strange disturbance.

'A rounded back and tail appeared,' he said later, 'and a 40-ft-long creature churned the water, throwing up a cloud of spray.'

NESSIE IDENTIKIT
Eyewitness reports have built up the following picture of Nessie:
Length: **More than 50 ft.**
Body: **At least 30 ft long with a 12-ft girth.**
Head: **Snail-like and very small compared with the body.**
Neck: **About 4-7 ft long, graceful, and as thick as an elephant's trunk.**
Tail: **Rather flat, blunt at the end.**
Flippers: **Two small ones at the front, two large ones at the back.**
Skin: **Snail-like – grey, silver and black.**

Gray's photograph of the monster was sent to Kodak for analysis. The firm agreed that the film had not been tampered with, but the shadowy image was unconvincing as evidence.

A photograph regarded by many experts as still the best was snapped in April 1934 by Robert Kenneth Wilson, a London surgeon of unquestioned character and veracity. Wilson and a friend were driving alongside Loch Ness at the start of a holiday during which they hoped to take wildlife photographs – but the pictures Wilson took that day were of a form of wildlife he had never dreamed existed.

The surgeon and his companion had driven through the night and decided to stop for a rest near Invermorriston. As Wilson stretched his legs beside the loch, he became aware of a small head peering out of the water. He dashed back to his car, grabbed his camera and took a series of snaps. They showed an elegant head and neck, with the faint outline of a body remaining beneath the surface.

These photographs – and the hundreds taken since – were inevitably dismissed by the debunkers of the Nessie legend as showing tree trunks, seals, birds, otters or upturned boats. But whatever the truth, those first reports and pictures of the Loch Ness Monster caused a world-wide sensation.

The loch was soon crawling with tourists, scientists, big-game hunters, schoolboys and hoaxers. Villagers did a roaring bed-and-breakfast trade. Circus-master Bertram Mills offered £20,000 to anyone who could deliver the monster to him alive. Questions were asked in parliament about Nessie's safety. Eventually, a law was passed protecting any creature in the loch from being 'shot, trapped or molested'.

The one thing lacking was a serious, scientific examination of the evidence pouring out of Loch Ness day by day. The main reason for this was that a series of hoaxes – phoney sightings, touched-up photographs and the like – were rapidly turning Nessie into a joke. The canny Scots, it was said, had found a great way of extracting money from the purses of gullible foreigners.

One of the earliest hoaxes involved big-game hunter Michael Wetherell, a Fellow of Britain's highly-respected Zoological Society. In December 1933, he found what appeared to be the monster's footprint on the shore of the loch. Wetherell said: 'It is a four-legged beast. It has feet or pads about eight inches across. I judge it to be a powerful animal about 20 ft long.'

Amid intense excitement, plaster casts of the footprint were sent to London's Natural History Museum. Experts there identified the print as 'resembling that of a hippopotamus'. And then it was found that a mounted, dried foot of a hippo was missing from the museum at Inverness, only a few miles from the loch.

Of the three most sensational sightings reported in 1933 and 1934, two were by locals, the third by a London businessman.

This is how Alexander Campbell, a local freelance journalist, described what he saw on a June day in 1934:

> As I left my cottage close by the loch, the creature rose from the water like a prehistoric monster. It was 30 ft long with a long, snake-like neck and a flat tail. Where the neck and body joined there was a hump. The monster basked in the sunshine until the noise of a boat from the Caledonian Canal disturbed it. It lowered its neck and dived, leaving a minor tidal wave behind it.

A few weeks before Campbell's sighting, a monk, Brother Richard Horan, of St Benedict's Abbey, Fort Augustus, reported:

> I saw the monster rise out of the waters of Loch Ness, and watched it for 20 minutes. The head and neck protruded from the water at an angle of 45 degrees. It had a thickset neck, the lower side of which was silvery in colour. It had a snub nose. When a motor-boat came within earshot the monster sank, slowly.

London company director George Spicer told of a somewhat different but equally fantastic encounter with the monster:

> My wife and I were motoring along the loch-side when we saw an extraordinary animal crossing the road about 200 yards ahead. It had a long neck a bit thicker than an elephant's trunk and a large body about five feet high. It had dark skin of a loathsome texture and it moved in a jerky sort of way. I speeded up, but the creature vanished into the thick undergrowth.

Other monster-hunters reported seeing the beast open and shut its mouth. Some said it had a mane, like a horse's. One spotter claimed to have been close enough to see drops of water falling from scaly skin as the monster shook itself.

By the summer of 1934 Nessie's fame had spread far enough to interest John Earnest Williamson, an American who was a leading expert in underwater photography. He arrived at Loch Ness with a contraption he called a photosphere – a submersible, windowed globe, in which he sat in an armchair taking underwater photographs.

What Williamson did not know before he reached Loch Ness was that below 30 ft the water is first dark brown and then an inky black that dims the most piercing lights. This murkiness is caused by particles of peat which for many thousands of years have been washed down the mountains into the loch. Williamson abandoned his plan and went home.

Each year up to the outbreak of World War Two, scores of sightings were reported and many more photographs taken. But during the war years there were no tourists. The roads round the loch were used only by a few locals and the armed forces. Nessie stopped making news.

It was not until 1947 that she reared herself into the front pages again. In that year, the clerk to Inverness County Council and three of his friends reported that they had seen humps of a beast that was swimming in the loch. The monster-hunting season had opened once more.

In 1951, local woodsman Lachlan Stuart rose early and stepped out of his

The Loch Ness monster at Castle Urquhart.

croft door to milk his cow. He glanced towards the loch, stopped in his tracks, then dashed back into his croft to grab a camera. He ran with it down to the shore and took one picture before the shutter jammed. His photograph showed three huge humps sticking as much as four feet out of the water. Out of the frame, but described by Stuart, was a neck topped by a head like that of a sheep, except that it was blackish and had no hair, wool or scales. From his description, corroborated by a friend who also rushed to the water's edge, the monster must have been between 50 and 60 ft long.

Recorded sightings over the succeeding years included the following:

1953: Several men cutting timber by the side of the loch reported that they had watched the monster for two minutes.

1954: A fishing boat entering Loch Ness from the Caledonian Canal, the waterway which links the loch with the sea, received on its echo sounder the imprint of a huge creature moving through the water at a depth of nearly 500 ft. Its length was 'at least 50 ft'.

1959: Automobile Association patrolman James Alexander stopped his motorcycle and sidecar at a phone booth on the edge of the loch. Alexander, who had his back to the loch, suddenly got a creepy feeling that he was being watched. He turned – and there, he claims, was the monster's head and neck sticking seven feet out of the water. He flagged down a passing truck, and the driver confirmed his story.

1960: Torquil MacLeod and his wife were driving near Invermorriston when they saw a large creature basking on a beach on the opposite shore. MacLeod watched it through binoculars for nine minutes before it flopped into the water. He described it as having grey, elephant-like skin and large paddle-like flippers. He estimated its length as 60 ft.

1960: Aviation engineer Tim Dinsdale took the first movie film of the monster. The four-minute sequence showed a humped-back creature zigzagging through the water at ten miles an hour. Dinsdale was so convinced by what he filmed that he gave up his career to live by the loch and hunt for Nessie.

1961: More than a dozen guests at a loch-side hotel claimed to have watched a beast 30 ft long, with two humps, rise out of the water and remain in view for six minutes.

1962: World-famous British naturalist Peter Scott helped launch the Loch Ness Phenomena Investigation Bureau to organize a serious study of the mystery. For ten years, bureau volunteers and one or two full-time workers kept watch on the loch. Their cameras were at the ready round the clock. They logged many sightings of their own and put on record scores of eye-witness stories. But the only prize worth having for such an effort eluded them. They, too, failed to get the definitive photograph of Nessie.

Perhaps the most useful thing the bureau did was to send films of what was claimed to be the monster to the Joint Air Reconnaissance Intelligence Centre, for independent analysis. The centre reported that one film showed an object which was neither a boat nor a submarine but which appeared to be 'an animate object, 12 to 16 ft long, 3 ft high and 6 ft wide'. Another film showed a similar object 6 ft wide and 5 ft high.

But the Loch Ness Phenomena Investigation Bureau failed to grasp its greatest chance of solving the mystery. In 1971, Tim Dinsdale was directing a 100-strong bureau team when a black, snake-like creature reared from the water. Dinsdale had five cameras but was too astonished to use any of them.

Frank Searle is another of the small number of fanatics who have taken up monster-hunting as a profession. In 1969, this Cockney ex-paratrooper gave up his job as a grocery-store manager, bought some first-rate photographic equipment and went to live in a tent by Loch Ness.

Searle then sat watching and waiting for his chance to make a fortune. For he reckoned that if his patience was rewarded with the first totally convincing pictures of Nessie, they could be worth £250,000 in world-wide publication fees.

Searle claims to have seen the monsters – he estimates there is a colony of at least 20 of them – 24 times. He says: 'They're bulky, 12 to 16 ft long with a sheep-like head and a 7-ft neck. They have paddle-like flippers.'

In 1972 and again in 1976, Searle took photographs which he claims were of the monsters. They were published round the world and described as 'the most amazing yet'. But a Glasgow zoology professor said of them: 'My first impression is that this is the carcass of an animal which has been in the water for some time. Or a tree.'

Throughout the 1960s and the 70s, monster-hunting continued as a major British sport. And Nessie became the Scottish Tourist Board's biggest single asset.

A diver who went down to recover a drowned man's body from the loch reported an eerie sight. He had seen huge rock ledges piled high with eels 'as thick as a man's torso'.

A frogman working in the loch claimed that Nessie had surfaced only 30 yards away from him. He said: 'It was about 30 ft long, with a long neck, an otter-like tail and four fins. I shouted to my mate, and it dived out of sight.'

Various ways of cornering or enticing Nessie were suggested. Dragging the loch with steel nets at a cost of £200,000 was ruled out. So was a scheme to induce Nessie to bask in water warmed by giant hot plates sunk in the loch. Proving tests on a British mini submarine took it 450 ft below the loch's surface. Its occupants saw nothing. 'It's as black as hell down there,' they said.

In 1969 the American invasion of Loch Ness began. Dan Taylor, a former

US Navy submarine crewman from Atlanta, Georgia, had spent five years and £20,000 building a tiny yellow glass-fibre submarine which he named *Viperfish*. He planned to fire darts from it to remove a sliver of Nessie's flesh. Taylor claimed to have picked up Nessie on his echo sounder, but never for long enough to track her. He also said that *Viperfish* had been sucked into a 130-ft-deep hole. But he repeated John Williamson's mistake of 35 years earlier. He had not realized that the loch's waters are impenetrably dark below 30 ft. He packed up and went home.

In 1970 Dr Robert Rines, president of the Academy of Applied Science, in Belmont, Massachusetts, spent two weeks at Loch Ness. He headed a four-man team equipped with sonar gear, underwater cameras and a 'sex cocktail' made from the reproductive essences of creatures such as sea cows, eels and sea lions. The team also had tapes, to be played underwater, of the sounds made by a variety of water creatures mating, fighting and 'talking'.

Rines later claimed that the sex cocktail had enabled him to make contact with creatures 'one hundred times the size of any fish in the loch'. They lived, he said, on a shelf 200 ft from the loch's shore. Two years later, in Boston, Rines produced colour and black-and-white photographs taken in the loch and showing what appeared to be a very large flipper attached to a cow-shaped body.

Almost at the same time as Rines' expedition, another US team reached the loch. This one, sponsored by the Cutty Sark whisky firm, was led by Professor James Ullrich, of the Smithsonian Institute. Ullrich had taken the precaution of paying £15 to insure himself at Lloyds for £5,000 against being bitten or maimed by the monster. He said: 'The monster is no longer a myth, but a scientific reality.' And a member of his team was just as certain: 'There's no question. There is a monster. Nobody seriously believes, do they, that the thing is a drainpipe, eight tree roots, or a biscuit crumb on the lens of somebody's camera? Because if it is, I don't think I can stand it.'

Cutty Sark had arranged with Lloyds of London for payment of £1 million to anyone who caught the monster alive and unharmed before May 1972. There were no serious claimants, and Ullrich's team, using much the same techniques as the Rines expedition had employed, including sex lures, failed to get any better evidence than its predecessors to support or crack the legend.

Then the Japanese jumped on the Nessie bandwagon. In 1973, Yoshiou Kou, the 36-year-old showman who had brought Muhammad Ali and Tom Jones to Japan, led a 15-strong team to Loch Ness. A Japanese business consortium had raised the cash, and Kou announced that his team would use two submarines which would arrive soon from Tokyo. But when Kou's divers saw how inky the loch water was, they cancelled their mission.

Meanwhile, the amateur monster-watchers seemed to be having more success. In 1974, truck driver Andy Call and his mate Henry Wilson were driving alongside the loch when the water foamed and a creature surfaced. Call says: 'It was black, 50 or 60 feet long, with a horse-like head. We watched it for 15 minutes. It submerged three times.'

The following year, two female university graduates from Munich claimed to have seen several humps moving around in the water. Ten days later, four French girls reported a similar sighting. They were joined by a party of English tourists who supported their story.

In 1978, lorry driver Hugh Chisholm and his wife Mhairi were driving along the loch towards their home at Inverness when they saw the monster. Mrs Chisholm said: 'It was really huge, with the head and one hump clearly visible. When it vanished underwater, it left large waves behind.' She said that on a previous occasion her husband had claimed to have seen Nessie – and she had laughed at him.

However, perhaps the most convincing evidence of the existence of a monster in Loch Ness has come as a result of a second expedition to Scotland by Dr Rines. On 20 June 1975, his team lowered two underwater cameras into the loch near ancient Urquhart Castle. They were at depths of 40 ft and 80 ft and they took 2,000 pictures at intervals of 75 seconds, aided by immensely powerful strobe lights. The resulting photographs appeared to depict a reddish-brown beast with a fat body about 12 ft long and an arching neck about 8 ft long. The head of the creature was hideous, with gaping jaws and two tube-like protruberances on top of it.

It at last convinced veteran monster-hunter Sir Peter Scott of Nessie's existence. He said: 'There are probably between 20 and 50 of them down there. I believe they are related to the plesiosaurs.'

The plesiosaur has not been seen on earth for 7 million years. The monster-hunters believe, therefore, that Nessie's ancestors may have been cut off from the sea when the loch was formed at the end of the last Ice Age. Loch Ness is up to 1,000 ft deep – deeper than the North Sea – and its vastness and remoteness would have allowed the creatures to flourish undisturbed as survivors from another millennium.

But why the spate of sightings from 1933 onwards? The monster-hunters have an explanation for that, too.

The road that John Mackay and his wife were driving along when they first spotted Nessie on 14 April 1933 had only recently been built and was the first to skirt the loch-side. To construct it, thousands of tons of rock had been blasted into the loch, and dense vegetation which for centuries had shrouded its banks had been cut down. This blasting, the experts say, destroyed the monsters' primeval underwater lairs – and left them, for the first time, homeless wanderers in the loch.

Curse of 'The Flying Dutchman'

Many have sighted the ship doomed to sail on forever

What was – or is – *The Flying Dutchman*? And why has a seemingly far-fetched sailor's yarn maintained such a fascination over the centuries – even for those who don't go to sea? The cautionary tale of the ship's captain who made a pact with the Devil was well known to seamen long before Wagner's famous opera. A fanciful story, certainly, but every few years, even to this day, the legend reappears as a weird and frightening warning.

The legend originated in the 17th century, when an unscrupulously greedy Dutchman, Captain Hendrik van der Decken, set sail from Amsterdam to make his fortune in the East Indies. All went smoothly until his ship tried to round the Cape of Good Hope. A fierce storm blew up, ripped the sails to shreds and battered the ship's timbers day after day.

At this point in the story, legend becomes mythology – the Devil is reputed to have appeared before the captain and asked him if he were willing to challenge God's will and head straight into the storm. The impatient Dutchman agreed, and brought down upon himself the curse of the Almighty – that he and his ghostly ship should roam the seas ceaselessly until Judgement Day.

It is a tale that does not beg to be taken too seriously. And yet, over the centuries, there have been numerous sightings of strange, old ghostly ships resembling the battered East-Indiaman, many of them from the area where *The Flying Dutchman* originally disappeared. Not only that, but the mariners' belief that anyone who sees the phantom ship will soon encounter bad luck has regularly been fulfilled.

Some of the witnesses of the nautical apparition have been of the utmost respectability. On 11 July 1881, Prince George, a 16-year-old Royal Navy midshipman who was later to become King George V, made an historic entry in his log book aboard *HMS Inconstant* off the coast of Australia. He wrote:

At 4 am *The Flying Dutchman* crossed our bows. She emitted a strange phosphorescent light as of a phantom ship all aglow, in the midst of which light the masts, spars and sails of a brig 200 yards distant stood out in strong relief as she came up on the port bow, where also the officer of the watch from the bridge saw her, as did the quarter-deck midshipman, who was sent forward at once to the forecastle, but on arriving there no vestige nor any sign whatever of any material ship was to be seen either near or right away to the horizon, the night being clear and the sea calm.

It is obvious that the young prince was deeply impressed by the vision, which was seen by 13 other men aboard the *Inconstant* and two sister ships. Later that day, the seaman who had first sighted *The Flying Dutchman* fell to his death from a mast. The death of the admiral of the fleet followed shortly afterwards.

The Flying Dutchman has been logged by several ships off the Cape of Good Hope, but perhaps the most astonishing sightings have been made by people standing on dry land.

In September 1942, four people were relaxing on the terrace of their home at Mouille Point, Cape Town, when they spotted an ancient sailing ship heading into Table Bay. They followed its progress for about 15 minutes before it disappeared from view behind Robben Island.

Three years earlier, in March 1939, almost 100 people saw the phantom East-Indiaman. They were sunbathing on Glencairn beach in False Bay, south-east of Cape Town, when a fully rigged sailing ship appeared out of the heat haze. It passed across the bay with its sails full, although there was not a breath of wind. The ship seemed to be heading for a distant, isolated beach. But, as the crowd of excited witnesses looked on, *The Flying Dutchman* vanished as suddenly as it had appeared.

Other parts of the world also have their own 'Flying Dutchman'.

Britain's phantom ship haunts the Goodwin Sands, the sandbank in the English Channel that has claimed 234 wrecks. It was on the Goodwins that the *Lady Lovibond* ran aground on 13 February 1748. The ship had left London for Oporto, Portugal, with its newly married skipper, Captain Simon Peel, his bride and some of the wedding guests. But, according to legend, a jealous mate, who was also in love with the bride, killed Peel and steered the ship on a suicide course on to the Goodwins. The entire company was drowned.

On 13 February 1798 – 50 years later to the day – a three-masted schooner identical to the *Lady Lovibond* was seen heading for the Goodwins. The crew of a fishing boat followed and heard the sounds of a celebration and women's voices. The schooner hit the sands, broke up – and vanished.

The same vision was reported by another ship's crew exactly 50 years later. It was seen again, by a group of watchers near Deal, Kent, on 13 February 1898. Does the phantom appear every 50 years? Watchers were on the lookout on 13 February 1948. Visibility was poor and they saw nothing.

North America's 'Flying Dutchman' lurks off the coast of Rhode Island. Its name is the *Palatine*, and it left Holland in 1752, packed with colonists heading for Philadelphia. But a winter storm blew the ship off course, the

captain was lost overboard, and the panicking crew mutinied. The passengers spent Christmas Day in confusion and terror. Two days later, the *Palatine* ran aground on rocks off Block Island and began to break up. As the storm abated, the doomed ship began to slip back off the rocks, drawn out to sea again by the tide. But before it could do so, dozens of local fishermen descended on the *Palatine*, took off the passengers and looted the ship.

When their frenzied rampage had ended and they had stripped the *Palatine* of everything of value, the fishermen set it on fire and watched it drift, ablaze from bow to stern, to the open sea. But even the tough fishermen were struck with horror when they saw a woman appear from her hiding place on the *Palatine* and stand on the deck screaming for help until the flames engulfed her.

For more than two centuries since, the *Palatine* has reappeared off the New England coast, a battered sailing ship swept by blood-red flames.

Chapter Three

Mysteries of The Skies

Ever since man looked to the heavens and envied the power of birds to fly, the mysteries directly above his head have intrigued him – the sky, the stars, infinity . . . What is the secret of the black holes in space? Where do flying saucers come from? And was a holocaust that once devastated part of Siberia caused by visitors from space? Man may have conquered the skies but he is a long way from solving their deepest mysteries.

Encounters of the third kind

The case for UFOs is backed by astronauts – and the US President

When Barney and Betty Hill told their story, no one believed them. Barney, an American social worker, told how he had been driving with his wife along a lonely road in New Hampshire when a spaceship landed in front of their car and a strange figure got out. There followed a lost two hours which were totally erased from the Hills' memories. The next thing they recalled was looking at their watches and finding themselves on the same road but 30 miles further on.

The couple's story was intriguing but unbelievable – until they were put under hypnosis and questioned about their missing two hours. The stories they then told were identical. They said they had been taken aboard the spaceship and subjected to tests. They also drew pictures of the walls of the craft, which were covered in star maps.

The maps were shown to astronomers, who found them puzzling. For the charts included distant stars which were not known to astronomers at that time – but which have since been discovered.

The Hills are just two out of millions of people round the world who have seen what are now termed UFOs – Unidentified Flying Objects. And among those millions are the chosen few – the people who claim to have encountered the occupants of such spacecraft face to face. Such witnesses risk being labelled cranks, drunks or liars when they report their strange encounters. But nowadays scientists are loth to dismiss such evidence. After all, US President Jimmy Carter claims to have seen a UFO: 'an advancing and receding object which changed from blue to red, shining with a luminous glow'.

Astronaut Gordon Cooper says: 'Intelligent beings from other planets regularly visit our world. The US government and the space agency have a great deal of evidence of such visits, but they keep quiet so as not to alarm people.'

Ed Mitchell, who was the sixth man on the moon, says: 'I am completely convinced that some UFO sightings are real. The question is not whether there are UFOs, but *what* they are.'

The Royal Air Force's late Air Chief Marshal Lord Dowding was a staunch believer in 'flying saucers'. As early as 1954, he said: 'I have never seen a flying saucer, yet I believe they exist. Cumulative evidence has been assembled in such quantity that, for me at any rate, it brings complete conviction. There is no alternative to accepting the theory that they come from an extra-terrestial source. For the first time in recorded history, intelligible communication may become possible between the earth and other planets.'

Although Dowding admitted never having seen a flying saucer he would have received numerous reports of UFO sightings by the fliers under his command during World War Two. But UFO reports began a long time before our present airborne age. One of the firmest sightings of all time, for instance, was made more than 700 years ago. . . .

On New Year's Day 1254, a group of English monks at St Albans stared skywards in awe at 'a kind of large ship, elegantly shaped and of marvellous colour'. Thirty-six years later, monks at Byland Abbey, Yorkshire, recorded the sighting of 'a large, round silver disc' in the sky. And in 1566, one of the most spectacular UFO phenomena in history occurred when a host of glowing discs covered the sky over Basle, Switzerland.

But it is within the last century that the UFO mystery has really captured the imagination. The sightings seem to have run in phases.

A vintage year was 1897, when a rash of reports came out of the United States. A large 'space object' landed at Carlinville, Illinois, but took off at speed when curious townspeople approached. More than 10,000 people saw a mysterious 'airship with flashing lights' hover over Kansas City for ten

---

THE FIRST 'SAUCERS'

On 24 June 1947, a clear and sunny day, American civilian pilot Kenneth Arnold was flying over Mount Rainier in Washington State, when he saw in the distance a formation of nine glistening objects. At first he thought they were fighter planes, but as they darted towards him and skimmed the mountain tops at incredible speed, Arnold realized that they were 'like nothing I had ever seen before'. He watched them move erratically across the horizon and estimated their speed at 1,300 miles an hour. When he landed he sought words to describe the mystery objects . . . and came up with the phrase: 'like saucers skimming over water'. Thus was the term 'flying saucers' born.

minutes before shooting off into space. In the same year, a member of the House of Representatives, Alexander Hamilton, watched an enormous object land outside his home near Le Roy, Kansas. He described it as 'cigar-shaped, some 300 ft long, transparent and brilliantly lighted'. Six strange creatures were visible within the craft, but, when approached by members of Hamilton's staff, it took off and flew out of sight at amazing speed.

There was another spate of sightings in 1909, this time in Britain. Within two months, there were reports of spacecraft from 40 towns. The most dramatic was from Caerphilly, South Wales, where a large cylindrical object was seen to land. Two creatures got out, but, when approached, dashed back inside and took off. There was a similar spate of UFOs in New Zealand that same year, and in Ontario, Canada, four years later.

The advent of air travel led to a dramatic increase in the number of UFO reports. Perhaps the first air-to-air sighting was by pioneer aviator Francis Chichester, later to become famous as a round-the-world yachtsman. Chichester was flying his plane *Gipsy Moth* from Australia to New Zealand when a strange airship appeared alongside him. It was circular and glowed brightly. It followed him for some miles before accelerating into the distance.

There were many UFO sightings during World War Two – not surprisingly, considering the increased aerial activity – but a security veil was drawn over most of them. It was after the war that the dossiers on UFOs and flying saucers really began to bulge.

1947: American pilot Kenneth Arnold sights flying saucer formation (see panel).

1948: Hundreds see huge white object in the sky over Madisonville, Kentucky. Three P51 Mustangs are sent up to investigate. One of the pilots gives chase as the object speeds away. The wreckage of his plane is found later that day.

1952: Amateur astronomer George Adamski, of Palomar, California, produces the most famous (but nowadays generally disregarded) photographs of a UFO. Taken through his reflecting telescope, they purport to show a flying saucer hovering half-a-mile up.

1952: Mysterious glowing craft lands and then lifts off vertically from Marseilles airport, France.

1952: Mysterious lights over Washington DC, labelled by the press as the Washington Invasion (see panel).

1953: US Air Force F89 jet chases a UFO over Lake Superior. Trackers watch the pursuit on radar, see the plane catch up then disappear from the screen. UFO speeds north out of radar net. Searchers fail to find any trace of the jet.

1953: L. Gordon Cooper, later to become a US astronaut, sees a UFO while

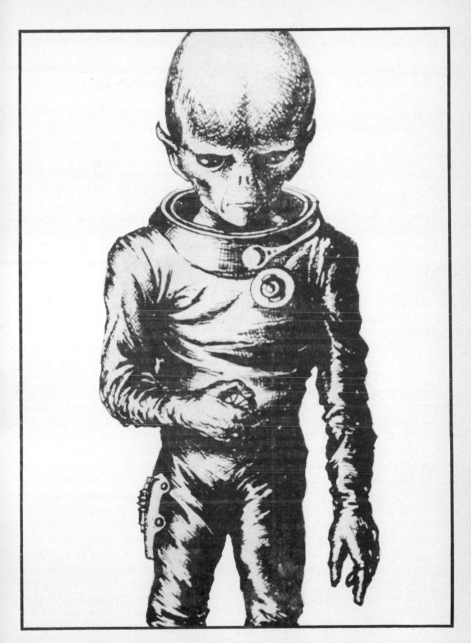

A popular image of a UFO occupant.

piloting a jet over Germany. He says: 'I now firmly believe in extra-terrestial craft.'

1953; Pilot of DC-6 airliner flying from Wake Island in the Pacific to Los Angeles radios to report UFOs approaching. Radio falls silent. Searchers later find wreckage and 20 bodies.

1954: Crew and passengers of a Boeing Stratocruiser flying from New York to London watch a formation of seven craft travelling alongside the airliner for several minutes. The UFOs appear to be six flying saucers and a larger 'mother ship'.

1956: Glowing UFOs are seen by dozens of eyewitnesses over eastern England. Confirmed by radar trackers at Lakenheath air base, Suffolk.

1958: Two men in a car approach a 100-ft-long glowing, egg-shaped object hovering above a bridge near Baltimore, Maryland. It shoots skywards in a flash of light and heat. The men's faces later show signs of radiation burns.

From the early 1960s, a wholly inexplicable plethora of UFO reports began to be noted – all from rural areas of Britain. Over the years, a pattern developed and two of the areas have become famous for their space visitations. One is centred on Warminster, in Wiltshire, and the other is a part of Wales that has become known as the Broadhaven Triangle. The people who live in these and other UFO-prone areas of Britain have not always emerged unscathed from their encounters with the spacecraft.

It was one o'clock in the morning when Mrs Pauline Coombs had her close encounter in the Broadhaven Triangle. She was sitting with her husband in their lonely farm cottage when she glanced towards the window. Mrs Coombs stifled a shriek of terror when she saw framed in the window 'a towering 7-ft figure. . . . It was dressed entirely in silver and was surrounded by a luminous glow, but it had no face – no features at all, just an empty black hole'.

Terrified, the young wife was at first speechless. When she regained her voice, she screamed at her husband, Billy, who was sitting with his back to the window. He phoned neighbours for help but by the time they arrived the figure had vanished. Mrs Coombs said: 'We were sweating, trembling and crying with fear. Our dog, which normally barks at the slightest sound, just ran around in circles and later refused to leave the house.' A local farmer who was first on the scene said: 'The couple were terrified – scared out of their wits.'

They had reason to be. Only three days earlier the Coombs family had been out for a drive when their car was pursued by what they described as a glowing ball in the sky which chased them back to their cottage in Ripperton, Dyfed.

A year later the family had their most extraordinary encounter of all. They were out with two of their five children when a silver disc appeared in the sky. It circled them, then headed off towards the nearby coast and seemed to disappear into a large rock. The family followed the path the UFO had taken.

'When we got to the rock,' said Mrs Coombs, 'we saw two tall figures in glowing silver suits. They walked around for a while, then just vanished into the rock.'

UFOs have picked out the Broadhaven Triangle for no apparent reason. One of Mrs Coombs's neighbours, housewife Josephine Hewison, looked out of her bedroom window one morning and saw what she claims was a 50-ft silver spacecraft standing beside her greenhouse. After about ten minutes, it took off and flew away.

Louise Bassett, wife of a restaurant owner from Ferryside, Carmarthen, said: 'I was driving home one night when my radio went dead. At the same time I saw flashing lights in the sky. I took a detour to avoid them but they appeared again three miles further on.' When Mrs Bassett's radio cut out, so did dozens of other people's radios and televisions in the area. Mrs Bassett's

---

'THEY'RE TELLING THE TRUTH'
American medical experts have used hypnosis to test the truth of stories told by people claiming to have had personal encounters with alien beings. The results have often been startling.

A 16-year-old high school boy, who claimed to have seen a tall, green-eyed creature in his garden, agreed to tests at the South-west Montana Mental Health Centre, Anaconda. The youth had forgotten what happened after he encountered the creature, but under hypnosis he said that three aliens had dragged him into a spacecraft. They had examined him, then told him he would forget the entire incident.

Dr Kent Newman, who conducted the experiment, said: 'I believe that the boy honestly reported what he had experienced.'

A similar view is taken by Dr Leo Sprinkle, of the University of Wyoming, Laramie, whose tests revealed that most space encounters took place against the subjects' wills and that they were generally terrified and highly emotional. They often experienced physical effects and amnesia. Dr Sprinkle said: 'I don't know whether these people experienced physical or out-of-the-body encounters, but my personal and professional bias is to accept their claims as real.'

Dr Alvin Lawson, of California State University, Long Beach, is more cautious. After placing under hypnosis several witnesses who claimed to have been abducted, he said: 'Their stories are at least partially true. But that does not mean that their experiences are necessarily "real" physical events - any more than hallucinations are.'

dog was in the car with her at the time. 'He has never been the same since that night,' she said.

Shop assistant Stephen Taylor was out walking near his home ten miles from the Coombs's cottage late one night when he saw a glowing object in the sky. He said: 'It was 40 or 50 ft across and the light seemed to be coming from the underneath. Suddenly a dog shot out of some bushes ahead of me. Then a tall figure popped up right next to me. It was dressed in silver. I was terrified, so I took a swing at it, then fled. When I got home that night my pet dog started snarling at me. It wouldn't let me get near it.'

Perhaps the most convincing witnesses of all are the children of Broadhaven Primary School. Fifteen of them – 14 boys and a girl – were playing football when they rushed inside to tell their headmaster that they had seen a spaceship in the sky. The head, Ralph Llewellyn, split them into groups and asked them to draw pictures of what they had seen. He compared the finished results and was astounded by their similarity. Over years of questioning, the children stuck to their story.

A similar sighting was made at Wawne Primary School, 250 miles away in Humberside. Twenty children aged six and seven dashed to the study of headmaster Michael Yates and told him they had seen a strange object in the sky. The children described a classic UFO – 'like a dish upside down and with a hump on the top'.

At Elgin, in north-east Scotland, two ten-year-old girls described 'a silver-coloured saucer with a bump on the top' which they had seen hovering in a wood. The craft glowed with a red light, they said, and a silver-suited man stood beside it. Mrs Caroline McLennan, mother of one of the girls, said: 'When my daughter told me about it, I remembered having heard a strange whirring noise and saying to my neighbour: "Sounds like a flying saucer." The girls led us back to the wood and we found a big patch of flattened grass. The leaves on the trees nearby were scorched.' A saucer-shaped craft with a beam of light shining down from it was independently witnessed by several people in the same area on the same night.

Karen Iveson, a young tax officer, saw it while out with her boyfriend in Parley Cross, Dorset. She said: 'It was like nothing I had ever seen in my life before. It was a large silvery disc-shaped object with a conical silvery green light beam shining down from the centre of it. The ship hovered over a field for ages, then sped away at a fantastic speed just above tree level. We both panicked a bit.'

The same vision startled Mrs Pauline Fall and a friend. Mrs Fall said: 'It looked like the underneath of a dinner plate, and out of the centre of it came a cone of silver light. The light was shining straight on to my car, and the craft was getting lower and closer to us all the time. My stomach went ice cold.

Then the craft vanished. The car has never worked quite the same since that night.'

A little to the north of the Dorset sightings lies the UFO 'capital' of the world – Warminster, in Wiltshire – UFO-watchers in this small town started an information centre and newsletter to keep their members informed of the latest sightings. Dozens of reports have been registered of a glittering flying saucer known as the 'Warminster Thing'.

Neil Pike and his wife, Sally, are two of the Warminster UFO-watchers, and they claim twice to have seen spacecraft and spacemen. On one occasion the couple were with a party of sky-watchers on a hill near Warminster when they spotted what they thought were two UFOs. Mrs Pike said: 'Suddenly the air became warmer and two shadowy figures appeared. They were very tall and we could see their outlines – but they appeared to be made out of mist or smoke. They had no features.' Her husband, a bank security officer, walked towards the figures. They faded from his vision. But Mrs Pike said: 'The rest of us watched as he walked straight through the figures and out the other side.'

Though Warminster may be the 'UFO capital' it is the United States which claims to have recorded the biggest and the most startling appearances of alien spacecraft.

1964: Police patrolman Lonnie Zamora sees a UFO land near the town of Socorro, New Mexico. He races to the spot and encounters two strange figures, which he describes as 4 ft high, standing beside a glowing, oval spacecraft. They flee inside and take off. Indentations that could have been made by the UFO's landing gear are later discovered.

1965: James McDivitt, in orbit 100 miles above the earth in Gemini 4, sees cylindrical object with antennae protruding. Starts photographing it but McDivitt and fellow astronaut Ed White become alarmed that craft will collide with theirs and they prepare to take evasive action. Before they can do so the UFO disappears.

1965: William Howell and his family, of Foggy Hill, Texas, are out in their car when an amazingly bright blue light appears overhead and keeps pace with them. As Howell accelerates, so does the light. Eventually, the UFO shoots away at incredible speed.

1965: Farm workers at Kelly, Kentucky, report shooting at alien creatures 100 yards away. Whenever one of the creatures is hit by a rifle bullet it keels over – then floats upright again without making any sound.

1972: Muhammad Ali is on a training session in New York's Central Park when he encounters a UFO. He says: 'I was out jogging just before sunrise when this bright light hovered over me. It just seemed to be watching me. It was like a huge electric light bulb in the sky.'

1973: John Gilligan, governor of Ohio, reports seeing a UFO near Ann

Arbor, Michigan. He describes it as 'a vertical shaft of light which glowed amber'.

1973: Jimmy Carter, then governor of Georgia, is sitting on a verandah with 20 other people after an official dinner at Thomastown, Georgia, when, according to Carter, they witness a UFO 'which looked as big as the moon and changed colour several times from red to green'.

1973: Astronauts Jack Lousma, Owen Garriot and Alan Bean, 270 miles up in Skylab 2, photograph a rotating red UFO for ten minutes.

1973: Police chief Jeff Greenshaw, of Falkville, Alabama, drives up to a 6-ft-tall metallic figure on the road. The figure flees up the road, pursued by Greenshaw in his patrol car. The creature outpaces the car and vanishes into the distance.

1973: Off-duty shipyard workers Charles Hickson and Calvin Parker are fishing near Pascagoula, Mississippi, when, according to the two anglers, a 100-ft-long silvery craft hovers before them. A hatch opens and three grey-coloured aliens float out. They have wrinkled skin, claw-like hands and a single slit for an eye. The anglers are miraculously lifted off their riverbank and join the space creatures, who float back inside the craft. Once inside, the two men are laid on their backs on a table and a camera descends from the ceiling to examine them. After about 20 minutes the two friends are released by the aliens and then report their experience. They are hypnotized and given lie-detector tests but their stories remain the same.

1975: Forestry worker Travis Walton is a passenger in a truck with five friends near Snowflake, Arizona, when they see a bright light hovering above some trees. Driver Mike Rogers pulls up. Walton leaps out and runs towards the UFO, but before he gets far there is a bright flash and he falls to the ground. His friends drive on to get out of the firing line but return shortly afterwards to rescue Walton. He has disappeared. Five days later he reappears in the nearby town of Heber and claims to have spent the time with 'weird creatures like human foetuses'. Walton is given a lie-detector test which indicates that he is telling the truth.

1977: Two off-duty nurses are out walking on Staten Island, New York, when they see a cigar-shaped object land in a lightly wooded area. Thoroughly shaken, they stop a police patrol car which goes to the scene – just in time to see a UFO 'bigger than the Goodyear airship' shoot into the air and speed away. The police chase it across the state line into New Jersey, but it vanishes in a silver blur.

1978: Sir Eric Gairey, prime minister of Grenada, tries unsuccessfully to have the United Nations officially investigate UFOs. He says he has seen one – 'a brilliant golden light travelling at tremendous speed'.

1978: German-born movie actress Elke Sommer is in the garden of her Los

Angeles home when a shiny orange ball, about 20 ft in diameter, appears out of the blue 'glowing and floating about like a big moon'. It hovers towards her and she flees into the house. When she reappears it has vanished.

In that same year, 1978, two of the world's great mysteries merged into one for just two hours. That was the length of time that radar operators managed to keep track of a UFO as it zigzagged around the Bermuda Triangle, a mysterious offshore graveyard of ships and planes that have disappeared without trace.

THE WORLD'S GREATEST MYSTERIES

The UFO was also seen by eye-witnesses. It was a circular craft emitting red, green and white light and travelling in an incredibly erratic manner. No civilian or military aircraft were in the vicinity at the time. Experts at the Pinecastle electronic warfare range, near Astor, Florida, struggled to track the strange craft as it kept abruptly changing direction. One moment it would be stationary, the next it would accelerate to 500 miles an hour.

One of the radar operators said: 'It manoeuvred in such a manner and at such speeds that it could not have been an airplane or a helicopter. I've never seen anything like it and I don't want to see anything like it again.'

The most remarkable spate of UFO sightings in recent years began in the closing days of 1978. An Australian television team were flying over the Kalkoura area of New Zealand's South Island on New Year's Eve following earlier UFO reports by airline pilots. The newsmen took the first worthwhile television film of a UFO – one of several round objects marked with bright orange rings which darted around their plane.

At the same time as the sighting, air traffic controllers at Wellington recorded a series of erratic blips on the control tower radar. They moved around the screen at remarkable speed for more than three hours. One of the operators said: 'Six pilots have seen UFOs in the past ten days, and there has been a host of radar sightings. There is obviously something strange out there.'

Not to be outdone by the Australians' TV scoop, a New Zealand camera team took to the skies in the same area of South Island early in January, 1979.

THE WASHINGTON INVASION
Flying saucers and UFOs normally seem to shun densely populated areas. But one of the most famous visitations of all time happened directly over the capital of the USA. The press labelled it the Washington Invasion.

On the evening of 19 July 1952, five strange, strong lights zigzagged across the sky, watched by thousands of people. A week later, on 26 July, they appeared again - with reinforcements. This time, they were between 6 and 12 of them, and their speedy, erratic movements ruled out the possibility that they were aircraft.

Three F94 jet fighters were sent up to buzz the mystery objects. Two of the interceptors could find no trace of the UFOs but the third pilot flew straight into a cluster of brilliant bluish-white lights. The lights, he said, travelled alongside him for 15 seconds before dispersing at remarkable speed.

The pilot returned safely to base, and the lights were never seen again.

They filmed an object which they described as 'an illuminated ping-pong ball, rotating, pulsating and darting around'.

While all this activity was going on in Australasia, similar sightings were being reported from all corners of the globe. In Britain, eyewitnesses from Scotland to the south coast were terrified by white balls in the sky. Some people claimed that they were 'buzzed' by the objects.

In Israel, a rash of close encounters with red balls and flashing lights was reported. In northern Italy, dozens of villages on the slopes of Gran Sasso Mountain were plunged into darkness after a UFO was seen hovering over a hydro-electric plant. Technicians said the instruments suddenly went haywire and machinery stopped. In South Africa, a young mother met 'six darkish skinned spacemen' on a country road near Johannesburg. They spoke in high-pitched voices but fled in a glowing spacecraft when she became excited.

Around the world, scientists and astronomers scorned suggestions of a space 'invasion'. They attributed the sightings to meteors or space debris burning up on entering the earth's atmosphere. Sir Bernard Lovell, director of Britain's Jodrell Bank radio astronomy station, dismissed the sightings as 'pure science fiction'.

Many people over the years have poured similar scorn on UFO sightings. Few have felt able to back the claims of the sincere and often frightened people who have had close encounters with objects from the skies. Yet the sightings continue, growing daily. The UFO riddle is a mystery that simply refuses to go away.

The black holes phenomenon

Even giant suns are sucked into these vast whirlpools in space

Beyond the earth's atmosphere lies an infinity of space that man has only just begun to explore. Its secrets are being tapped, one by one. Yet with every discovery made comes a new and often greater mystery.

One of the most baffling that scientists have ever faced is the phenomenon known as black holes. They cannot be seen, and the only evidence that they exist is the effect that they have on other objects. They are like whirlpools in space. Any debris plunging its way through space that may stray too near a black hole is sucked into its dark maw. Where it goes, scientists can only guess. What happens to it no one knows. Atomic particles, galactic dust, even giant suns can disappear without trace. Do they cease to exist? Or do they travel in some strange fashion through time and space to another dimension?

Scientists do not have the answers. American physicist John Wheeler calls black holes 'the greatest crisis ever faced by physics'.

Black holes are giant stars which have suddenly collapsed inwards. According to one theory, the process is infinite. It goes on and on, with the star getting smaller and smaller and more and more dense. A star ten times bigger than the sun would end up as a black hole only 40 miles across. A spoonful of this matter would weigh millions of tons. Because the gravitational pull of this relatively small, dense object is so great, nothing, not even light, can escape from it. And all the normal scientific laws no longer apply.

The first black hole was identified on 16 May 1973. Scientists were already investigating 'dead' stars. These include the so-called white dwarfs – which our own sun will become when it cools down in about 8,000 million years. Larger stars die in a different way and become what are known as neutron stars. Others are called pulsars because of the regular signals they emit. But, scientists asked, what happens to the biggest stars of all?

The key to the mystery came from the constellation Cygnus, The Swan. A super-giant star in this constellation was behaving in an odd way. Further investigation showed that the star was being affected by the gravitational pull of an invisible neighbour. Although it could not be seen, all the evidence pointed to its powerful existence. Then some intense study by three English scientists – Peter Sanford, Fred Hawkins and Keith Mason – provided proof that this invisible force was what was termed a black hole. Similar investigations were launched to prove the existence of another black hole in the Speilon Aurigae star system.

Study of the super-giant in The Swan constellation has shown that great clouds of gas are being drawn from the star into the black hole. As the star approaches the 'event horizon' – the point of no return after which it cannot be seen – the gravitational pulls of the star and the black hole conflict. Light emitted from this region travels so slowly that it seems almost to stand still.

In theory, if a man entered a black hole he would be stretched out, the part nearest the hole being attracted more quickly than the part furthest away. His image would linger for millions of years, even though his fall into the black hole would take only a fraction of a second. The tremendous force of gravity would finally break him down into atoms. But, by this point, time and space would have lost their conventional meanings. He would have entered what scientists call a singularity – the point where an infinitely small object has infinite density and gravity.

Some scientists have asked what would happen if a man could avoid destruction on entering a black hole. One answer they have come up with is that, because black holes defy all normal physical laws, when he emerged on the other side, he could find himself in a different universe – or even travelling backwards through time.

Another theory holds that man could eventually tap unlimited sources of energy from black holes by dumping rubbish into them and trapping and storing the gravitational energy that would be produced. There is one snag to this, though. If the greatest care were not taken, the black hole could grow large enough to suck the earth – and eventually the whole universe – into oblivion.

Black holes may help solve another great mystery – what holds the universe together? According to the 'big bang' theory, the universe was created by a gigantic explosion and is constantly expanding. But in that case, what is stopping the universe from flying apart indefinitely? The great scientist Albert Einstein suggested that there must be enough mass in the universe to hold it together. This mass could be black holes, counteracting the effects of the 'big bang' and drawing other stars and their planets towards them. If this is so, then the process would over millions of years speed up, the black holes eventually consuming every heavenly body. And, instead of ending with either a bang or a whimper, the universe would simply be swallowed up.

Still no one knows why the 'Hindenburg' crashed

The cool, calm words of radio reporter Herbert Morrison were recording the arrival of the giant Zeppelin airship, the *Hindenburg*, as it nosed its way to the mooring tower at Lakehurst naval station, New Jersey. It was unlikely that his commentary would even be broadcast. After all, it was just a routine flight and there was nobody famous on board.

'The ropes have been dropped and they have been taken hold of by a number of men on the field,' Morrison said. 'The back motors of the ship are holding it just enough to keep it . . .'

Then suddenly his gentle voice broke into a scream: 'It's burst into flame!'

With a popping noise, a tiny flicker of flame had appeared at the rear of the *Hindenburg*'s giant gas balloon, then burst into a sheet of incandescence that

The smoking wreckage of the *Hindenburg* after the explosion.

swept along the airship. Morrison's words became an almost incoherent babble as he sat helplessly watching the catastrophe unfold before his eyes: 'This is terrible . . . the flames are 500 feet in the sky . . . it is in smoke and flames now . . . those passengers.'

Tiny figures tumbled from the holocaust, and Morrison sobbed: 'I'm going to step inside where I can't see it. I . . . I . . . folks, I'm going to have to stop for a while. This is the worst thing I've ever witnessed. It is one of the worst catastrophes in the world.'

When Morrison resumed his recording only seconds later, the disaster was virtually over. The airship – the pride of Hitler's Germany – was a mass of incandescent rubble.

It was 6 May 1937. And until then the *Hindenburg* had been known not only as the world's biggest-ever airship but as the safest. With unfailing regularity it had ploughed its way through rain, storms and fog across the Atlantic. It was 830 ft long, 125 ft high, and under its belly – beneath nearly 7 million cubic ft of highly inflammable hydrogen – it carried 35 passengers in luxurious comfort.

The *Hindenburg* had finally convinced the world, after earlier American and British airship disasters, that the age of airship travel had come to stay. German ingenuity and efficiency had overcome the dangers.

Ernst Lehmann, the first commander, who was travelling as observer for the captain, Max Pruss, had told a passenger: 'Don't worry, my friend. Zeppelins never have accidents.' And Chief Steward Howard Kubis told another passenger: 'We Germans don't fool with hydrogen.'

Safety precautions were stringent. All matches and lighters were taken from passengers when they came aboard, catwalks were covered with rubber to prevent sparks, crewmen working in possibly hazardous areas wore felt boots and asbestos suits devoid of metal fastening. And the air pressure inside the travelling quarters was sufficient to expel any leaking hydrogen.

The *Hindenburg* first approached Lakehurst at around 4 pm, but Pruss did not like the look of some dark storm clouds and, true to the Zeppelin tradition of never taking a chance, he decided to delay landing. Two hours later the storm clouds had disappeared and preparations were made for what looked like being a routine arrival. The passengers were even handed back their lighters and matches. Radio officer Willy Speck was telling the *Hindenburg*'s sister ship, the *Graf Zeppelin*, that there had been a safe landing.

Then disaster struck.

Pruss stayed at his controls until his cabin hit the ground. He was badly hurt, but not so terribly as Lehmann, who was found slouched in the rubble murmuring over and over again: 'I can't understand it.' He clung on to life for another two days, and just before he died he was asked: 'What caused it?' His last word was: 'Lightning.' But a puzzled frown crossed his face, as if he doubted his own words.

Altogether 20 crewmen, 15 passengers and one member of the ground staff died, and a dozen more people were badly injured. But, miraculously, the rest of the 97 people on board escaped unharmed.

The inquiry officials seemed as puzzled as everyone else about what had caused the disaster, but finally blamed a freak electrical charge in the atmosphere.

Thirty-five years later, author Michael Macdonald Mooney, in his book *Hindenburg*, placed the blame on crew member Eric Spehl, a young rigger. Mooney said that Spehl, encouraged by an anti-Nazi mistress, placed an incendiary bomb aboard the *Hindenburg*. It was due to go off after the Zeppelin had landed, but Spehl had been unable to foresee the delay caused by the weather. . .

Several other crew members certainly believed that the inferno was caused by sabotage, motivated by a desire to dent the prestige of Hitler's Germany.

There had been hints of the impending disaster: the German ambassador in Washington had received a letter warning him that a bomb had been planted aboard the airship; before the *Hindenburg*'s departure from Frankfurt, one of its officers had suddenly begged to be allowed to say farewell to his wife 'for the last time'; and another officer had been told by a clairvoyant that he would die in a burning airship.

But whether the disaster was caused by sabotage or misfortune, one thing is certain – the *Hindenburg*'s demise also spelled the end of the most magnificent form of air travel the world had ever seen.

How did Glenn Miller really die?

Ever since band leader Glenn Miller's military aircraft disappeared on a flight from England to France on 15 December 1944, theories about his fate have abounded. It is a mystery which today still intrigues millions of music lovers all over the world.

Miller was 40 and at the peak of his career when he vanished. His unique big-band sound had made huge hits of numbers like 'In the Mood', 'Moonlight Serenade', 'American Patrol' and 'String of Pearls'. Their popularity swept the world, and the band was soon earning more than £1 million a year.

America's entry into the war led to Miller's enlistment as a captain and then his promotion to major, leading the United States Air Force Band in Europe. It was in this role that he was to visit Paris to prepare a Christmas broadcast – although such an arrangement would normally have been taken care of by the band's manager.

Despite fog warnings, Miller took off in a single-engined Norseman D-64 aircraft from Twinwoods airfield, Bedfordshire. With him were the pilot and another American officer. The aircraft and its occupants were never seen again. Despite repeated searches, no bodies or wreckage were found.

The most widely accepted theory at the time was that the light aircraft iced up and dived into the English Channel, drowning those trapped inside. Many people, however, refuse to accept this official and seemingly logical conclusion, and as the name and music of Glenn Miller has continued to live on in the world, his disappearance has become the subject of various strange theories.

One of the more recent and most startling claims has come from the most dedicated Miller fan of all time. English businessman and former RAF pilot John Edwards has devoted more than 12 years and about £10,000 in attempts to solve the Miller mystery. One of his claims is that Miller was not aboard the Norseman aircraft when it crashed. He says he has evidence that the band leader was murdered in Paris three days after the plane disappeared. He believes that Miller, known to be a womanizer, died of a fractured skull in the Pigalle, then the haunt of Paris prostitutes and criminals. Authorities covered up this scandal by claiming that Miller was on board the lost aircraft.

Edwards has spoken to a man who claims he saw Miller land safely in the ill-fated Norseman after making only a short flight to an airfield at Bovingdon, Hertfordshire. The band leader then switched to a Dakota and took off again.

The Dakota reached Paris safely.

Edwards also supports his theory of an official cover-up by pointing to the lack of a full inquiry. He said: 'I have met great difficulty in trying to solve this mystery. Records have been reported burned. Other information, like the aircrew report, is unaccountably vague. Even the weather conditions were listed as unknown.

'But pieces of information I collected over the years eventually all fell into place. I have evidence that an American military doctor in Paris signed Miller's death certificate. A retired US Air Force lieutenant-colonel recalls being told by the provost marshal's police office in Paris that Miller had been

Major Glenn Miller giving a US private some tips.

murdered. And I know a man in Miller's band who stated that it was common knowledge to those close to him that his boss was murdered in Paris.'

In an eerie seance session at the now-derelict Twinwoods airfield, an English medium, Carmen Rogers, claimed that she was able to look into the past and see what happened to Miller.

'I could see him walking to the aircraft with two other men,' she said. 'Miller was disturbed and worried about his domestic and other affairs. He did not want to make the trip to Paris. He felt sick and afraid. After they took off, Miller asked the pilot to land. The pilot put down as soon as possible, and let Miller get out. The aircraft touched down on the Essex side of the Thames estuary. Then Miller got out and made a phone call to London and arranged his own disappearance.'

Countless other theories about Miller's fate have been put forward over the years. He was a spy on a top-secret mission which went wrong. He was so terribly mutilated in the aircraft crash that he preferred to live in secret. He was an amnesia victim. He was mistakenly shot down by a British fighter over the Channel . . . and so on.

Various wrecked wartime aircraft have been discovered in the Channel, each prompting the hope that here, at last, was the Norseman that could provide the answers to the Miller mystery. But the plane has never been discovered.

So the death of the man who set the world humming to his big-band hits remains shrouded in controversy. But for some people the attempt to solve the riddle has a special incentive. It is thought that when the band leader left England he took with him a briefcase containing the original scores of Glenn Miller music that had never been played. Anyone finding them intact would certainly strike it rich.

How do birds migrate?

The world's cleverest navigators leave man in the dark

It is one of the oldest unsolved mysteries. It has baffled man since the dawn of civilization. How does a fragile bird with a tiny brain find its way twice a year from one side of the world to the other?

Every spring and autumn millions upon millions of birds are on the move. Some fly as far as 12,000 miles and as high as 30,000 ft. Where they go and where they come from was a mystery for centuries. It was only in our own age

MORE MIGRANTS

It is not only birds that migrate vast distances with unfailing accuracy. Fish, insects, reptiles and mammals all have strong homing instincts which appear to be lacking only in man.

Green turtles leave the beaches of South America every year to swim 1,500 miles to tiny Ascension Island in the Atlantic. Somehow they manage to make the necessary allowance for changing tides and sudden storms to reach their target, which is only five miles wide.

Eels from both Europe and North America head annually for the drifting weed masses of the Sargasso Sea. There, they breed before returning up to 2,000 miles to their familiar river-beds. The navigation of the eels - and of salmon, which perform a similar remarkable feat - has been partly explained by their acute sense of smell.

Butterflies, notably the Monarch and the Painted Lady, fly annually between Canada and the Mexican border, always returning to the same nesting sites.

The lemmings of Scandinavia, which breed at an incredible rate, have their own method of population control. As if at a single command, they migrate from the hills in a vast living unstoppable river, passing through homes and across streams. Eventually they tumble into the sea. One theory is that their mass movement is prompted by an instinct to migrate from Scandinavia to Britain - an instinct implanted in their senses before the Ice Age bridge between the two land masses melted.

Even domestic pets retain an inexplicable homing instinct, as is evidenced by the numerous stories of dogs and cats returning to their owners after long journeys. A hardy fox terrier made its way through the burning heart of Australia from Darwin to Adelaide, and a pining cat pursued its owners from New York to California. These are just two of the feats by man's best friends that even man cannot comprehend.

that their journeys were charted by attaching rings to the legs of the birds and recording the point and date of their departure and arrival.

The results of such experiments astounded ornithologists. They discovered, for example, that geese migrate regularly between Siberia and India, flying over the Himalayas at heights of up to 30,000 ft – higher than Mount Everest. An Arctic tern was ringed in Greenland and recaptured in South Africa – a journey of almost 10,000 miles in less than three months.

In fact, Arctic terns are the migratory record holders. They fly from their

THE WORLD'S GREATEST MYSTERIES

An arctic tern and its migratory path.

Arctic breeding grounds in Canada, Siberia and northern Europe across the globe to their winter haunts in Antarctica – and then they fly back again. Their life is almost perpetual motion. They are on the wing, 24 hours a day, for eight months of the year, and each bird covers up to 24,000 miles.

Why do they do it? They are not following any particular climatic or feeding pattern. On the appointed day for migration they all set out, even if feeding conditions remain excellent. Equally, if the time for migration has not arrived, they will stay put, even in the most appalling conditions.

How do they do it? An airline pilot takes years of training and a fortune in equipment before he can find his way from one vast airport to another. A bird can make a journey of the same length, without altering its course for a moment, until it arrives at the very same nest that it left the previous year.

Great shearwaters, for instance, gather four million strong every year to fly from Newfoundland, Greenland and northern Europe to lay their eggs in their traditional and only nesting grounds 6,000 miles away. They make their way unerringly to the tiny island of Tristan da Cunha, a mere dot in the vast southern Atlantic, almost 2,000 miles from the nearest land.

Ornithologists captured a Manx shearwater on the coast of Wales. They placed it in a darkened box and airfreighted it across the Atlantic to Boston, Massachusetts, where it was released. It found its way back to its nest on a Welsh cliff 12 days later. How could it have plotted its course so precisely without ever having made the journey before?

Birds rarely begin their long migratory journeys in overcast conditions. So perhaps they are guided by the sun or by the shadows that it makes on the ground. Yet ornithologists have discovered that during the seasons of migra-

94

tion, more birds are in flight at night than during the day. The sun could not be helping them then. So are birds also able to 'read' the map of the stars?

Such feats would require amazing ingenuity – for the sun's height and angles change by the minute, and the stars alter their pattern in the skies nightly. The information that a bird would need to contain in its tiny brain would be literally astronomical. So, in this respect, do birds know more than man? If so, the term 'bird brain' is a slur on some of the cleverest little creatures in the world.

The Siberian fireball disaster

How a 40-mile-wide track of the earth was utterly devastated

Even in northern Siberia, with its freezing winters and scorching summers, the early hours of a June morning are a time to be enjoyed. And farmer Sergei Semenov had taken a break from his wheat fields to snatch a few moments' rest in the sunshine on the porch of his farmhouse.

It was just after 7 am on 30 June 1908 and to Semenov, miles away from the revolutionary fever that was beginning to sweep parts of the country, it seemed a good time to be alive.

At precisely 7.17 am his reveries were brought to an abrupt halt. An enormous explosion rent the horizon with a blinding light.

He said later: 'There appeared a great flash. There was so much heat, my shirt was almost burnt off my back. I saw a huge ball of fire that covered an enormous part of the sky. Afterwards it became very dark.'

It was then that the enormous force of the blast threw the farmer from his porch and knocked him unconscious. When he regained his senses, a mighty, thundering noise swept across the tundra. 'It shook the whole house and nearly moved it from its foundations,' he said.

Farmer Semenov was lucky. If he had been nearer the centre of the holocaust he would not have lived to tell his strange and frightening tale. And but for the fact that the disaster occurred in the remote Tunguska River valley, the devastation would have been even more appalling than it was.

The inferno laid waste an area the size of Leningrad. Herds of reindeer were incinerated. Virtually all the trees in an area more than 40 miles across were ripped from the earth and thrown from the centre of the blast to lie like the spokes of a giant wheel. Nomad tribesmen 45 miles away were hurled to the ground, their tents ripped away by a searing wind.

What was the cause of this awesome devastation? And could something like it happen again?

It was not until 22 years after the explosion that anyone got close to finding out the answers. In 1930, Professor L. A. Kulik, of the Soviet Academy of Science, spent almost a year in the area with a small team of investigators. It was his third attempt to reach the scene of the blast. His two previous expeditions had been abandoned because the marshy forests were impenetrable.

Professor Kulik eventually found a landscape pock-marked with craters. He found nearly 2,000 square miles of uprooted, rotting tree trunks. And, most important of all, he found eyewitnesses of the blast. They told of a vivid ball of fire sweeping across the sky – 'so bright that it made even the light from the sun seem dark'.

People who had been more than 50 miles away from the centre of the explosion spoke of 'violent vibrations' followed by 'a fiery body trailing a wide band of light across the sky'. One said: 'I was washing wool in the River Kan when I heard a noise like the whirr of the wings of frightened birds. The water in the river began to form waves. Then there was a jolt so violent that one of my friends fell into the river.'

Some 250 miles away in the town of Kirensk, people had seen a pillar of fire followed by 'several thunderclaps and a crashing sound'. And even 600 miles away at Turukhansk, a witness reported 'three or four dull thuds, like distant artillery'. Many of the witnesses could have been describing a nuclear explosion. Several observers described a fireball followed by a mushroom-shaped pillar of smoke many miles high. But could an atomic blast have occurred nearly 40 years before the devastation of Hiroshima and Nagasaki?

Some scientists have indeed suggested that the explosion could have been nuclear. They put forward the startling theory that a spaceship of visitors from another planet became damaged on entering the earth's atmosphere. The nuclear fuel became critically overheated and set off an explosion equivalent to that of a 30-megaton nuclear bomb.

Australian journalist John Baxter and American scientist Thomas Atkins followed up the work of Russian scientists and supported the exploding-spaceship theory with the following evidence:

- In a nuclear explosion, the earth's magnetic field is disturbed. After the Siberian blast, it was.
- Nuclear blasts leave a particular pattern of destruction. The Russian explosion did just that.

Atomic fungus over Hiroshima after the explosion.

THE WORLD'S GREATEST MYSTERIES

- The atomic bombs dropped on Japan in 1945 caused weird plant mutations. The Siberian disaster caused similar mutations.
- Nuclear explosions leave behind tiny green globules of melted dust called trinitites. These were found after the Russian blast. And, according to Russian experts, these trinitites contained traces of metal not normally found in the Tunguska region, and not usually part of the make-up of meteorites.
- Finally, the two refer to eyewitness evidence from people who saw a large bluish, cylindrical object racing through the sky with a roaring sound, leaving a vapour trail behind it, just before the blast.

Other, less extraordinary, solutions put forward by scientists include:

The comet theory. Comets are thought to be giant balls of frozen gases and debris. One could have entered the earth's atmosphere – although there were no reported sightings – and generated such heat that it exploded in mid-air.

The anti-matter theory. Some scientists think that a mass of anti-matter – material that corresponds to that found on earth but made up of positive particles (positrons) instead of negative particles (electrons) – could have plunged into the earth's atmosphere. As soon as it came into contact with atoms of ordinary matter there would be an enormous explosion.

The black hole theory. Black holes are thought to be stars which have collapsed to a tiny size. Because of their immense mass – the weight of the earth could be contained in a black hole the size of a tennis ball – their gravitational pull is strong enough to prevent light escaping, so the objects cannot be seen – there is only a black hole in space where they exist. It has been suggested that a black hole hit Siberia.

The meteorite theory. One of the most popular theories, although it was at first discounted, is that a giant meteorite fell to the earth. Meteorites are entering the earth's atmosphere at the rate of 200 million every day, although most burn up before reaching the planet's surface. A meteorite that fell on Arizona in prehistoric times left a crater three-quarters of a mile across. Scientists at one time claimed that, as there was no crater in Siberia, the explosion could not have been caused by a meteorite. But it has since been discovered that a meteorite made of rock, rather than metal – which is more common – could explode just before hitting the ground, so causing extensive damage but no crater.

Whatever caused the Siberian blast, one thing is certain. The fact that it happened in a virtually uninhabited area was a stroke of good fortune. If the object from space had plummeted on to a major city the result would have been the greatest disaster in the history of mankind.

Comet Kohoutek, 4 January 1974.

Chapter Four

Mysteries of the Mind

The mind is a largely uncharted world, a system of
unimaginable complexity and extraordinary powers.
And despite the surgeons, despite the psychologists,
it remains as much of a mystery today as ever.
How, for example, do some people have the power
not to feel pain? How can some seers foretell the
future so accurately? And how are spiritualists
apparently able to communicate with the dead?

World War Three, 1999

The prediction of two amazing fortune-tellers

Four hundred years ago, a French physician predicted that a great world war would break out before the turn of this century, reaching its destructive peak in 1999. More recently, an American housewife predicted exactly the same thing. Nothing too alarming about such wild warnings, you might think. But the predictions came from perhaps the two best-known prophets of doom of all time.

The Frenchman was the remarkable Nostradamus. The American was Jeane Dixon. And the predictions of both these seers have so far proved amazingly accurate.

Nostradamus was born Michel de Nostredame in St Remy de Provence on 14 December 1503. His family was Jewish but Michel was brought up as a Catholic. He decided to change his name to Nostradamus during his term as a brilliant student of medicine at Montpellier.

In 1529, he became famous for his treatment of victims of a plague which had ravaged Provence for four years and which had claimed the lives of his wife and two sons.

But despite his renown as a physician, Nostradamus's real interest lay in astrology and clairvoyance. With his family dead, he wandered through France, Corsica and Italy, making predictions which almost invariably seemed to be fulfilled.

He once stayed at the Lorraine castle of the Seigneur de Florinville, who expressed a strong cynicism about his guest's powers. One day, as the host stalked through the estate's farmyard, he asked: 'What does the future hold for those two pigs?' Nostradamus answered: 'You will eat the black one but a wolf will devour the white one.'

To prove the futility of such prophecies, the seigneur ordered the white pig to be slaughtered for dinner that night. When the meal was served, the host told Nostradamus that he was eating the white pig – but the seer insisted that it was not so. To settle the argument, the cook was called in. He admitted that, while leaving the kitchen unattended earlier that day, a wolf cub had made off with the white pig. He had thus been forced to kill the black pig to fill the dinner table.

While in Italy, Nostradamus one day fell down in the dust in front of a young priest who was walking towards him along a country lane. The startled man, Felici Peretti, thought that the French stranger was a lunatic. But almost 50 years later, that same obscure peasant priest was ordained Pope Sixtus the Fifth.

In 1547 Nostradamus ended his wanderings and remarried. He settled down as a doctor in Salon, Provence, and began composing his major prophecies. They were published in 1555 – the first of ten volumes covering seven centuries. The forecasts, written in more than 1,000 cryptic verses, were veiled in riddles and symbolism. According to the author, this was because he did not wish to worry his readers unduly – or, perhaps more importantly, to be accused of witchcraft. So he 'wrote down everything under a figure rather cloudy than plainly prophetic'.

> *The Young Lion shall overcome the old*
> *In a warlike field in single fight*
> *In a golden cage, he will pierce the eye;*
> *Two wounds in one, then die a cruel death.*

That was Nostradamus's prediction for Henri II of France. And in 1559, Henri took part in a joust with the captain of his Scottish guard, Montgomery. The Scot's splintered lance pierced Henri's cage-shaped visor and gouged into his eye. He was also wounded in the throat – 'two wounds in one'. The king died in agony ten days later.

> *The rejected one shall accede to the throne;*
> *Her enemies shall be found to be conspirators.*
> *Her time shall triumph as never before.*
> *At 70, she shall surely die, in the third year of the century.*

That was the prediction for Queen Elizabeth I, who died in her 70th year (she was 69 and six months) in 1603.

> *The great plague of the maritime city*
> *Shall not cease until death is avenged*
> *For the blood of the just, taken and condemned though innocent,*
> *And the great dame, outraged by feigning saints.*

So wrote Nostradamus, predicting the Great Plague that ravaged London in 1665. 'Dame' was his term for a cathedral, in this case St Paul's, 'the just' was how he referred to the executed King Charles I, and the 'feigning saints' were the Puritans.

> *The blood of the just shall be required of London*
> *Burned by fire in thrice-twenty-and-six.*
> *The old dame shall fall from her high place*
> *And many edifices of the same sect shall be destroyed.*

Nostradamus was accurately predicting the Great Fire of London in 1666. The 'old dame' is again St Paul's, destroyed in the fire.

Nostradamus then looked forward into the 18th century and wrote of 'an emperor born near Italy who will rule France for 14 years' before 'exchanging his empire for a small place'. Whom could Nostradamus have been talking about but Napoleon, the Corsican-born emperor who was exiled to St Helena.

In many cases, Nostradamus gave not only dates but names. He referred to medical scientist Louis Pasteur when he wrote: 'Pasteur will be renowned as a godlike man.' And he wrote about the two foes of the Spanish Civil War, General Franco and Primo de Rivera, in these terms: 'From Castille, Franco will bring out the assembly, and the people of Rivera will be in the throng.' He also foresaw the emergence of Adolf Hitler, whom he called 'Hister'. He wrote of him:

> *In the mountains of Austria near the Rhine*
> *There will be born of simple parents*
> *A man who will claim to defend Poland and Hungary*
> *And whose fate will never be certain.*

Elsewhere, he wrote of:

> *A leader of great Germanies*
> *Who will come to give help which is only counterfeit.*
> *He will stretch the borders of Germany*
> *And will cause France to be divided into two parts . . .*
> *Living fire and death hidden in globes will be loosed,*
> *horrible and terrible.*
> *By night, the enemy will reduce cities to dust.*

Finally, Nostradamus predicted a war to end all wars. A 'yellow race' would invade Europe and 'blood and corpses' would cover the land. The carnage would culminate 'in the year 1999 and seven months, when from the sky will come the great king of terror'.

Nostradamus also forecast his own death. He wrote: 'I shall be found dead beside my bed and my bench.' Eleven years later, on 2 July 1566, he was found dead on a bench which had been set beside his sick-bed to help him ease himself in and out.

The prophecy of an international holocaust which Nostradamus made four centuries ago is mirrored by another startling view of the future by the

The actress Carole Lombard who did not heed Jeane Dixon's warning.

extraordinary American prophetess Jeane Dixon. The wife of a real estate agent in Washington DC, she has been consulted as a clairvoyant since the age of nine.

Mrs Dixon has forecast a world war beginning in the late 1980s and culminating in 1999 – the same year quoted in the works of Nostradamus. But Jeane Dixon's most remarkable predictions were about President John F. Kennedy.

In 1952, just 11 years before the President's death, Mrs Dixon was in St Matthew's Cathedral, Washington, when she had a vision of 'a blue-eyed Democrat entering the White House'. She saw a date: 1960. She also saw a warning – that the President would be assassinated.

Her prediction was reported at the time, then forgotten. But early in November 1963, three years after Kennedy's election, Jeane Dixon began to have a series of further visions about the President.

While lunching with friends, she suddenly interrupted the conversation and said: 'He's going to be shot.' When asked whom she was talking about, she replied: 'Why, the President, of course.'

Over the next couple of weeks, Mrs Dixon made repeated attempts to warn Kennedy of the danger he was in, but without success. On 19 November, she cried out aloud: 'The President has been shot.' And on the morning of Friday, 22 November, she said: 'This is the day it will happen.' That afternoon, John F. Kennedy was gunned down in Dallas, Texas.

Jeane Dixon accurately predicted the deaths – and the successes – of many other statesmen and famous personalities. Comedian Bob Hope once tried to test her skills by asking her how many strokes he had made during a game of golf earlier that day. He did not mention the name of his partner in the game, for that was a closely guarded secret. Without hesitation, Jeane Dixon answered: 'You took 92 strokes, and President Eisenhower took 96.'

It seems that it can be dangerous to ignore Mrs Dixon's warnings. She once told a famous film star who consulted her not to travel by plane within the following six weeks. The actress, Carole Lombard, replied that she would have to do so in three days' time and was unwilling to change her plans on the strength of a clairvoyant's warning. Mrs Dixon was so insistent, however, that the film star agreed to toss a coin to decide the matter. 'If it's heads I'll cancel the flight. If it's tails I'll go ahead.' The coin landed tails. Three days later, Carole Lombard died in a plane crash.

The warnings Caesar ignored

The level-headed Romans allowed prophecies virtually to rule their lives. The most famous prediction of all time was made to Julius Caesar: 'Beware the Ides of March.' The warning was made in 44 BC by the eminent seer Vestritius Spurinna.

Caesar had also been warned by a prophet to 'beware of Cassius' – one of the plotters then scheming his death. And on the eve of 15 March – the Ides of March – Caesar's wife Calphurnia dreamed that her husband was being stabbed. She pleaded with him in vain not to go to the forum that day.

On the way to the forum, Caesar again saw Vestritius Spurinna and said to him: 'Well, the Ides of March have come.' The seer answered: 'Aye, Caesar, but not gone.' Just before midday, Caesar was stabbed to death.

Seventeen years later, Caesar's heir, the Emperor Augustus, built a Temple of Peace and asked the famous Oracle at Delphi how long it would stand. The answer was: 'Until a virgin gives birth to a child and yet remains a virgin.' Augustus was well pleased with the answer, which he took to mean that the

---

MOTHER SHIPTON'S WARNINGS

Britain's most famous seer was born Ursula Southell at a place known as the Dropping Well, near Knaresborough, Yorkshire. Despite her dwarfish appearance, she found herself a husband - a carpenter, Toby Shipton. Until her death at the age of 73 in 1561, Mother Shipton, as she came to be known, issued a remarkably accurate series of prophecies.

Among them were King Henry VIII's routing of the French, Cardinal Wolsey's arrest for treason, the Caesarean birth of Edward VI, the reign of a maiden queen (Elizabeth I), the beheading of a widowed one (Mary Queen of Scots), the execution of Charles I and the Great Fire of London.

Looking even further ahead, Mother Shipton appeared to foretell the invention of radio, submarines, cars and metal ships. She wrote:

> *Around the world thoughts shall fly*
> *In the twinkling of an eye.*
> *Under water men shall walk,*
> *Shall ride and sleep and even talk.*
> *Carriages without horses shall go*
> *And accidents fill the world with woe,*
> *In water, iron shall float*
> *As easily as a wooden boat.*

But there are two further lines which are a bit too close to the predictions of Nostradamus and Jeane Dixon for comfort. They are:

> *The world to an end will come*
> *In nineteen-hundred and ninety-one.*

temple would last forever. But at around the time of the birth of Jesus of Nazareth, the Temple of Peace unaccountably collapsed on its foundations.

It is also recorded that, shortly before the collapse of the temple, Augustus consulted a prophetess known as the Tiburtine Sibyl. He asked her whether he should accept the senate's offer to confer on him the title God of the Nations.

As the Sibyl deliberated, a meteor crossed the sky. She immediately said: 'A child has just been born who is the true god of the world. He is of humble birth and from an obscure race. He will work miracles but he will be persecuted. In the end, however, he will be victor over death, rising from where his killers entombed him . . .'

Premonitions that were fulfilled

Countless dreams have foretold dramatic events in history

Many men and women who never thought of themselves as psychic have had sudden visions of what lies ahead. Usually, they are premonitions of disaster. But not always.

On 7 October 1571, Pope Pius V suddenly interrupted a mundane meeting of his treasury officials and announced: 'We must go and give thanks to God. Victory has gone to the Christian fleet.' A secretary made a note of the Pope's comment and added the time: 5 pm. Two weeks later, news reached Rome that the combined fleets of Spain, Venice and Genoa had overwhelmed a Turkish fleet in the Battle of Lepanto on the afternoon of 7 October.

The *Titanic* in dock at
Southampton. *Opposite*
Jackie and Bobby Kennedy.

THE WORLD'S GREATEST MYSTERIES

Many premonitions come in dreams. In 1812, as Napoleon's armies advanced on Moscow, the wife of the Russian general Count Toutschkoff dreamed three times that her husband had died at a place she had never heard of before – Borodino. After each dream, Countess Toutschkoff searched maps in vain for such a name. On 7 September of that year, the retreating Russians finally turned and routed Napoleon's armies at an insignificant village called Borodino. One of the casualties was Count Toutschkoff.

A second famous case of premonition occurred in the same year. Again, the warning came in three separate dreams. Cornish mine owner John Williams told friends that in the dreams he had seen a man shot dead in the lobby of the House of Commons, and that when he had asked who the victim was he had been told: 'The chancellor of the exchequer.'

Nine days later, on 11 May 1812, Spencer Perceval, who was both prime minister and chancellor of the exchequer, was assassinated. Williams's description of the killing had been exact in every detail – even down to the cut of the victim's waistcoat and the colour of the buttons on the killer's coat.

Another leader, President Abraham Lincoln, was given an unhappy glimpse into the future in a dream, in March 1865. He told his friend, Ward Hill Lamon, about it in these words:

There seemed to be a deathlike stillness about me. I heard subdued sobs, as if many people were weeping. I feel that I left my bed and walked downstairs. I went from room to room. No living person was in sight, but the same mournful sounds of distress met me as I passed along.

I kept on until I arrived at the East Room, where I met with a sickening surprise. Before me was a catafalque, on which rested a corpse wrapped in funeral vestments. Around it were guards and a throng of mourners, many weeping pitifully.

'Who is dead in the White House?' I demanded of one of the soldiers.

'The President,' was his answer. 'He was killed by an assassin.'

On 14 April 1865, Lincoln was shot dead at a Washington theatre. His body was laid in state at the White House – in the East Room.

One of the most celebrated instances of unconscious premonition occurred in a novel published in 1898 by American author Morgan Robertson. It recounted the story of the biggest and most luxurious liner ever built . . . of how it set out from Southampton on its maiden voyage to New York . . . of how it hit an iceberg in the Atlantic . . . of how its hull was torn open beneath the waterline . . . of how it sank with appalling loss of life because there were not enough lifeboats. And the name Robertson gave to his ship was the *Titan*.

Fourteen years later, on 10 April 1912, almost every word of that fictional tragedy came true when the *Titanic* sank to its doom.

Another giant of international travel, the airship R101, slipped its moorings on 4 October 1930 and set off on its maiden flight from England to India. As it passed over London, Harold Ceazer and his wife watched from their garden and saw its shape change to that of a coffin. They had a strong premonition of death. So did the son of one of the airship's riggers, and the wife of the captain, Flight-Lieutenant Carmichael Irwin. The captain's wife told friends: 'We both knew he was not coming back again.' Early next morning the R101 crashed into a hillside near Beauvais, France, killing all but six of the 54 people aboard.

A Californian paint-firm owner, Jack Swimmer, amazed newsmen with his predictions of voting figures in the 1952 presidential elections which swept Dwight D. Eisenhower to power. But in 1956, Swimmer really wrapped up the election in advance. He handed over to Los Angeles police for safe keeping a list of the votes he believed would be cast for Eisenhower. They were: nationwide 33,974,241, California 2,875,637, Los Angeles 1,218,462. After the election results were announced, Swimmer's figures were found to be precisely accurate.

A less happy prediction was made in 1966 by South Wales schoolgirl Eryl Jones. She told her mother she had dreamed that she had walked to school in Aberfan but that the school was no longer there. 'Something black had come over it,' she said. Two days later, on 21 October, a black slag heap slid down a mountainside on to the school, burying it along with 144 children and teachers.

An airliner which crashed into a hillside near Perpignan, France, on 3 June 1967, was one passenger short. The seat reserved for Gina Beauchamp was empty because, as she waited for an airport bus in London, she had a premonition of disaster. She told her mother that they must cancel their holiday flight to Spain. Mrs Mary Beauchamp insisted on continuing. Her daughter stayed – and survived.

On the day President John F. Kennedy was assassinated, he told his wife: 'If someone wants to shoot me from a window with a rifle, I can't stop him. So let's not worry about it.'

Although he was predicting the manner of his own death only hours later, Kennedy had no conscious foreboding of it. But five years later, in 1968, Kennedy's widow, Jackie, had a very firm premonition – of the death of her brother-in-law. She said sadly of Robert Kennedy, then launching his campaign for the Presidency: 'I know he is going to be shot – just like my husband was.'

On 5 June, the young senator was shot dead in a Los Angeles hotel. The premonition was only one of dozens recorded around the world – all inexplicable forewarnings of tragedy that were to come true.

Men with a strange power over pain

Pain – it's what we all feel and what we all fear. But need we? Our pain thresholds drop when we expect pain – when we feel tense, frightened, over-aware. But some people can 'programme themselves' to feel no pain – and no one knows how they are able to achieve it.

There are extremely rare cases (about a dozen have been recorded) of people who have virtually never experienced pain in their lives – even breaking limbs without knowing it. Such a seemingly pleasant immunity is not to be envied, however. For pain is the body's early warning system of danger.

More common is the occasional ability to persuade oneself – or others – that an experience is not painful. In an experiment at Harvard University's medical school, more than 150 patients were given injections of pure water following operations. They were told, however, that the injections were of pain-killing drugs. In half of the cases, the patients said that their pain had been eased.

Such powers of self-persuasion are taken to extremes in the case of fire-walkers, whose mastery over pain has baffled scientists for centuries. The fire-walking cult was already old when it was recorded by Virgil and Plato. In modern times it has been practised in India, Sri Lanka, the Balkans, Japan, and notably in the Fiji Islands. There, a pit is dug, 20 ft wide and up to 5 ft deep, and is filled with logs which are set alight. Stones are added until the pit is a carpet of glowing stones. The priest then leads the fire-walkers slowly across it. In most cases, the fire-walkers seem to be in a mild trance, but this is not always the case. In the Shinto fire ceremonies in Japan, the fire-walkers are often fully aware and utterly casual about their ordeal.

In 1935, London University held a scientifically controlled experiment involving a young Indian who walked calmly across coals at a temperature of 800° Fahrenheit and experienced no ill effects.

In the 1950s there appeared two remarkable reports on fire-walking. One was by an American doctor, Harry B. Wright, who witnessed a ceremony on Biti Levu, Fiji. Immediately after the fire-walking, he prodded the feet of the participants with a pin and a lighted cigarette. They all felt normal pain.

The other case involved a British professor of English literature, Edward Stephenson, who took part in a fire-walking ceremony in Tokyo. He was not in a trance and had been in no elaborate ritual. Yet the only pain he felt was when he trod on a sharp stone and scratched the sole of his foot.

How are fire-walkers able to work such miracles? If it is a simple case of their feeling no pain, that might be explained by their being in a hypnotic trance. But this is not always the case. And it does not explain how they achieve not only a mental but an even stranger physical immunity to the carpets of fire they tread.

Voices from the dead

Rosemary Brown at the piano.

Sceptics cannot explain away the amazing feats of spiritualists

Few mysteries have troubled the minds of rational men as much as spiritualism. Doubters have debunked the idea that the living can communicate with the dead. Yet they offer no rational explanation of how a middle-aged widow in Balham, London, has composed classical music in the style of the masters . . . of how a Royal Marine with no interest in history pinpointed the hidden ruins at ancient Glastonbury . . . and of how an American housewife in St Louis, Missouri, wrote a novel in authentic medieval English.

Spiritualism was born in March 1848, in a small wooden house in Hydesville, New York. It was the Wayne County home of Methodist farmer John Fox, his wife, and their daughters Margaret, 15, and Katie, 12. Strange knocking sounds began in the night. Almost by accident, the girls discovered that if they snapped their fingers or tapped on a table, they were answered by similar sounds.

When Katie gave a series of silent waves, she heard the same number of knocks. And when Mrs Fox asked for the ages of her children, she received two series of the correct number of taps, plus three more. Her youngest child had died at the age of three.

The family devised a code of knocks for communicating with the force behind the sounds. In this way, they claimed to have learned that the force was the spirit of a pedlar called Charles Rosma, murdered by a previous tenant for the contents of his pack and tin trunk – $500. Nothing was found when, on tapped instructions, the cellar floor was dug up. But in 1904 a cellar wall fell in – to reveal a skeleton, a tin trunk and the remains of a pedlar's pack.

Claims of the family's ability to talk to the dead spread like wildfire at a time when Charles Darwin's theory of man's evolution from apes was challenging the Church's preaching of life after death. Soon mediums claiming similar powers sprang up on both sides of the Atlantic, passing on messages through tapping, speech under self-induced trance, and so-called automatic writing.

Author Sir Arthur Conan Doyle, renowned for the logical reasoning of his detective creation, Sherlock Holmes, became a fervent believer. Britain's leading scientist, Sir William Crookes, president of the Royal Society, also became a convert. Queen Victoria went to seances to contact her dead husband, Albert, and came away convinced that she had done so.

The unscrupulous spotted a perfect chance to cash in on the gullible, and many fake mediums and photographers were exposed by scientists and journalists. But despite adverse publicity, when the spiritualist movement celebrated its 100th anniversary, there were 50,000 members in Britain and 250,000 in America. And more than 100,000 people were buying *Psychic News*, the weekly chronicle of spiritualist activity. For the revealed trickery of charlatans was more than balanced by the inexplicable achievements of serious mediums – achievements like those of Mrs Rosemary Brown.

Mrs Brown bought a piano just after World War Two but gave up lessons after only a year. Neighbours in Balham, South London, said she showed little interest in music. She could just about struggle through a hymn. But in 1964 she produced a piano work which could have been written by one of the classic masters.

Indeed, she claimed that it was – that composer Franz Liszt, who died in 1886, had guided her fingers to the notes and had told her: 'I shall return. We have much work to do together.'

Over the next few years, Mrs Brown produced 500 new compositions all in the styles of the masters. They included a 40-page 'Schubert' sonata, 12 'Schubert' songs, and a fantasia impromptu in three movements 'by Beethoven'.

Mrs Brown said each composer communicated in a different way. Liszt and Chopin guided her fingers to the keys, and she later wrote down the work. Schubert tried to sing, but had an indifferent voice. Bach and Beethoven simply dictated the notes. All spoke to her in English, but relapsed into the vernacular when irritated. Beethoven exclaimed, 'Mein Gott!' when the doorbell rang one day while they were hard at work.

In 1970 a long-playing record of some of the works was released. Critics were divided over its merit, but all agreed that the styles were authentic.

Queen Victoria (George Hayles).

THE WORLD'S GREATEST MYSTERIES

And composer Richard Rodney Bennett said: 'You couldn't fake music like this without years of training. I couldn't fake some of the Beethoven myself.'

Glastonbury, in Somerset, has been a historic site for centuries. Legend has it that King Arthur and Queen Guinevere are buried there, and that the Holy Grail — the chalice used at Christ's Last Supper – is buried under the spring on the Tor. Each year thousands of tourists flock to look at the ancient ruins, unaware that spiritualism was responsible for uncovering many of them. The archaeological work was inspired by a manuscript in medieval script, ostensibly written by a monk but actually produced in a trance by an officer of the Royal Marines. He knew nothing of the subject or how the script was produced, and was not particularly interested in it once it was.

In 1924, medical professor's daughter Geraldine Cummins felt an unseen hand guiding her pen. Over a month, it produced more than a million words of automatic writing. Investigators from Edinburgh and St Andrews universities in Scotland examined the documents, said to be a true account of the life of the Apostles after Christ's death, written by a 1st-century Christian convert, Cleophas. The researchers agreed that the stories contained insights that could have come only from a contemporary of the Apostles. Miss Cummins had never studied theology, and knew nothing of the subject of which she wrote.

In 1957, Miss Grace Rosher was sitting at home in Kensington, London, writing to friends. Suddenly, the pen in her hand began to move of its own accord, scribbling: 'With love from Gordon . . . it is me, Gordon.' Four days later, it began again, describing how Gordon Burdick had died in Canada 15 months earlier.

Miss Rosher knew who he was. He had been on his way to England to marry her when he died. But she could not have known the details that were now down on paper. And when the Churches' Fellowship for Psychical Study sent the writings to a graphologist, together with letters from Burdick, he concluded that they were all written by the same hand.

Direct contact with a spirit like this is rare. Most people rely on the use of mediums like Lilian Bailey. It was she to whom Australian speech therapist Lionel Logue turned when his wife died in London in 1945. A double surprise awaited him.

Twenty years earlier, Logue had been asked by King George V to coach his son the Duke of York (later to become George VI), to help him master his stammer. Eight years later, Lilian Bailey told Logue: 'King George V is here. He asks me to thank you for what you did for his son.' Logue then received messages from his wife. He became convinced they were genuine when, after he had asked where they had first met, the correct reply came back: 'Charlie Sparrow's house, Fremantle.'

Tricksters have made conclusive proof of spiritual contact almost impossible. And trick photography has made proof by camera suspect. But no one has yet explained away the ingenious evidence provided by Polish medium Franek Kluski between 1919 and 1923. Kluski, described as King of the Mediums by Dr Gustav Geley, director of the Institute Metapsychique Internationale de Paris, persuaded spirits, channelled through him, to plunge either their face or their hands into boiling wax, then cold water. This produced wax-likenesses which could later be turned into plaster casts. Comparison of the wax gloves made at his seances with the hands of those in the room showed that none matched. And the wrists of the gloves were so small that no one could have drawn his hand out without destroying them.

The Church has often investigated spiritualism, and has refused to publish its findings. In 1937, Cosmo Lang, Archbishop of Canterbury, kept secret a report by seven of a ten-strong committee under the Bishop of Bath and Wells. The report said: 'Certain outstanding psychic experiences make a strong *prima facie* case for survival and the possibility of spirit communications. We think it probable that they proceed in some cases from discarnate spirits . . . there are quite clear parallels between the miraculous events recorded in the Gospels and modern phenomena attested by spiritualists.'

But what Archbishop Lang refused to publish during his life, he was seemingly prepared to comment on after death. In 1959, 14 years after he died, his voice, through medium Leslie Flint, said: 'Where spiritualism was concerned I was afraid. But it is vital and important that all peoples should know about . . .'

Then his voice tailed away. The message has never been completed.

The three lives of Glenn Ford

Hollywood star joins the ranks of those who claim to have lived before

In 1978 Hollywood film star Glenn Ford got the shock of his life – his third life, that is. For when a doctor hypnotized him, he spoke emotionally of a previous existence as a Colorado cowboy. Later, at another session, he recalled being a piano teacher in Elgin, Scotland.

Listening to tapes of both sessions was a surprise in itself for Ford. But he was amazed when researchers discovered evidence that both his previous 'incarnations' had actually existed – and at about the times the actor had indicated. 'I'm very confused about it all,' Ford said. 'It conflicts with all my religious beliefs. I'm a God-fearing man and proud of it, but this has gotten me mixed up.'

Ford is not the first person to produce evidence of reincarnation. Indeed, Buddhists believe that man goes through a series of lives, both human and animal, before reaching the bliss of nirvana – the extinction of individuality and absorption into the supreme spirit. But Ford's is one of the best-documented cases on record of life after death.

The actor's first hypnosis session was at his home in Beverley Hills, California. Then aged 61, he spoke vividly about working as a cowboy, Charlie Bill, for a rancher called Charlie Goodnight, and of being ambushed and shot. Researchers from the University of California in Los Angeles went to Colorado and uncovered evidence of both Bill and Goodnight.

The second session, again tape-recorded, took place at the university. This time, equally vividly, Ford spoke of life as Charles Stuart, and said : 'I teach the piano to young flibbertigibbets,' a dated term for frivolous children. Ford also played the piano under hypnosis, though as he admitted later : 'I can't play a note.'

When University of California researchers visited Elgin, they found the grave of a Charles Stuart, who died in 1840. They showed a photograph of the grave to Ford. 'That shook me up really bad,' he said. 'I felt immediately that it was the place I was buried.'

Ex-British Army Captain Arthur Flowerdew retired to a cottage in the Norfolk village of Bramerton. Born and brought up in rural England, he had led a quiet life and had never travelled further than Europe. Yet this contented grandfather was convinced that he, too, had lived before – as a soldier in the rock-hewn Jordanian city of Petra, 2,200 years earlier.

Flowerdew told researcher Joan Forman, who was writing a book on the subject, that since childhood strange unexplained visions had invaded his mind. As a boy at the seaside, he had picked up red and amber stones, thinking : 'This is the colour of the rock of that city.' Later came mental pictures of a city cut out of the cliffs, men in long Biblical robes, golden treasure hidden in a temple, tombs carved in pink and amber rock, a narrow gorge running down to a desert, a battle as he and ten other men defended the gorge against a horde of invaders, and, finally, the pain as a spear thrown by a giant Syrian crashed into his chest.

Miss Forman checked what he told her against the known facts on Petra, and found that much of it tallied. She was further amazed when she introduced him to a local schoolteacher who had taken colour slides of the ruined

Glenn Ford.

city during a holiday in 1964. The teacher said: 'He could tell me more than what could be seen. He was able to describe what was next to certain pillars, off the edge of the photograph.'

Flowerdew said: 'I'm not the sort of chap to day-dream, and I have never understood how I received these pictures of my city. If pushed, I think I would come down on the side of reincarnation, but I can't see how it could happen.'

Dorothy Eady was born into a wealthy South London family in 1903.

When she was three, she tumbled down stairs and was declared dead by the family doctor. But when he and a nurse returned to lay out the body, they found the little girl alive. All was not well, however. Dorothy took to hiding under tables and behind furniture, demanding to be taken 'home'.

When the family visited the Egyptian rooms at the British Museum, she ran wild, kissing the feet of statues, hugging mummy cases, and screaming that she wanted to be left with 'my people'. When she was later shown a photograph of the temple to the god Osiris, built beside the Nile by Pharaoh Seti I, she told her father that the temple was her real home, that she had known Seti and that he was a kind man.

In 1930, Dorothy married an Egyptian and went to live in his country. When they had a son, she called him Seti, and herself Um Seti, 'mother of Seti'. It was 22 years before she visited Abydos, site of the ancient temple to Osiris, and when the train stopped near a range of limestone hills she said that she was 'home'. In 1954 she returned to live at Abydos, helping to look after the temple, praying daily to Osiris, and persuading the temple curators to let her be buried in the grounds when she died.

Flowerdew and Dorothy Eady are both unusual in that their visions of previous lives did not rely on hypnosis.

Many hypnotherapists and psychiatrists have cases on their files similar to the two recorded by Welsh hypnotist Arnall Bloxham, of Cardiff, in 1956. One was of a teenager who, under hypnosis, spoke vividly of a previous existence as a man in a land where people were decorated with scars and teeth. The other was a woman who claimed to be the daughter of Charles I and Queen Henrietta Maria. She knew little of history, but could describe accurately the court of King Louis XIV of France, where she and her 'brother', the future Charles II, stayed during the royal family's exile after the English Civil War.

American amateur hypnotist Morey Bernstein described the curious claim of a Colorado housewife in his book *The Search for Bridey Murphy*, published in 1956. Bernstein was taking Mrs Ruth Simmons, born in the mid-west in 1923, back to her childhood under hypnosis when she started talking as Bridey Murphy. She said she had been born in Cork, Ireland, on 20 December 1798, had married a lawyer called Sean McCarthy when she was 17, and had moved to Belfast. She had died after a fall in 1864 and could describe her own funeral and tombstone.

Researchers in Ireland found much of her story difficult to corroborate, but her descriptions of the Antrim coastline and a journey from Belfast to Cork were accurate, and records were found of a grocer called Farr, at whose store Bridey claimed to have shopped. Mrs Simmons had never been to Ireland, and her normal voice had no trace of an Irish accent.

The man who lived two lives at once

On 17 January 1887, American carpenter and local preacher Ansel Bourne left his home in Rhode Island, drew $551 from his bank and set off to visit his nephew in Providence to discuss buying some land for a farm.

On the morning of 14 March, he awoke with a jolt in a bed at the back of a small confectionery and stationery store in Norristown, Pennsylvania, with no idea of what he was doing there.

His landlord explained that he was A. J. Brown, that he had rented the store in early February and had run the business and attended the local Methodist Church. But Bourne could recall nothing of what had happened after he had left his nephew's home two months earlier and 230 miles away. He had no idea why he should set up a business he knew nothing about and had no interest in.

Three years later, Bourne was hypnotized by Professor William James of Harvard and said his name was Albert John Brown. He detailed the journey to Pennsylvania on 17 January and described the setting-up of the shop. He was confused about his life before 17 January and could remember little after 13 March.

Professor James decided that Brown and Bourne were two distinct people, each with his own mannerisms, gestures and handwriting. Further hypnotic treatment caused Brown to fade away, never to return. But there was no explanation how, for two months, he had taken over another man's life.

Chapter
Five

Mysteries of Science and Discovery

Science boasts an ever-increasing fund of knowledge, but for every scientific breakthrough, there remains a blank page. How did life begin on earth? Who built Stonehenge – and why? Is the image on a shroud truly that of Christ? Until these and many other questions can be answered, science can only stand humble in the face of so much that remains beyond explanation.

The riddle of human spontaneous combustion

Victims who have for no apparent reason suddenly burst into flames

Widow Mary Reeser was a plump woman of 67 who lived quietly in a modest but pleasant apartment in St Petersburg, Florida. On the morning of 2 July 1951, a telegram arrived for her. The landlady, who lived in the same building, tried to deliver it but could get no reply from Mrs Reeser. She tried the doorknob. It was so hot to the touch that she cried out in pain.

Two painters were working nearby, so the landlady called them over and asked them to break in. They put their shoulders to the door and, with a splintering of woodwork, it swung open. The landlady and the workmen reeled back under a blast of furnace-hot air. But when shortly after they crept inside the apartment there was no sign of the conflagration they had expected. All they could see was a feeble flame flickering on the partition wall which separated them from the apartment's small kitchen. They easily put it out, and peered round the partition into the kitchen.

The landlady expected to see Mrs Reeser, perhaps sleeping in her armchair. But all she saw of the armchair were a few springs – and all she saw of Mrs Reeser were a few unrecognizably charred bones, a skull shrunken to half-size by intense heat, and a single satin carpet slipper containing a left foot burnt off at the ankle. . .

Plastic utensils in the kitchen had been melted and a mirror had been shattered by the heat. But the only other sign that there had been a fire was a small area of scorched floor. A newspaper lying near by was quite untouched.

At an inquest held into Mrs Reeser's death, experts professed themselves utterly baffled. The blaze which had consumed her body had been more intense than the 2,500° Fahrenheit needed to dispose of the corpses in the city's crematorium. Yet the fire had not spread by more than inches from the old woman's body. No cause could be found for the blaze, and a police suggestion that Mrs Reeser had fallen asleep while smoking and had set fire to her clothing was laughed out of court by the pathologist.

The experts admitted defeat. Their only other course would have been to admit the possibility of one of the strangest and most argued-about scientific phenomena of all time – spontaneous combustion, the sudden bursting into

Spontaneous combustion in Dickens's *Bleak House*.

flames of a human body, during which the clothing is sometimes not even scorched.

The unfathomable case of Mrs Reeser is only one of the more recent cases of spontaneous combustion. Such 'human torch' blazes have been discussed for centuries. (Charles Dickens referred to one in *Bleak House*.) But because 20th-century scientists are highly sceptical about the phenomenon, cases of it are seldom well documented and rarely studied. Even so, apart from the death of Mrs Reeser, there are some other well-substantiated cases.

THE WORLD'S GREATEST MYSTERIES

In 1880, an eminent physician, Dr B. H. Hartwell, was among several witnesses to the death of a woman at Ayer, Massachusetts. Flames suddenly burst from the woman's torso and legs, and she sank to the ground and died in a horrifying blaze.

In England, in 1919, a well-known author of the day, J. Temple Thurston, died at his Kent home, his body horribly burned from the waist down. The inquest verdict was that he had died from heart·failure. But no one could explain how he came to be burned over half his body when there was no sign of fire in his room and when the rest of his body was untouched, and how his body had blazed away beneath his clothes without even singeing them.

In 1922, Mrs Euphemia Johnson, a 68-year-old widow, was burned to a pile of blackened bones at her home in Sydenham, London. The fire that consumed her body must have been as intense as that of a furnace – yet her clothes were untouched.

Two similar, horrifying cases of spontaneous combustion occurred in England in the 1930s. The first involved a 19-year-old secretary, Maybelle Andrews, who was dancing with her boyfriend at a club in London's Soho. Flames suddenly shot from her chest and back, consuming her within minutes and resisting all attempts by other dancers to beat them out. At the inquest no solution was offered to the mystery of her death. Her numbed boyfriend, William Clifford, said: 'The flames seemed to come from within her body.' The inquest verdict: death by misadventure, caused by a fire of unknown origin.

The second case was reported in 1938. Phyllis Newcombe, 22, was leaving a dance hall at Chelmsford, Essex, when blue flames suddenly engulfed her body. She was reduced to a pile of ashes within minutes. The coroner who investigated her death said: 'In all my experience I have never come across anything as remarkable as this.'

Another case in England that same year was investigated by biologist Ivan Sanderson, who founded the Society for the Investigation of the Unexplained, in New Jersey. This was the case of Mrs Mary Carpenter, who was with her family aboard a boat on the Norfolk Broads on a hot summer's day. Suddenly, as her husband and children watched in horror, she burst into flames and was reduced to ashes.

Two of the best-authenticated cases of spontaneous human combustion in recent years have occurred in the United States. The first involved Billy Peterson, who was sitting in his parked car in Detroit when flames apparently burst from his body. When rescuers pulled out his charred corpse they found that the heat inside the car had been so intense that part of the dashboard had melted. Yet Billy Peterson's clothes had not even been singed.

The second and equally remarkable phenomenon occurred on 5 December

1966. Early that morning Don Gosnell started his working day reading gas meters in Coudersport, Pennsylvania. One of the first houses he called at was the home of Dr John Bentley, a 92-year-old retired family physician. Knowing that the old man could move around only with the help of a walking frame, Gosnell was not particularly surprised when no one answered the front door. He let himself in and walked downstairs to the basement to read the meter. There he found a neat little heap of ashes on the floor. Gosnell wondered how it had got there but did not think to look up at the ceiling, where a charred hole gave a clear view into the bathroom. The ashes had fallen like powder through the hole.

Gosnell read the meter and walked back upstairs, calling out for Dr Bentley. Traces of smoke hung in the air and as Gosnell walked down the hallway to investigate he sniffed 'a strange, sweetish smell'. He opened the bathroom door and fell back in horror.

The doctor's soot-blackened walking frame lay on the floor, overhanging a gaping hole, its edges scorched by fire. Also on the floor lay all that remained of Dr Bentley – a right foot, still in its carpet slipper and burnt off at the calf.

At the inquest which followed, the coroner recorded a verdict of 'death by asphyxiation and 90 per cent burning of the body'. All the comment he would make later was: 'It was the oddest thing you ever saw.'

The curse of Tutankhamun
Death struck down those who disturbed the sleep of the Pharaohs

In an English country house in the middle of the night a dog suddenly started howling. The constant, pitiful noise awoke the sleeping household. The wretched animal would not be comforted, and the howling continued until, breathless at last, the dog lay down and died.

This strange occurrence took place at the Hampshire home of a titled amateur archaeologist, 57-year-old Lord Carnarvon. At the moment the dog started howling, Carnarvon was himself drifting towards death, thousands of miles away in a room at the Hotel Continental, Cairo. The curse of the Pharaoh boy king Tutankhamun had claimed its first two victims. Many more were to follow.

The curse of the Pharaohs had been well known to Carnarvon, a fanatical Egyptologist. He had been reminded of it while still in England planning his latest and biggest expedition to Egypt to seek the fabled, treasure-packed tomb of Tutankhamun. He had received a cryptic warning from a famous mystic of the day, Count Hamon. The message read: 'Lord Carnarvon not to enter tomb. Disobey at peril. If ignored will suffer sickness. Not recover. Death will claim him in Egypt.' Carnarvon was so concerned about the warning that he twice consulted a fortune-teller, who each time forecast his impending death in mysterious circumstances.

Nevertheless, Carnarvon went ahead with the expedition, which was the culmination of a dream that had inspired him for years. When he arrived in Egypt he even affected a jaunty bravado and made light of the curse that was having such a profound influence on the frightened native diggers at the excavation site at Luxor. One of his close associates on the expedition, Arthur Weigall, was driven to remark: 'If Carnarvon goes down into the tomb in that spirit, I don't give him long to live.'

On 17 February 1923, Carnarvon and his team broke through into the funerary chamber of the boy king. Inside, Carnarvon and his American partner, Howard Carter, found treasures even they had never dreamed existed – gold, precious stones and gems as well as the solid-gold coffin containing the mummified body of Tutankhamun. Above the tomb was an inscription, which they translated. It read: 'Death will come to those who disturb the sleep of the Pharaohs.'

Two months later, the now-famous Lord Carnarvon awoke in his room at the Hotel Continental and said: 'I feel like hell.' By the time his son arrived, Carnarvon was unconscious. That night he died. Carnarvon's son was resting in an adjoining room at the moment of his father's death. He later recalled that 'the lights went out all over Cairo – we lit candles and prayed'.

Carnarvon's death was attributed to an infected mosquito bite, which debilitated him and caused the onset of pneumonia. Strangely, the mummified body of King Tutankhamun was said to have had a blemish on the left cheek in exactly the same spot as Carnarvon's mosquito bite.

Shortly afterwards there was another death at the Hotel Continental. American archaeologist Arthur Mace, one of the leading members of the expedition, complained of tiredness and suddenly sank into a coma. He died before his doctors could decide what was wrong with him.

The deaths of other Egyptologists followed one upon another. A close friend of Carnarvon, George Gould, rushed to Egypt as soon as he heard of the earl's death. Gould visited the Pharaoh's tomb. The next day he collapsed with a high fever. He died 12 hours later.

Radiologist Archibald Reid, who X-rayed Tutankhamun's body, was sent home to England after complaining of exhaustion. He died shortly afterwards.

Carnarvon's personal secretary on the expedition, Richard Bethell, was found dead in bed from heart failure.

British industrialist Joel Wool was one of the first visitors invited to view the

Lord Carnarvon and Howard Carter on the site of the excavation.

tomb. He died soon afterwards from a mysterious fever.

Within six years of the excavation of Tutankhamun's tomb, 12 of those present at the discovery had died. And within seven years only two of the original team of excavators were still alive. No fewer than 22 others connected with the expedition had died prematurely, including Lady Carnarvon and the earl's half-brother. He apparently committed suicide while temporarily insane.

One of the lucky survivors was the expedition's co-leader, Howard Carter. He continued to scoff at the legendary curse, and died of natural causes in 1939.

But the curse of the Pharaohs was still taking its toll years later. In 1966, Egypt's director of antiquities, Mohammed Ibraham, was asked by his government to arrange an exhibition of the Tutankhamun treasures in Paris. He argued against the decision and had a dream that he would face personal danger if the Pharaoh's treasures were to leave Egypt. As he left a final, unsuccessful meeting with government officials in Cairo, Mohammed Ibraham was knocked down by a car and killed.

Three years later, the sole survivor of the Tutankhamun expedition, 70-year-old Richard Adamson, gave an interview on British television to 'explode the myth of the curse'. Adamson, who had been a security guard with Lord Carnarvon, told viewers: 'I don't believe in the myth for one moment.' Later, as he left the television studios, his taxi crashed, throwing him out on to the road. A swerving lorry missed his head by inches. It was the third time that Adamson had tried to put paid to the legend. The first time he spoke out, his wife died within 24 hours. The second time, his son broke his back in a plane crash.

After his road accident, Adamson, recovering in hospital from head injuries, said: 'Until now I refused to believe that my family's misfortunes had anything to do with the curse. But now I am not so sure.'

Fear of the Pharaohs' curse was revived in 1972 when the golden mask of Tutankhamun was crated in Cairo for an exhibition at London's British Museum. In charge of the Cairo end of the operation was Dr Gamal Mehrez, who, as director of antiquities, was a successor to the ill-fated Mohammed Ibraham.

Dr Mehrez did not believe in the curse. He said: 'I, more than anyone else in the world, have been involved with the tombs and mummies of the Pharaohs, yet I am still alive. I am the living proof that all the tragedies associated with the Pharaohs have been pure coincidence. I don't believe in the curse for one moment.'

The doctor was at the Cairo Museum to organize the removal of the treasures on the day the shippers arrived to load the priceless cargo on to

The mask of Tutankhamun.

lorries. That evening, after watching the operation, Dr Mehrez died. He was 52. The cause of death was recorded as circulatory collapse.

Unperturbed, the organizers of the exhibition continued with the arrangements. A Royal Air Force Transport Command aircraft was loaned for the job of conveying the relics to Britain. Within five years of the flight, six members of the plane's crew had been struck by death or ill fortune.

Flight-Lieutenant Rick Laurie, chief pilot aboard the Britannia aircraft, and Flight-Engineer Ken Parkinson were perfectly fit men. But both were soon to die. Parkinson's wife said that her husband suffered a heart attack every year after the flight, each one at the same time of year. The last one, in 1978, killed him at the age of only 45. Chief pilot Laurie had died two years before him, also of a heart attack. At the time his wife said: 'It's the curse of Tutankhamun – the curse has killed him.' Laurie was just 40.

During the flight, Chief Technical Officer Ian Lansdowne had jokingly kicked a box containing Tutankhamun's death mask, saying: 'I've just kicked the most expensive thing in the world.' That leg was later in plaster for five months, badly broken after a ladder inexplicably collapsed under Lansdowne. The aircraft's navigator, Flight Lieutenant Jim Webb, lost all his possessions after his home was destroyed by fire. A girl aboard the plane had to quit the RAF after a serious operation.

A steward, Sergeant Brian Rounsfall, disclosed, 'On the flight back we played cards on the coffin case. Then we all took it in turns to sit on the case containing the death mask and we laughed and joked about it. We were not being disrespectful – it was just a bit of fun.' Rounsfall was 35 at the time. In the following four years he suffered two heart attacks.

Is there any logical explanation for the mysterious deaths and misfortunes of so many people connected with the Tutankhamun relics? Journalist Phillip Vandenburg studied the legend of the Pharaohs' curse for years. He came up with two remarkable suggestions. In his book, *The Curse of the Pharaohs*, he says that the tombs within the pyramids were perfect breeding grounds for bacteria which might have developed new and unknown strains over the centuries and might have maintained their potency until the present day.

He also points out that the ancient Egyptians were experts in the use of poison. Some poisons do not have to be swallowed to kill – they can be lethal by penetrating the skin. Poisonous substances were used in wall paintings within the tombs, which were then sealed and made airtight. For this reason, those who raided tombs in ancient days first bored a small hole through the chamber wall to allow fresh air to circulate before they broke in.

The most extraordinary explanation of all for the curse of the Pharaohs was put forward in 1949. It came from the atomic scientist Professor Louis

Bulgarini. He said: 'It is definitely possible that the ancient Egyptians used atomic radiation to protect their holy places. The floors of the tombs could have been covered with uranium. Or the graves could have been finished with radio-active rock. Rock containing both gold and uranium was mined in Egypt 3,000 years ago. Such radiation could kill a man today.'

A FATEFUL CARGO

In 1912, a liner was crossing the Atlantic with a valuable cargo - an Egyptian mummy. It was the body of a prophetess who lived during the reign of Tutankhamun's father-in-law, Amenhotep IV. An ornament found with the mummy bore the spell: 'Awake from the dream in which you sleep and you will triumph over all that is done against you.'

Because of its value, the mummy was not carried in the liner's hold, but in a compartment behind the bridge, on which the captain stood. The captain's name was Ernest Smith, Commodore of the White Star fleet. And it was partly because of his errors of judgment that the liner he commanded rammed an iceberg and sank with the loss of 1,513 lives.

The liner was the *Titanic*.

Sciences of the ancients

Is the story of mankind one of erratic but certain progress from ignorant savagery to civilized enlightenment? Or are we only now rediscovering marvels that our forefathers took for granted thousands of years before the birth of Christ?

In China a belt-fastener has been found which is made of high-grade aluminium, a metal supposedly first discovered in 1803 and not refined in a pure form until 50 years later. The fastener has been examined by scientists and is said to be nearly 1,700 years old.

The Egyptians and Palestinians of 5,000 years ago possessed building implements and ornaments made of bronze hardened to a degree that cannot be duplicated today.

Utensils, tools and ornaments, thousands of years old from Asia, Europe and North and South America have been found which show a skill and accuracy in their manufacture that would today require precision machinery, and sometimes enormously high smelting temperatures.

Ancient Hebrew legend tells of a glowing jewel that Noah hung up in the Ark to provide a constant source of illumination and of a similar object in the palace of King Solomon about 1000 BC. Other legends of the Middle East tell of jewelled lights illuminating tombs with an almost limitless source of power. These stories suggest that some form of nuclear power might have been harnessed all those years ago.

Evidence of electro-plating, a process long thought to have been developed in the 19th century, has been found in Egypt and Iraq on ornaments that date back 4,000 years.

Just before World War Two, a German archaeologist, Dr Wilhelm Koenig, discovered small clay pots in Iraq which were about 2,000 years old. Each contained cylinders of copper and iron rods and were sealed with bitumen. They showed evidence of having contained some sort of acid. Dr Koenig recognized them as electric cells. When later tested with an acid solution, they produced $1\frac{1}{2}$–2 volts of power.

As archaeologists unearth ever-more startling discoveries, it is worth pondering whether our gifted ancestors might have developed some of their own highly advanced sciences which 20th-century man can only now match?

The secret of Stonehenge

Was it a massive Stone Age observatory?

Gaunt and hauntingly remote, the megaliths of Europe – massive, monumental stones – rear up in a giant's chain. From Sweden and the Shetland Isles in the north to Spain and Malta in the south, they stand as mysterious monuments to the imagination, ingenuity and skills of our distant ancestors – people once dismissed as ignorant savages.

There are at least 50,000 sites, where great stones form rows, circles, ovals, crosses or horseshoes, sometimes amazingly precise in their geometry. Some stones still stand, but many more have toppled over. Countless others have been destroyed by man or nature.

None could have been more imposing than the Grand Menhir Brise at Lochmariaquer, in Brittany, which once stood 150 metres high and weighed between 300 and 400 tons. Now it lies split into four pieces. At nearby Carnac, uniform rows of stones, more than 3,000 of them, stretch away beyond the horizon.

Early European man's obsession with raising these giant pillars of stone

The megaliths of Stonehenge.

spanned a period of more than 2,000 years, coming to an end around 1500 BC. But the questions they arouse have never been satisfactorily answered. Who were the people who spent so much time and effort on hewing the great rocks and dragging them to selected sites? And why did they do it?

In earlier times the stones were thought to have been raised by legendary creatures – giants, wizards, demons, even the Devil. More recently, a popular myth linked the megaliths with the Celtic priests called Druids and their pagan rites – although it is now certain that they were built centuries before the time of the Druids. Yet another theory suggests that survivors from the lost city of Atlantis inspired this curious and widespread surge of building.

Another widely held belief was that ancient cultures of the eastern Mediterranean – advanced civilizations like those of the Greeks and Egyptians – had spread their influence westward by means of voyaging merchants or missionaries. But modern scientific techniques have cast serious doubts on this theory, and it is now known that stone monuments were being set up in Brittany possibly 1,000 years before the Egyptians built the Pyramids.

To underline the point, scientific dating methods show that the earliest megaliths are those on the fringe of the Atlantic seaboard and that the stone monuments become younger as they move eastward inland.

Experts who have studied the way primitive peoples live today think that the megaliths may have been used for a number of social and religious purposes: as rallying points, markets, temples, or a combination of all three. Certainly many of the stones marked Stone Age burial sites, and investigation of bones that have been preserved indicates that the sites were used as family vaults. Ancient tribes may have started the process by building stone cairns over their dead. And it is not difficult to imagine how different communities would want to erect bigger and better monuments as each tried to enhance its prestige over its neighbours.

But could the mystery of the megaliths have a more profound explanation?

Recent thinking has focussed on the astonishing connections between many of these stones and the heavenly bodies. Some scientists claim that the sites were astronomical observatories, used to provide information of practical value to farming and seafaring peoples. If this is the case, then our 'primitive' ancestors must have been men of remarkable knowledge and intellect.

At the heart of the observatory theory stands the vast, brooding enigma of Stonehenge, not the largest but easily the best known and most impressive of 900 or so sites scattered across the British Isles. This great stone circle, rising from the bleak expanse of Salisbury Plain, holds a special place among prehistoric sites because it is the only one where the blocks have been cleverly shaped and fitted together to form a carefully planned whole.

In the early 1960s, an American astronomer, Professor Gerald Hawkins, claimed to have solved the Stonehenge riddle. He made a close study of the numerous sight lines between the sun and moon and various points in the stone circles. When he fed his information into a computer the startling results showed that the site was indeed a huge observatory and could be used for extremely complex calculations and predictions. Stonehenge, in fact, was itself a kind of giant Stone Age computer.

These exciting ideas are by no means universally accepted among scientists and astronomers. But there is no doubt at all about the incredible feats of engineering design and technology that went into the building of Stonehenge.

There were three distinct stages in the development of the site, covering more than 1,000 years. And none of the three groups of builders quite managed to complete its task – leaving yet another mystery.

The first builders were Neolithic people who worked on the site around 2700 BC. They set out the encircling ditch and bank and the famous Heelstone, which lines up with the Midsummer's Day sunrise from the central point of the circles. These Stonehenge pioneers also dug the curious Aubrey Holes, named after the 17th-century writer who discovered them. The 56 shallow pits, which form a ring just inside the bank, contain cremated bones and were apparently filled in soon after being dug. Their purpose is still a matter of guesswork.

Stonehenge II was built some 800 years later by the Beaker People, so called because they buried pottery with their dead. Their almost incredible achievement was to bring to Stonehenge by sea and river 60 to 80 giant bluestones, each weighing more than four tons, from the Prescelly Hills in South Wales – a journey of 200–250 miles. In a further tremendous feat of strength

---

IS THERE A STONEHENGE 'LIFE FORCE'?
Could all the stone circle sites of Europe be linked together by a strong but indefinable 'life force'? Many of the circles are undoubtedly designed to line up with particular points on the horizon, and in some cases with each other.

This has led some investigators to put forward the theory of ley lines, lines of force that sent a powerful, beneficial energy across the countryside – energy which could be felt by people who were more in tune with the rhythms of nature than is modern man.

Supporters of this theory believe that although the system is no longer active, the ancient stones have not completely lost their 'magical' properties. Some photographs seem to show light radiating from the stones, and, in other experiments, people claim to have received electric shocks from the stones.

and skill, the Beaker People went on to set up the bluestones to form a double circle inside the earlier enclosure.

Still more breathtaking was the building of Stonehenge III, probably around 1500 BC, when the gigantic sarsen stones, nowadays the most familiar feature of the site, were placed in position. These huge standstone boulders, each weighing up to 50 tons, were transported more than 20 miles from the Marlborough Downs to the north.

All this was taking place at a time when there were no wheeled vehicles. Everything had to be moved either by water, where possible, or even more laboriously by primitive sledges hauled overland by large teams of men.

The builders of Stonehenge II (whose work was later to be uprooted by the third group) must have been possessed of a rare determination even to contemplate shifting their bluestones from the south-west corner of Wales all the way to the heart of southern England. It involved a journey of daunting complexity. First they probably had to drag the great stones from the mountains down to the coast, then manhandle them on to rafts to carry them up what is now the Bristol Channel. For the remainder of the journey they would have had to transfer the massive loads to canoes, lashed together for two separate river passages and further hauls by sledges.

Although the sarsen stones used in Stonehenge III had to be moved only 20 miles or so, this was an even more formidable problem. For these 50-ton monsters would have needed as many as 1,000 men at a time to heave them by rope across country on sledges and rollers.

Even when the last generation of Stonehenge builders had managed to bring their raw materials to the site, their task was far from complete. They then had to chip and pound the colossal blocks into shape, using chunks of the same stone – and sarsen is the toughest of all British stones to work.

Next came the positioning of the pillars, possibly achieved by raising the stones bit by bit on timber ramps or scaffolding until they could be tipped into their prepared holes. Finally, the great stone lintels would have been lifted on to the tops of the towering 21-ft uprights, again by means of a gradually raised timber square.

While we marvel at the brute strength expended on this massive project, we must also admire the expertise of craftsmen who fashioned accurate peg-and-socket joints to fit the slabs together, who had the geometric and architectural vision to cut the horizontal blocks with gentle curves that joined to form one continuous curve, and who balanced them with delicate precision on a sloping hill site.

How did 'primitive' man learn such skills? And how can it be explained that Stonehenge shares with scores of other sites throughout Europe a standard unit of measurement – the 'megalithic yard' of 2·72 ft? How, too, was the impetus to build maintained over so many years? No one can be sure how long the builders of Stonehenge laboured on their vast undertaking, but one estimate is 1½ million man-days.

What compelling force drove men to spend hundreds of years virtually moving mountains? And why did they suddenly abandon their project?

Finally, perhaps a still more intriguing puzzle: if Stonehenge was planned and built by men of such skill and learning – pioneering engineers, architects, mathematicians and astronomers – why did they never create anything else (the wheel, for instance) to further man's development?

Is this the face of Christ?

The image on the Turin Shroud has staggered the Christian world

Photography was a hobby only for the dedicated in 1898. Secundo Pia, an Italian archaeologist, was a mere amateur. But the photograph he took in the Chapel of the Dukes of Savoy at Turin Cathedral was of profound significance to Christianity. For the negative that Pia produced appeared to show the face of Christ.

The young archaeologist was the first person to be allowed to photograph the cathedral's most famous relic, the Turin Shroud, in which Christ is reputed to have been wrapped after the Crucifixion. The shroud had always been said to bear the faint outlines of Christ's body – although the same claim had been made for 40 or more other pieces of linen preserved in various churches around Europe. But when Pia took his photograph, the result was a clear negative picture of a crucified man.

Because scientific photography was a relatively untried medium, Pia's remarkable picture was not at first universally accepted as genuine. It was not until 1931 that the shroud was again properly photographed, this time by a professional cameraman, Guiseppe Enri. And it was his remarkable picture which converted many of the sceptics, as well as prompting world-wide interest in the relic.

Nowadays, following years of scientific investigation, the Holy Shroud of Turin can be 'read' almost like a book. It tells a story that spans almost 2,000 years.

The shroud is 14 ft long and 3½ ft wide. It is made of a mixture of cotton and linen, woven into a regular herringbone pattern in the style common in

Palestine during the 1st century AD. Swiss scientists have even analyzed pollen in the cloth and dated it to the same period. The cream-coloured material is marked by a faint brown outline of a man's body, with darker, rust-coloured stains of blood. The marks indicate that the man was naked, 5 ft 11 in tall and had shoulder-length hair and a beard. It is also clear that he had been tortured and crucified. The hands had been nailed through the palms and the feet had been fastened together by a single nail. The stains indicate that the body had received more than 100 lash marks, many inflicted with a scourge – a flail with heavy metal balls attached – and that the man's side had been pierced by a spear.

It is easy to accept that blood would have stained the shroud, but it is not so simple to understand how the outline of the body could have been dyed into the fabric and remained for so many centuries. One popular explanation is that the resurrection caused a supernatural release of energy which scorched the linen. More scientific is the theory that the stains were caused by gas from the skin (probably ammonia) or sweat, mixed with ritual Jewish burial spices.

The most recent and most startling theory, however, is that put forward by US Air Force scientists who believe that the image on the shroud was caused by a micro-second burst of intense radiation.

Much research was carried out to trace the journey of the shroud back to its origins. The first reference to the Crucifixion shroud comes in St Mark's Gospel, which states that the cloth in which Christ was wrapped was found in his empty tomb. Three hundred years elapsed before the shroud was next mentioned in the reports of pilgrims to Jerusalem. The cloth then found its way from Palestine to Constantinople, and from there to France, where it arrived in the 13th century.

In the late 15th century it was given for safe keeping to Louis I, who built a chapel at Chambéry to house it. But in 1532 fire swept the chapel and damaged the silver casket in which the relic was kept. It is assumed that this was when the folded shroud acquired the symmetrical burn marks which disfigure it. The fabric was carefully mended by nuns and was eventually moved to Turin Cathedral in 1572.

If the history of the shroud is so uncertain, why are so many Christians convinced that it represents the only true picture of Christ? Thousands of people were crucified by the Romans. Why single out this burial cloth as being that of Christ?

The answer has been provided by the scientists. They say that the imprint on the shroud indicates that the victim's hair was matted with blood and that blood had coagulated in scratches across his forehead. It is evidence that tallies with Biblical stories of the crown of thorns thrust mockingly on to the head of the 'King of the Jews'.

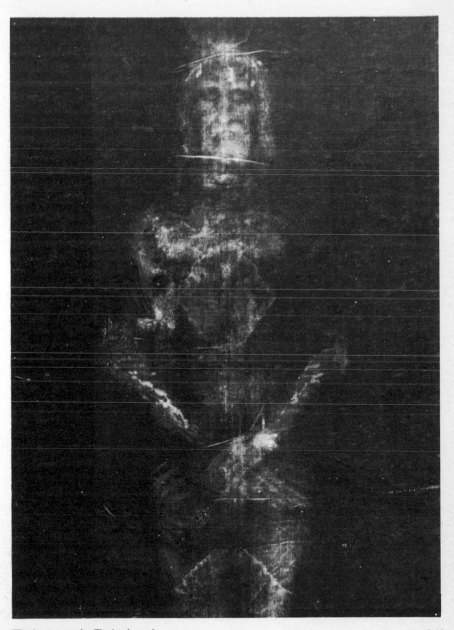

The image on the Turin shroud.

The great pyramid of Giza

A building whose construction would have daunted modern engineers

The Great Pyramid at Giza, in Egypt, was designed to be a lasting and fitting memorial to King Khufu, better known by his Greek name of Cheops – one of the most powerful rulers the ancient world had known. About 40 pyramids stand along the banks of the Nile, but none can compare with the Great Pyramid. It stands more than 450 ft high and covers an area of 13 acres – enough space in which to cluster together Westminster Abbey, St Paul's Cathedral and the great cathedrals of Milan and Florence.

The accurately cut blocks of stone used to build it – 2,300,000, each weighing from two to 15 tons – would provide more than enough material to construct all the cathedrals, churches and chapels built in England since the coming of Christianity. Napoleon's surveyors calculated that it contained enough stone to build a wall three yards high and a yard thick around the whole of France.

Its base is a perfect square, the four sides accurately facing the four points of the compass. The corners are almost perfect right angles.

Even today, it is difficult to imagine how awesome it is without standing in its huge shadow. But 5,000 years ago it was even more magnificent, when it was faced with gleaming white limestone – long since plundered for building material elsewhere – and topped by a 30 ft capstone of beaten gold.

But is the Great Pyramid merely a technological marvel, or something that has a much deeper, mystical significance?

As more and more is discovered about the ancient past, irrefutable evidence comes to light that ancient civilizations often reached astonishing levels of scientific expertise. Some seem even to have possessed knowledge that we lack today. How, for example, did the ancient Egyptians, who had not yet even discovered the wheel, raise the Great Pyramid with the aid only of levers and rollers? How did they carve their giant blocks of granite with such amazing precision? How did they harden their bronze tools to a strength that cannot be duplicated today? And how did they acquire the confidence to launch a project whose scale would daunt even the most adventurous of modern architects and engineers?

The Great Pyramid stands on a rocky plateau ten miles west of Cairo. It is thought that a perfectly level foundation was made for it by building a mud wall around the plateau and flooding the area. As the water was gradually drained, bumps were revealed and were cut away until a flat surface was left. On to this foundation, even more level than that beneath a 20th-century skyscraper, gangs of labourers hauled giant blocks of sandstone from nearby quarries. The facing surface of gleaming limestone had to be brought further, from quarries on the far bank of the Nile. The stones were drawn on sledges up gentle ramps. Once in position, teams of stonemasons took over, cutting them to perfection.

In case King Khufu should die before the work was completed, a tomb was tunnelled deep into the solid rock foundations beneath the pyramid, and later another was created within the pyramid itself but at a lower level than the planned burial chamber. This was placed in the heart of the pyramid, 138 ft above ground level. It was reached by a tiny passageway which opened out into a majestic 25-ft-high gallery. Huge granite 'plugs' were placed within the passageway so that it could be blocked forever once the priests had completed the rites inside the funerary chamber.

But despite all these elaborate arrangements, it seems that a body was never placed in the Great Pyramid.

Egyptologists who have studied the pyramids closely are basically divided into two groups – those who think the pyramids have some deep and mysterious significance and those who think they are merely tombs. But if the Great Pyramid is merely a tomb, why the absence of a body, and why the mathematical accuracy of every wall, slope, corridor and cavity?

As is shown by the tombs in the Valley of the Kings – where Tutankhamun's grave was found – bodies were normally buried surrounded by artefacts and valuables. Thieves, when they raided the tombs, would steal what was valuable and very rarely carry away the bodies. Yet, when the Great Pyramid was first breached in about AD 800 – by a young caliph of Baghdad, Al Mamun – nothing was found in it.

Al Mamun was, in fact, after knowledge, not plunder. He had heard legends that the Great Pyramid contained astronomical charts and maps, unbreakable glass and purest metals. After a hazardous and difficult assault on the tomb, which entailed his men carving out passages around the giant granite plugs, he finally reached the King's Chamber. All it contained was a lidless and empty sarcophagus, or stone coffin.

THE WORLD'S GREATEST MYSTERIES

It seemed impossible to the caliph, after he had seen the undisturbed granite plugs, that anyone could have been there before. He searched for evidence of forced entry or plundering – but in vain. Finally, he left, disappointed – and baffled as to why the vast monument had been built.

The Great Pyramid was then left virtually undisturbed for centuries until British and French scientists and mathematicians started to take an interest in it during the 17th and 18th centuries. In 1638, the Oxford scholar John Greaves explored the King's Chamber and marvelled at its accuracy 'even to a 1,000th part of a foot'. His findings attracted the attention of his fellows, including Sir Isaac Newton, and they laboured – unsuccessfully – to discover the secrets of the Great Pyramid.

In the 1830s an English adventurer, Colonel Richard Howard-Vyse, led a team which stumbled across two 9-in. conduits leading from the north and south walls into the King's Chamber. When these passages were cleared it was found that the temperature inside the chamber, regardless of the climate

THE 'POWER' OF THE PYRAMIDS

It has long been claimed that the pyramids contain mysterious forces that cannot be explained. There have been tests attempting to prove that the structures are magnets for cosmic rays, or that they are power-houses of static electricity. There are also many stories of visitors to the pyramids being able to foresee their own fates. Tourists sometimes go into shock or faint.

On 12 August 1799, Napoleon visited the King's Chamber inside the Great Pyramid. After some time, he asked his guide to leave him. When he finally emerged, Napoleon, the conqueror of Europe, was white and shaken. Asked what had happened, he said brusquely: 'I do not want this matter referred to ever again.' Later in his life, he hinted that he had foreseen the future while in the Great Pyramid. Shortly before his death on St Helena, he seemed about to reveal his secret to an aide. Then he said: 'No. What's the use? You'd never believe me.'

But the most extraordinary cases of pyramid power have been experienced by ordinary people with non-scientific minds who have never been anywhere in Egypt. They are the folk who claim remarkable successes by using cardboard, metal or plastic models built to the precise scale of the Great Pyramid. These models are said to keep razor blades sharp for great lengths of time, keep food fresh, promote feelings of peace and contentment, and even help shape the future.

During the 1850s, a Frenchman named Bovis visited the

outside, remained a steady 68° Fahrenheit – ideal for storing the scientific weights and measures that featured in the legendary tales about the tomb.

Another Englishman, John Taylor, the son of the editor and publisher of *The Observer* newspaper, made further discoveries 30 years later without even straying from his own study. He made a thorough examination of all that was then known about the Great Pyramid and, in his book *The Great Pyramid: Why Was It Built and Who Built It?* he reached the conclusion that the Egyptians 'knew the earth was a sphere and, by observing the motion of heavenly bodies over the earth's surface, had ascertained its circumference, and were desirous of leaving behind them a record of the circumference as correct and imperishable as it was possible for them to construct'.

His studies revealed that the height of the pyramid bore the same relationship to its perimeter as the radius of a circle does to its circumference. This seemed to show that the Egyptians knew of the value of pi, the invaluable mathematical principle that was not thought to have been discovered until

Great Pyramid. Inside, among the usual debris left behind by tourists, he found the body of a dead cat - a remarkably well-preserved mummified body. When he returned home, Bovis experimented with model pyramids, built to scale, and found they helped to keep food fresh.

A hundred years later, Czech engineer Karel Drbal read of Bovis's experiments. There was a shortage of razor blades behind the Iron Curtain, and Drbal wondered whether the pyramid power would extend to metal. He built a model pyramid and found that the razor blades he placed in it never became blunt. When he went to the patent office in Prague in 1959 he was not believed. But, after the chief scientist there tested the idea, Drbal was granted patent No. 91304.

Why the technique should work nobody knows. The only clue is the old World War One legend that razor blades left out in the moonlight go blunt. The edge of a razor blade is composed of minute crystals. If the energy generated by the rays of the moon can blunt a blade, could the energy said to be generated by a pyramid help keep it sharp?

There are certain rules to be followed for the pyramid to work. It must be built on a base-to-side ratio of 15.7 to 14.94 and its sides must be aligned with the four points of the compass. The razor blade must rest 3.33 units high, and the sharp edges must face east and west.

Nobody can explain the secret power of the pyramid, but there are thousands of people around the world who swear that it works.

3,500 years later. His findings were confirmed by the brilliant mathematician, Charles Piazzi Smyth, who became astronomer royal for Scotland.

Other theories then followed thick and fast. Some were inspired, some eccentric, some religious and deeply mystical, others practical and scientific. One idea put forward was that the Great Pyramid had been built as a giant clock. In 1853, the French physicist Jean Baptiste Biot deduced that the wide, level pavements adjoining the northern and southern faces were graduated shadow floors. In the winter, the pyramid would cast its shadow on the northern pavement, and in the summer, the polished limestone face would reflect the sun on to the southern floor. In this way the time of day and the day of the year could be seen. David Davidson, a British structural engineer from Leeds, and fellow-Yorkshireman Moses B. Cotsworth followed up Biot's idea and claimed that it was correct and that the Egyptians could measure the length of the year to within three decimal places.

Another idea was that the Great Pyramid is, in fact, a huge observatory. The 19th-century British astronomer Richard Proctor pointed out that the corridor known as the Descending Passage was precisely aligned with the Pole Star. The Pole Star in those days, because of the earth's slight shift on its axis over the centuries, was Alpha Draconis. But as the Great Pyramid has moved along with the earth, the Descending Passage is now aligned with Polaris, the present Pole Star. Proctor pointed out that the various slots and notches to be found in the Grand Gallery of the Great Pyramid could have been used to support movable benches and platforms for observers to study with their instruments the passage of the stars across the entrance opening of the Grand Gallery.

Members of the Institute of Pyramidology, in London, believe that the Great Pyramid accurately prophesies the future of humanity. They claim that it can be shown, through a complicated system of measurements and mathematics, that the Great Pyramid predicted the exodus of the Jews from Egypt, the Crucifixion of Christ, the outbreak of World War One – which, they say, was the beginning of the breakdown of the Old Order as foretold by both Daniel and Jesus – and the beginning of the Millennium in the autumn of 1979. This, the group says, marks the beginning of Christ's 1,000-year rule on earth which will end with Armageddon and the Day Of Judgment in 2979.

Author Peter Tompkins, who made an exhaustive study of the mysteries of Giza, wrote a book in 1971 which attempted to solve the enigma of the Great Pyramid. Tompkins claimed that the priests of Egypt promised Khufu a mighty tomb. But once the king had sanctioned and financed the building, they set about constructing not a tomb, but a monument to their scientific knowledge. And when he died, the deluded Khufu was not buried there.

With Dr Livio Strecchini, professor of ancient history at New Jersey's

Oxen threshing wheat at the foot of the Great Pyramid.

William Paterson College, Tompkins studied the scientific achievements of the pyramid builders and came up with the following conclusions:
- The Great Pyramid is a carefully located landmark from which the geography of the ancient world was worked out.
- It served as an observatory from which maps and tables of the stars were drawn with remarkable accuracy.
- Its sides and angles were the basis of all ancient map-making.
- Its structure incorporated a value for pi.
- It may have been a practical library of the ancients' system of weights and measures.
- Builders knew the precise circumference of the earth, and the length of its year, including its 'left-over' .2422 of a day. They may also have known the length of the earth's orbit around the sun, the specific density of the earth, the 26,000-year cycle of the equinoxes, the acceleration of gravity and the speed of light.

Could the ancient Egyptians, 3,000 years before the birth of Christ, have known all this? And if they did, how did they gain this knowledge, and why was it forgotten for centuries?

It is obvious to everyone who sees the Great Pyramid that an advanced civilization was responsible for building it. Did this civilization also possess powers that today we can only wonder at?

Did life begin with a 'dirty snowball'?

How did life begin on earth? What originated the myriad living forms of which man is the most sophisticated? Ever since Charles Darwin published his theories that man evolved from the ape, scientists have been delving further back into primeval history in an attempt to discover the origin of life itself.

The conventional view is that life emerged about 3,000 or 4,000 million years ago from what is termed 'primordial soup' and that flashes of lightning in the earth's early turbulent atmosphere created the correct mixture of chemicals to produce primitive cells – the first forms of life.

But more recently, another answer to the mystery has been propounded. The man behind the theory is Sir Fred Hoyle, an arch debunker of accepted scientific dogma. Hoyle, who was professor of astronomy at Cambridge University for 20 years, believes that life on earth began with a 'dirty snowball'. Our remote ancestors, he says, were born in dust clouds floating around our galaxy. According to Hoyle, these clouds contained viruses and bacteria. Some of them were picked up by a comet which later burst into the earth's atmosphere – 'seeding' the dead planet with life-giving cells. The tail of a comet is made up of gas and dust, but its tiny head also contains ice particles – life-giving water to nurture the bacteria it carries.

The theory was treated with disdain when Hoyle first expounded it in the 1940s. But since then, astronomers have turned up some strange finds in the dust clouds that float between the stars. These clouds contain chemicals crucial in the chain of life, including methylated spirits, formic acid, formaldehyde, and even something akin to neat gin. And recently there was an even greater boost for Hoyle's theory. It was discovered that the gas cloud known as Orion Nebula contains cellulose – a substance which, Hoyle claimed, makes up half of all living molecules.

If the professor's theories are correct, they may explain a seemingly superstitious belief held in medieval times. In those days, a comet in the sky was regarded as a harbinger of plague and death. Could this have been right? Is bacteria transmitted by comets that enter the earth's atmosphere? Could it be that the Great Plague was caused by a mere 'dirty snowball'?

Chapter Six

Mysteries of Ghosts and Ghouls

Ghosts, spectres, poltergeists. . . Many level-headed witnesses claim to have seen these apparitions from beyond the grave. And can every single one of them have been imagining things?
Who or what caused the eerie happenings at Borley Rectory? Is it the spirit of a brutally murdered Victorian actor who haunts Covent Garden to this day? Was it a ghost that offered 'Kojak' a lift? And what caused the repeated disturbances in a sealed tomb on Barbados?

Faces on the floor

Microphones picked up strange voices and agonized moanings

An old Spanish woman was looking after her grandchild in the kitchen of her tiny village home when the youngster suddenly cried out. The grandmother turned round – and got the shock of her life. For what had frightened the child was a sad, tormented face staring up from the faded pink tiles of the kitchen floor. When the woman had recovered her presence of mind, she tried to rub away the face. But the eyes only opened wider, making the expression of the face even more doleful.

After the incident, in August 1971, the old woman sent for the owner of the house, which is in Belmez, near Cordoba. He ripped up the tiled floor and replaced it with concrete. But three weeks later another face appeared, its features even more clearly defined. The local authorities were called in. They dug up the section of floor, and discovered underneath the remains of a medieval burial ground.

Now faces started appearing all over the kitchen floor – first one, then another, then a whole group. When the kitchen was locked and sealed, four more faces appeared in another part of the house, and ultra-sensitive microphones set up by investigators recorded sounds the ear could not pick up – agonized moans and voices speaking in a strange tongue. Then faces and sounds both melted away, as mysteriously as they had arrived, leaving no clue as to what they were or why they had come.

The unknown had invaded the known again – proving that even in an age of sophisticated technology and scientific research there are still mysteries of the spirit world that defy explanation.

Never have ghosts been subjected to such thorough investigation as they have in the last 40 years. Some have been proved hoaxes or genuine mistakes. Others have been rated doubtful. But there remain some phenomena that the experts cannot explain away.

Man has believed in ghosts since the Stone Age. Fear of the dead returning to harass the living prompted ceremonies to make sure the souls of the departed rested in peace. Ancient Babylonians, Egyptians and Assyrians all left ritual offerings in tombs to placate spirits. The Greeks and Romans also believed that the disturbed souls of the dead wandered the earth, haunted the wicked and terrified the good – particularly if the body had not been properly buried or burned.

Pliny, Roman consul at Sura, records the story of a long-haunted house in Athens. Eventually the philosopher Athenodorous moved into the house to keep watch himself. When a spectre dragging chains appeared, he followed it until it vanished in the courtyard. He marked the spot, and when it was dug up the next day, the skeleton of a man in chains was found. After a public burning of the bones, the ghost appeared no more.

In ancient India, people left food and other offerings in shrines to propitiate the 'bauta', gibbering spooks with small red bodies and lions' teeth believed to wander the land after dark. The Chinese left cakes out to placate their apparitions, which appeared in green light, the head first, then the feet, then the body. In Japanese folklore, dishevelled women in white robes and Samurai warriors, almost always legless, bore their earthly scars, and foxes turned into beautiful women, bewitching all who saw them. North American Indians did ghost dances to ward off spirits of the dead, who were said to chirp like crickets.

Even Christ spoke of a spirit dimension to life on earth. When his disbelieving disciples thought him a ghost after the Resurrection, Christ said, according to Luke: 'A spirit hath not flesh and bones, as you see me to have.'

So what is a ghost? For as long as man has believed in them, he has been trying to answer that question. French and German occultists once believed that ghosts were formed from salt in the body as it fermented and decayed after burial. Mediums suggest that when we die we remain earthbound until a guide directs us to our place in the 'afterlife'. How long we stay earthbound depends on our behaviour before death.

Another explanation put forward is that we have all lived previous lives, and any ghosts we may see are reincarnations of people we half-remember from our previous existences, dressed in the costume of that time. Others have pointed out that ghosts generally appear either after dark, when the mind is least prepared to reason and is most susceptible to loneliness and half-caught impressions, or at a time of extreme crisis or exhaustion, when hallucinations are likely.

Others suggest that time as we know it may not be the only form of time, that there may be several different levels of time existing side by side. If this is true, could it be that ghosts are merely travelling through time at a different pace, or in a different way, when we dimly glimpse them? Ghost chronicler Anthony Hippisley Coxe likens time to a long-playing record. We experience the results produced by one stylus. But what if there were to be more than one stylus on the record?

Today, many experts agree with the theory of Maurice Barbanell, editor of *Psychic News*, who believes ghosts are 'the timeless imprint left behind by people who died in trouble, difficulty or anguish, or by violence, producing an emotion so violent that it can impregnate a room'. The imprint is there as if on a sensitive film. But it needs receptive people at special moments in the right circumstances to discern the image.

Throughout the years, people have played hoaxes on those who believe in ghosts. Sometimes it is done out of mischief, as with the boys in the 18th century who tied candles to the shells of tortoises and set them loose in graveyards. Sometimes ghost stories are fabricated by those who want to deflect attention from their deeds, like the smugglers who spread stories of hauntings to keep honest folk out of the way. And sometimes ghosts are summoned up to help tricksters make money – tricksters like the fake mediums and picture forgers who tried to cash in on gullible spiritualists around the turn of the century.

Many ghosts may have been debunked, but the fact remains that the highly-respected Society for Psychical Research, founded in 1882, still has a list of 700 well-documented events in Britain alone for which no rational or logical explanation has ever been found. . .

Ghost 'capital' of the world

Every city, town and hamlet in Britain has its spirit

Every country of the globe has its ghosts and haunted sites. But nowhere is the spirit population greater than in Britain. It seems that in this land steeped in history and mystery, every city, every town, every hamlet, every historic building has its spirit.

Recent surveys reveal that about one in seven people in Britain claims to have seen a ghost. And they are in distinguished company. Over the years, kings, hard-headed scientists and scholars, sceptical authors like Sir Arthur Conan Doyle and Captain Marryat, bishops, and leading churchmen such as John Wesley have all been convinced by the evidence they have seen.

GHOSTS AND GHOULS

Ghosts have been seen in all kinds of places, from palaces and castles to humble farming crofts. Workmen busy at No. 10 Downing Street in 1960 claimed that they saw a misty figure in the garden. It could have been the ghost of the Regency politician said to haunt the house at times of national crisis.

The Tower of London, scene of many bloody deeds down the ages, possesses a veritable crowd of ghosts. The most frequent 'visitor' is Anne Boleyn, second wife of Henry VIII, who was imprisoned in the Tower and executed there in May 1536. In the 19th century, a guard attracted by a strange light in the chapel of St Peter ad Vincular, where Anne was buried, climbed a ladder to peer through a window – and saw a procession in Elizabethan dress file slowly up the aisle, led by a woman who looked like Anne. Then the eerie crowd suddenly vanished, leaving the chapel in darkness again.

In 1864, a sentry at the Tower was court-martialled for being found asleep on watch. He claimed a strange white figure had ignored his challenge. It wore a curious bonnet, but there was no head inside. And when he ran his bayonet into the figure, a fiery flash ran up his rifle. He fainted. Other soldiers and an officer testified to seeing the headless woman walk straight through the bayonet and the sentry. The court found the man not guilty.

Anne's ghost is said to arrive headless in a phantom coach at Blickling Hall, Norfolk, her childhood home, on the anniversary of her death, 19 May. It was also said to appear at the Tower on the eve of an execution. In February 1915, at 2 am, Sergeant William Nicholls and his watch all saw a woman dressed in brown with a ruff round her neck. She walked quickly towards the Thames, then disappeared into a 9-ft-thick stone wall. Just five hours later, a spy was shot in the Tower moat, one of 11 executed there during World War One. Anne was last sighted in 1933, when a sentry fled in terror after challenging, then bayonetting, the headless apparition.

But the unfortunate Anne is not the only mysterious visitor to the Tower of London. Two little children have been seen wandering the Bloody Tower hand in hand. They are said to be Edward and Richard, the princes allegedly murdered in the Tower by their uncle, so that he could take the throne as Richard III.

In 1817, Edward Swifte, Keeper of the Crown Jewels, whose family lived with him in Martin Tower, saw an apparition like a glass tube as thick as a man's arm, filled with white and blue liquid, hovering above his supper table. A few days later, a sentry saw what he thought was a bear coming out under a door to the Jewel Room. But when the keeper lunged at it with his bayonet, he only struck the wood of the door. He passed out from shock, and died a few days later.

Other historic buildings connected with British royalty are said to be haunted. In the 17th century, an apparition of the armour-clad Duke of Buckingham appeared at Windsor Castle three times before a terrified servant called Parker, and commanded him to tell the Duke's son that, unless he mended his callous ways, he had not long to live. The son, Sir George Villiers, took no notice and six months later was assassinated. Other apparitions said to have been seen at the castle include those of Elizabeth I, Charles I and George III.

Hampton Court is haunted by two of Henry VIII's unhappy wives, Jane Seymour and Catherine Howard. But the best-authenticated visitor is Mistress Sibell Penn, nurse to Edward VI. Sibell died of smallpox in 1562 and was buried in old Hampton Church. But in 1829, the church was pulled down and her remains scattered. Soon strange noises and mutterings were heard from the room in Hampton Court where the nurse had lived. Since then a tall, thin, grey-robed figure with a hood over her head has been seen several times, her arms outstretched in appeal. In 1881, a sentry saw her walk through a wall.

Glamis Castle, built on the site where Macbeth murdered King Duncan, is nowadays best known as the favourite Scottish residence of Queen Elizabeth, the Queen Mother, and the birthplace of Princess Margaret. But Glamis has for centuries been surrounded by legends of secret rooms and hideous monsters. Rumour has it that a workman who stumbled on a secret passage was paid a large sum to emigrate by the then Lord Strathmore. The present earl denies all knowledge of a ghoulish creature haunting the castle, but there have been many reports of guests being awakened in the night by the howling and snarling of an animal.

One guest told of seeing a pale face with large mournful eyes staring at her from a window across the courtyard. It disappeared. Then she heard appalling screams, and saw an old woman scurry across the yard carrying a large bundle. Another guest was awakened by the sound of hammering – and learned later that, since the hanging in 1537 of Janet Douglas, wrongly convicted of witchcraft and treason, ghostly hammering foretells the death of someone in the household.

In 1869, a Mr and Mrs Monro were guests in the castle. In the middle of the night, Mrs Monro awoke to feel a beard brush her face. Someone, or something, was standing over her. As she fumbled for a light, the figure moved into the adjacent dressing room, where their son was sleeping. His screams of terror sent both parents racing to his bedside, and the boy explained that he had seen a giant. Then they all heard a thunderous crash. At breakfast next morning, other guests said they had heard the crash. And one said her small dog had awakened her with mournful howls. But no one had any explanation for their troubled night.

London's historic St Paul's Cathedral has its own strange ghost story. A

The Tower of London.

wooden box containing jewels was unearthed by workmen digging the foundations for a new building alongside the cathedral. The jewels were deposited with the British Museum, and an expert took them home to clean, polish and value them. As he and his daughter worked away, they puzzled over why the room suddenly grew cold.

A psychic visitor found an answer. He saw a tall, thin man in Elizabethan clothes standing behind the couple, angry that his booty had been disturbed. When the jewels went on display at the museum there was another surprise. A woman inspecting them fainted. When she revived, she said she had seen blood on one gold necklace. Although attendants could see nothing, the woman remained adamant that the person who last wore the necklace had been murdered.

Theatres are traditional haunts of ghosts. More than 50 cleaners at the Theatre Royal, in London's Drury Lane, claim to have seen a man in a long grey coat and a powdered wig wandering round the dress circle, often on the eve of a successful run. Could this 18th-century dandy be connected with a skeleton found bricked up in a hollow wall in 1860? The skeleton, discovered by workmen, had a dagger in its ribs.

Strange happenings at the Adelphi Theatre, Covent Garden, are blamed on the ghost of William Terriss, an adventurer turned actor, who was stabbed to death outside the theatre in December 1897, after playing the lead in a thriller called *Secret Service*. Curious tappings, the sound of footsteps, the moving of mechanical lifts and the switching on and off of lights are all ascribed to his restless spirit. In 1928 a comedy actress using his old dressing room felt her couch lurching as though someone was trying to move it. Then her arm was seized, leaving a bruise. She knew nothing of the stories of a ghost until her dresser arrived.

Terriss's strangest appearance came in 1955, when Jack Hayden, a ticket collector at Covent Garden underground station, saw a tall, distinguished, grey-suited figure with white gloves at the station. When Hayden asked if he could help, the figure vanished. But four days later it returned and put its hands on the head of 19-year-old porter Victor Locker. He screamed and ran. Pictures of Terriss were shown to both men, and both recognized him instantly. Hayden and Locker later asked for transfers. But since then, other London Transport staff on the Piccadilly line have spoken of a strange presence at Covent Garden. And in 1972 a stationmaster, signalman and engineer there all claimed to have seen the man in grey.

Another London landmark that once had a ghost was Smithfield Market. In 1654 butchers complained that the ghost of a lawyer called Mallet glided through their stalls every Saturday evening, pulling joints of meat off their slabs. When they went for the mischievous spirit with cleavers and carving

Borley Rectory.

knives, they hit nothing but air.

Ghosts also haunt family homes, often forcing the occupants to move out. That happened in the 1970s in Nottingham, where a lorry driver and his daughter both reported seeing the figure of what looked like a foreign legionnaire in their modest house. Psychic researchers moved in, and during their midnight vigil noted a sharp drop in temperature, a loud scream, hysterical sobbing and footsteps. At a seance it was concluded that the ghost was that of a window-cleaner in white overalls who had committed suicide after falling from his ladder and becoming paralysed. He had been in love with the lorry driver's daughter.

Perhaps the world's most famous haunted house was Borley Rectory, a gloomy mansion on the Essex-Suffolk border which was burned down in 1939. Built in 1863 for the Reverend Henry Dawson Ellis Bull, the 23-room redbrick house became a centre of controversy for those who believed in ghosts and those who did not.

As soon as the Bull family moved in, strange things started happening. Footsteps and tappings were heard in the night. Bells rang and voices answered. Ghostly chanting came from nearby Borley Church. One of the family's 14 children was awakened by a slap in the face. Another saw a tall man in old-fashioned clothes standing beside her bed. Twenty people saw a nun on the lawn. Servants saw a phantom coach and horses gallop through the grounds. A headless man and a woman in white were sighted.

In 1929, poltergeist activity began at the rectory. Pebbles, keys and medallions were tossed through the air for no apparent reason. A cook reported that a door locked the night before was found open every morning. Newspaper reporters kept vigil one night, and spotted an eerie light in a deserted wing of the building.

From 1930, the house was in the hands of the Reverend Lionel Algernon Foyster and his wife Marianne. But the strange happenings continued and messages began appearing on walls and on scraps of paper. One said: 'Marianne, get help.' Mrs Foyster also heard a phantom voice calling her name and, after she was attacked by an invisible assailant, the family moved out.

Ghost investigator Harry Price, founder of Britain's National Laboratory of Psychical Research, moved in with a team of volunteer helpers. They reported sudden, inexplicable drops of ten degrees in temperature, books moving, curious incense-like smells, and pebbles – and even cakes of soap – flying through the air. A Benedictine monk was hit by flying stones while trying to hold a service of exorcism.

First theories ascribed the hauntings to a monk and a nun from nearby Bures, who eloped, were caught and punished in the traditional manner – he beheaded, she entombed alive. But in 1937, London medium Helen Glanville was told 'by a voice from beyond' during a seance at her Streatham home that the rectory was haunted by Marie Lairre, a nun induced to leave her French convent at Le Havre and marry one of the Waldergraves of Borley Manor. Her husband strangled her in May 1667, on the site of the rectory.

In 1939, the rectory, now re-named Borley Priory by the new owner, Captain W. H. Gregson, was gutted by fire. Several people claimed that they saw a young girl at an upstairs window as the flames raged. And the village policeman declared that witnesses told him they had seen a grey-clad man slip away from the inferno.

Though in ruins, the building continued to be beset by curious happenings. Chauffeur Herbert Mayes heard the thunder of hooves as he drove past. And wartime air-raid wardens were called several times when lights were seen at the windows. In 1943, the site was excavated, and fragments of a woman's skull and skeleton were found four feet underground, together with religious pendants. Was this the unhappy Marie Lairre? Or were the remains, as sceptics suggested, those of a plague victim buried in 1665?

Whether or not the Marie Lairre theory is correct, the fact remains that things have happened at Borley which no one can explain. And still do happen . . . As late as 1961, car headlights, cameras and torches all failed during investigations at the site.

The spook that Kojak met

As a TV cop, Kojak, alias Telly Savalas, has rarely failed to solve a case. But one off-screen incident has baffled the famous actor for years. And Savalas admits that it would have made his hair stand on end – if he had had any.

Did he see a ghost? That is the question he has asked himself since the night in 1957 when driving in a rural area of Long Island, New York, he ran out of

Telly Savalas.

petrol at 3 am. He says: 'I went into a coffee shop to ask the way to a petrol station and was told to walk down the road towards a freeway. I had just started walking when I heard someone ask in a high-pitched voice whether I wanted a lift. I turned and saw a guy in a black Cadillac. I got in and he drove me to the petrol station. He even loaned me a dollar to buy the stuff. I insisted that I would have to pay him back, and he wrote down his name, address and phone number so that I could return the money. His name was Harry Agannis.'

Savalas says that soon afterwards he telephoned the number and asked for Agannis. 'A woman answered the phone. She told me that Harry Agannis was her husband – but that he had been dead for three years.'

Amazed and intrigued, Savalas decided to visit the woman. He took with him the piece of paper the man had given him. 'I showed it to her,' says Savalas, 'and she told me that it was definitely her husband's handwriting. I described the clothes the man in the Cadillac had been wearing, and she told me that they were the clothes her husband had been buried in.'

So did Savalas see a ghost? 'I just don't know,' he says. 'I'll never forget the incident but I doubt if I'll ever be able to explain it.'

Good and evil spirits

Ghosts can save lives – or take them

The deadliest spectral killer of all time was the 19th-century phantom of 50 Berkeley Square, London. No one knows what it was, because few who saw it lived to tell the tale. And those who did survive were generally reduced to incoherence by fright.

Sir Robert Warboys was one of its earliest victims. Challenged by friends to spend a night in the notorious house, he readily agreed. But the nervous landlord insisted on precautions. Sir Robert must take a gun. And if anything unusual happened, he must pull the cord which rang a bell in the room below.

At midnight, 45 minutes after Sir Robert had retired, the landlord and Sir Robert's friends heard the bell jangle violently. As they raced upstairs, they heard a shot. Sir Robert was dead when they burst into the room – but not from a bullet wound. His eyes stared out in terror, his lips curled away from clenched teeth. He had died of fright.

Years later, two sailors from Portsmouth wandered into Berkeley Square

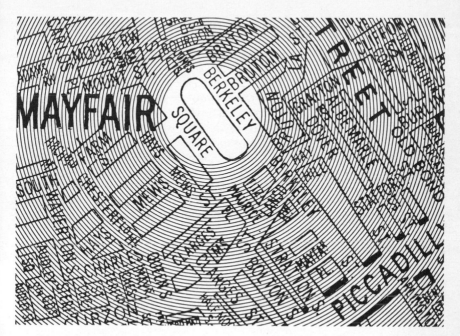

Berkeley Square in the heart of Mayfair.

and noticed a house hung with To Let signs. Edward Blunden and Robert Martin were not to know that the house contained a dreadful secret. To them it offered free lodgings for the night. They wandered through the disordered, neglected rooms and came at last to a relatively tidy top-floor bedroom. Martin soon fell asleep but Blunden was nervous. As he lay restlessly awake, he heard strange footsteps scratching their way towards the door. He woke Martin and the two men watched fearfully as the door slowly opened and something large, dark and shapeless entered.

The thing went for Blunden, trapping him near the window. Martin seized his chance to crash through the door and race downstairs into the street to obtain help. He blurted out his story to a policeman and they hurried back to the house. But they were too late. The shattered body of Blunden, his neck broken and his face fixed in a terrified grimace, lay on the basement stairs.

Other victims of the ghoul of 50 Berkeley Square included a girl guest at the house who went mad with terror, a man who slept there one night and was found dead the next morning, and the maid of a family renting the house who died in hospital after being found crumpled on the floor, whimpering: 'Don't let it touch me.'

Intrigued by these and other stories about the haunted house, a courageous 19th-century peer resolved to get to the bottom of the mystery. He was ghost-hunter Lord Lyttleton – a descendant of the man whose dead mistress told him he was doomed to die in three days' time (see page 170). Lyttleton resolved to spend a night in the haunted room. He took with him two guns, one filled with shot and the other with silver sixpenny pieces – charms to ward off evil spirits. During the night he fired a barrel of the silver coins at a shape which leapt at him. Perhaps the charms worked, for Lyttleton lived to tell the tale in his book *Notes and Queries*, published in 1879. In the volume he wrote that he had no doubt that the room was 'supernaturally fatal to body and mind'.

Today, however, the ghost seems to have given up its deathly vigil. Number 50 Berkeley Square is a bookshop, and the square itself has become better known as the haunt of a singing nightingale.

Breckles Hall, in Norfolk, is haunted by a strange scream for mercy. In addition, doors bang, mysterious footsteps are heard, and sometimes spectral dancers stage a ghostly ball.

Early this century, a body was found outside the front door of the hall. It was that of local poacher Jim Mace. He and another man had got drunk in a local public house and decided to bag a few partridges in the hall grounds. They knew the hall was empty and had been told that some nights the windows lit up to reveal a ghostly ballroom full of dancers. Their birds bagged, the two men went hunting for ghosts. They saw nothing and were turning for home when a coach and four horses swept silently into view at the bottom of the drive. Rooted to the spot, they watched the phantom coach come to a halt and a beautiful woman step out, decked in jewels. As she stared into Mace's eyes, he slumped to the ground with a piercing scream.

His friend raced to the nearest houses to get help, but no one would venture to the hall that night once he had told his story. It was the next morning before the vicar led villagers to the spot – and found the poacher, his face paralyzed with fear, his body stiff and cold.

Residents of Norfolk Island, in the Pacific Ocean 900 miles off the east coast of Australia, claim to have seen ghosts of shipwreck survivors, who lived for a while on the island, as well as the spectres of Irish convicts, hanged when the island was a British penal colony. The islanders also tell the story of Barney Duffy's curse. The giant Irishman had escaped from the colony's jail, but was found hiding in a hollow tree by two soldiers. 'If you take me back,' Duffy threatened, 'you'll die violently within a week of my hanging.' The soldiers ignored his warning. Two days after the execution, they went fishing near the hollow tree. Their beaten bodies were washed up next day on the tide. No one ever found out how they had died.

In 1804, a white phantom brought terror to Hammersmith, London, and cost two lives. It first appeared to a woman crossing a local churchyard. She fled but it followed her and seized her arms. She fainted and, though she was brought round, she never got over the shock and died at home a few days later. After 16 people travelling in a cart all fled from the ghost, local vigilante groups kept watch on the churchyard. And on the fourth night, Francis Smith, a customs officer, spotted a figure in white coming down a nearby lane. Smith shot at it and the figure fell. But it was not the ghost. It was bricklayer Thomas Milwood, coming home late from work in white overalls. Smith was sentenced to death for manslaughter but, on appeal, the sentence was commuted to a year in jail.

A spectre that killed was the phantom No. 7 bus seen racing around the

A London Transport bus of the Thirties.

THE WORLD'S GREATEST MYSTERIES

Ladbroke Grove area of London in the early hours of one morning in 1936. The story was told at a West London coroner's court to explain why a car had swerved into a wall, killing the driver. A witness said the bus was ablaze with lights and it had vanished when the car hit the wall. Other drivers said they too had seen the bus. And a bus inspector swore he had seen it pull silently into his depot, then disappear. The bus has not been seen since.

Among the good spirits is one recorded by ghost-hunter Lord Halifax. A sailor, whose ship was ploughing through the North Atlantic somewhere off the Canadian coast, saw a strange man writing in the captain's cabin. When the log-book was checked, an unknown hand was seen to have written: 'Steer to the north-east.' The captain did so, and after some hours he came across a ship in trouble. As the survivors came aboard, the sailor recognized the man he had seen writing in the log. When this man rewrote the words that had appeared mysteriously in the log-book, the two specimens matched exactly.

During World War One, a driver of the 42nd Field Ambulance was taking a badly wounded soldier from Ypres to a casualty station at Poperinge. A flare lit the night sky, and the driver saw the silhouette of a sentry standing directly in front of him. He stopped. But when he looked again, the sentry had vanished. All the driver saw was a vast shell crater, only yards from his front wheels. The phantom sentry had saved two lives.

Dr S. Weir Mitchell, an eminent 19th-century nerve specialist of Philadelphia, USA, was dozing after a hard day's work when he heard a knock at his door. He opened it and saw a thin girl in a shawl who begged him to come and treat her desperately ill mother. Dr Mitchell followed the girl through a snow blizzard to the house where her mother lay. He soon saw that she had pneumonia. After he had sent for medicine and made her comfortable, he mentioned her daughter's mission. The woman looked surprised. 'My daughter died a month ago,' she said. The girl was now nowhere to be seen. Her shawl was hanging in a nearby cupboard, and there was no trace of snow on it.

In the 1880s, Britain's ambassador to Paris, Lord Dufferin, was staying with friends in Ireland. One night he awoke to see a hunched figure with an ugly, grizzled face carrying a coffin across the lawn. When he called to the man, the vision vanished. Dufferin's host was mystified when told the story at breakfast, and over the years the ambassador forgot the incident.

But years later, attending a diplomatic reception at the Grand Hotel, Paris, Dufferin walked towards the lifts and saw the ugly, grizzled man again – in servant's uniform. Dufferin refused to take the lift, and so missed death. When the lift reached the fifth floor its cable snapped and it plummeted to the bottom of the shaft. All those inside were killed.

The ghosts of an airline pilot and his flight engineer succeeded in grounding

A World War I soldier.

A Lockheed TriStar air-bus.

a plane belonging to one of the world's biggest airlines a few years ago. Pilots and cabin staff of Eastern Airlines in America said they had been warned not to fly the plane by the ghosts of Captain Bob Loft and Flight Engineer Don Repo, killed when their Lockheed TriStar crashed with the loss of 101 lives in Florida's Everglades in 1972.

After that crash, ground staff claimed that Repo's ghost helped them trace faults in other TriStars. Stewardesses reported sudden drops in temperature in some TriStars and a mysterious airline captain who vanished when spoken to. Repo was also said to have appeared on the flight deck of TriStar 318 to warn of a fire; hours later, the plane had to return to the airport with a blazing engine. In 1974, the warnings stopped as mysteriously as they had begun.

Good spirits can be more generous in death than they are in life. In 1780, a serving woman who went to Powys Castle, in Wales, to look for work was, as a joke, put in a haunted bedroom. But the woman had the last laugh. For she claimed that an elegantly dressed ghost led her to a locked iron box, showed her the key hidden in a nearby crevice and told her to send it to the owner of the castle in London. The owner returned to the castle and took the old woman into his care, offering her any money she wanted and letting her stay at his home. The secret of the box was never revealed.

A well-known miser called Mrs Webb died in the village of Barby, Northamptonshire, in March 1851. Few mourned her passing. But a month later, strange knocking sounds were heard from her house, along with the sound of furniture being moved. They continued even after a family rented the cottage from the nephew to whom she had left it. Then one of the tenant's children saw a tall woman standing over a bed. When neighbours heard the story, they agreed to keep watch with the tenant's wife, Mrs Accleton. Three of them were with her when a ball of light suddenly leapt into the air towards a trap-door in the ceiling. They told the nephew, who agreed to search the loft. There he found two bags, one holding a bundle of property deeds, the other full of coins and notes.

But Mrs Webb had not finished her business. As the knockings, moanings and strange noises went on, unpaid bills were discovered. And only when the nephew had paid the last creditor were the Accletons left in peace.

Lost lives and loves

Strange happenings at the moment of death

Many ghosts seem to appear only once – at the very moment their earthly body is dying. One of the earliest recorded apparitions of this kind was seen in 1250, when a skeleton-like knight appeared to the Abbess of Lacock in England. From the insignia on its shield, she knew it was her son William Longespee, at that time away on a crusade. She told her friends of the visitation, but no one was prepared to believe her – until, six months later, a messenger arrived from Egypt with word that Longespee had been hacked to death by Saracens on the day the ghost had appeared.

On 22 June 1893, Lady Tryon was giving a party at her home in Eaton Square, London. Shortly after 3.30 pm, several guests saw her husband, Admiral Sir George Tryon, walk silently across the drawing room. When they told his wife she was puzzled. 'You must be mistaken,' she said. 'My husband is in the Mediterranean commanding his ship on an exercise.' At exactly 3.34 pm that day, Admiral Tryon's ship *Victoria*, the Royal Navy flagship, was rammed and sunk by another ship, the *Camperdown*, when, on Sir George's orders, two columns converged. Survivors heard him cry as the ship went down: 'It's all my fault.'

In 1774, during the American War of Independence, two British officers were waiting for the return of an overdue foraging party led by a Major Blomberg. They heard footsteps outside the tent, and a voice told them to go to a house in Westminster on their return to England. There they would find papers to be passed on to the major's son. When the two men scrambled outside to see who was talking, there was no one near the tent. Then a group of soldiers emerged from the forest carrying a body. The major had been shot ten minutes earlier.

THE WORLD'S GREATEST MYSTERIES

A year later two young soldiers, John Sherbroke and John Wynyard, were reading late in their quarters on Cape Breton Island, Canada, when a thin man of about 20 suddenly appeared, stared at them morosely, then went out the door. Wynyard went pale. He had recognized his brother, whom he knew to be in England. When he next received a letter from his family in England, Wynyard learned that his brother had died at the moment he had made his sudden appearance in Wynyard's quarters.

In his autobiography published in 1871, Lord Brougham tells of a macabre deal he struck with a fellow student at Edinburgh University. Whoever died first was to appear to the other, to settle their argument about life after death. The two drifted apart. Brougham's friend moved to India, and when Brougham published his book he had heard nothing of him for years. Then, on the evening of 19 December 1883 Brougham reached for a towel on getting out of his bath – and saw his friend sitting in the bathroom chair. When he recovered from the shock, the vision had vanished.

Some time later a letter arrived from India announcing that his friend had died – on 19 December.

Mary Goffe was still alive when her own ghost appeared in 1691. Dying at her parents' home, Mary pleaded to be taken to see her children one last time, but was told the exertion of the journey would be too much for her. She fell into a coma. Next day she died, but not before telling her mother she had seen her family. The mother thought she had been dreaming. But then a nurse who was looking after the children in Rochester, Kent, told how at 2 am on the day that Mary died she had seen her silently looking down on her offspring for about 15 minutes. Then she had vanished.

Two strange stories surround the death of Lord Thomas Lyttleton, which occurred in November 1779. One morning at breakfast he revealed that during the night he had been visited by the spectre of a girl who had killed herself after he had seduced, then deserted, her. She had told him he would be dead in three days to the minute. That was on 24 November. Later that day, he made a magnificent speech in the House of Lords. He was determined to ignore the fatal warning. But on the third night, as the clock struck 11, he put his hand to his side and collapsed into the arms of his valet.

Lyttleton had been due to spend the weekend with a member of parliament, Peter Andrews, but instead had returned to his own home in Epsom, Surrey, forgetting to cancel the arrangement. Andrews waited up for him, and finally went to bed a little annoyed. At 11 pm, he awoke to see Lyttleton by his bed in the dressing gown Andrews had left for him. Andrews took his guest to task for arriving so late, but Lyttleton only replied: 'It's all over with me, Andrews.' The member of parliament followed the figure out of the room, and found Lyttleton's bedroom empty – with the dressing gown still on its hook.

Love, lost or unrequited, has created many ghosts. A pamphlet, published in 1709, recalled sightings of a Guildford man, Christopher Slaughterford, who was hanged for murdering his sweetheart, Jane Young, though he protested his innocence all the way to the gallows. After his death Slaughterford was seen in Marshalsea Prison, Southwark, where he was held during the trial, and in the nearby White Lion Inn, where he waited to die. He also appeared to his servant, Joseph Lee, and a friend, Roger Voller, 'with a rope around his neck, a flaming torch in one hand and a club in the other, crying: "Vengeance, vengeance." '

A ghostly bridal procession in medieval dress has been seen several times over the years between Haltwhistle and Alston, in Northumberland. The bride is said to be Abigail Featherstonhaugh, who fell in love with a handsome pauper. Her father, a powerful noble, would not hear of such a match – some said because the boy was his illegitimate son. Instead, he chose a husband with wealth and status. One version of the legend says the spurned lover ambushed the wedding party, killed both bride and groom, and that the unhappy couple still wander the area, their nuptial finery stained with blood.

Another tragic love story lies behind the girl said to appear at Holywell, Huntingdonshire, each 16 March. It is the forlorn figure of Juliet Tousley, who hanged herself from a willow tree by the River Ouse after a lovers' tiff in the 11th century. Juliet was buried under a stone which is now in the bar of the Ferry Boat Inn, and at midnight is said to walk sadly from the inn to the river. One landlord recalled that, when a party of ghost-spotters asked a day early if they would see Juliet, he replied: 'Tomorrow – she'll not show herself tonight.' Then a tankard was wrenched from its hook by an unseen hand and dashed to the ground.

In Mexico City the ghostly La Llorona, the 'wailing woman', has been seen and heard for four centuries, wandering the streets at midnight in a blood-stained gown, crying out for her children. She is said to be Dona Luisa de Olveros, a beautiful 16th-century Spanish-Indian who became the mistress of a nobleman and bore him two children. But after a time he tired of her. Dona Luisa's dreams of being his wife were finally shattered when she found him celebrating his marriage to a Spanish noblewoman. Out of her mind with fury, she went home and stabbed her babies to death with a dagger. She was arrested and hanged, her body left aloft for six hours as a final humiliation.

Not all ghosts of love are tragic figures. In Ramsbury, Wiltshire, they still talk about the ghost of Grandfather Bull, a case investigated by the Society for Psychical Research. Samuel Bull, a chimney sweep, died at his small cottage in June 1931, after being ill for four years. Soon afterwards his widow, Mary Jane, also fell ill, and her married daughter moved in to care for her. The daughter brought along her husband and five children. The old cottage was now too crowded for comfort, and part of it was too damp to live in. It was a worry for the whole family – and seemingly a worry too for the spirit of Samuel Bull. Eight months after he died, the children screamed when they saw him walking up the stairs to his old room.

Mrs Bull, however, was not startled. She said she had seen him many times. And the family were all to see him again and again as he climbed the stairs and stood by his wife's bed, often putting his hand on her brow. They thought he looked sad that his loved ones had to live in such sorry conditions. And they could have been right. For when the local authorities found them a new and bigger house, Samuel Bull was never seen again.

Pleas from the afterlife

Ghosts who bring messages to the living

Why do phantoms appear to the living? The vast majority seem to be 'ghosts of conscience', often victims of injustice appealing to the living for a decent burial, or for their wishes to be kept, or just for sympathy. Some seek peace. Others protest that their peace has been disturbed.

Raynham Hall, a magnificent stately home near Fakenham, Norfolk, has been haunted for nearly 300 years by a woman dressed in brown. She is believed to be Dorothy Walpole, sister of Sir Robert Walpole, who became Britain's prime minister in 1721.

Dorothy's father, also called Robert and also a member of parliament, was made guardian of a 13-year-old viscount, Charles Townshend. And as Dorothy and Charles grew up together they fell in love. But when they wanted to get married, Dorothy's father refused. He feared people would think the Walpoles were after the Townshend fortunes and estates.

Charles resigned himself to his fate and soon married a baron's daughter. But Dorothy could not shake off her feelings so easily, despite a wild whirl of parties. She went to London, then Paris, scandalizing the social set by setting up house with a rakish lord.

In 1711, when Dorothy heard that Charles's wife had died, she hurried home to Raynham, and within a year they were married. For a while they were blissfully happy. Then gossip about Dorothy's escapade in Paris reached Charles. He was furious and confined her to her rooms. She was not allowed out and no one was allowed in. Ten years later she died. The records said it was smallpox, but local rumour blamed her death on a push from behind at

King George III.

the top of the hall's grand oak staircase. Her ghost was soon seen by servants, family and guests alike.

In 1786, King George III was staying at the hall. He awoke in the middle of the night to see a brown-clad woman, her hair dishevelled, her face ashen, beside his bed. He fled the room in his nightgown and nightcap and stormed round the house, rousing everyone with his wrath. He vowed not to stay an hour longer.

Alarmed at upsetting so honoured a guest, the Townshends ordered a nightly watch by gamekeepers. And a few nights later, they too saw the woman in brown, walking down a corridor. One man moved out to challenge her – and she walked right through him. He felt an icy cloud pass into his bones and out again.

In 1835 she appeared again. Colonel Loftus, brother of the then Lady Townshend, saw her on consecutive nights at Christmas – always a popular time with ghosts – and described her as a stately woman in rich brown brocade with a cap-like head-dress. Her face was clearly defined. But where her eyes should have been, there were only black hollows. The woman appeared to several other guests in the days that followed, and cut short the Christmas merrymaking.

A few years later, Dorothy startled another distinguished guest. He was Captain Frederick Marryat, author of *Mr Midshipman Easy* and *The Children of the New Forest*, a tough seagoing man who scoffed at the story of the hauntings. Invited to see Dorothy's ghost for himself, Marryat stayed at the hall in a room where a portrait of the formidable woman was hanging. Late that night, he and two other guests saw the ghostly shape of Dorothy walking a corridor. They scuttled into a side room as the phantom approached. It stopped outside the open door and grinned wickedly. Marryat was unnerved enough to grab his pistol and fire a shot. It went straight through the still-smiling spectre and crashed into the door opposite.

Dorothy was seen infrequently after that. But in 1936 she returned in dramatic manner. Two professional photographers, commissioned to take pictures of the hall for Lady Townshend, were setting up their camera to take shots of the oak staircase. Suddenly one saw a vapid form take shape, and urged his colleague to expose the photographic plate. This he did, without knowing why. The flash made the shape vanish – but when the plate was developed, there on the stairs was the outline of a woman in flowing veil and white bridal gown. Experts who examined the plate were convinced it was not a fake. Had Dorothy decided to let the world see what she had looked like on that fateful wedding day 224 years earlier?

The ghost of Chambercombe Manor, near Ilfracombe, Devon – a tall, smiling woman dressed in grey – is less malevolent. She has even been known to join tourist parties looking over her former home. But she has every reason to be as bitter as Dorothy.

Her story began with her grandfather, Alexander Oatway, of Chambercombe, one of the notorious West Country shipwreckers of 400 years ago. During storms he used to wave lanterns on the shore, to lure ships on to the rocks. Then he plundered them. One day his son William followed him and rescued a Spanish girl who had survived the wreck. Later they married and had a daughter, Kate. The family had left Chambercombe Manor by then, shamed by Alexander's wrecking activities, and William and his family lived on Lundy Island in the Bristol Channel. But when they heard that the manor was vacant again they moved back and rented it.

Shortly afterwards, Kate married an Irish sea captain called Wallace, and moved with him to Dublin. Years passed. Then one night a vicious storm blew up and William hurried down to the shore in case a ship was in trouble. He found a woman lying on the rocks. She had been hideously battered and disfigured by the sea. He carried her back to the manor house, where she died that night.

At this stage, temptation got the better of honest William. He realized that with the jewels and money from the belt the woman was carrying, he could buy the manor house outright. So when an admiralty man called two days later, making inquiries about a missing passenger from the wrecked ship, William said he knew nothing about the matter. But when the visitor mentioned the name – Mrs Katherine Wallace – William realized what he had done. Filled with remorse, he walled up her body in a secret room and moved from the manor.

His secret was discovered only 150 years ago, when a farmer living in the house found Kate's skeleton while rethatching the roof. Her bones were buried in a pauper's grave at Ilfracombe. But her spirit still wanders – her ghost has been seen as recently as 1976.

Spirit manifestations at the home of the Ewing family in Lynton, Devon, led to a much belated burial. In the 1930s guests staying in a room above the scullery were disturbed at night by the eerie crying of a child and the ghost of an old woman. Then Mrs Ewing's brother-in-law noticed that the guest room was much smaller than the scullery beneath. A walled-up cupboard was discovered, and in it were a quantity of bones and a child's box. Once the bones left for the mortuary, the haunting ceased.

At Bisham Abbey, in Marlow, Buckinghamshire, an old woman in black has been seen wandering round the Thames-side grounds, washing her hands in a bowl that moves before her. She is believed to be Dame Elizabeth Hoby, who died in 1609 in great distress. Her son was a slow learner and one day was locked in a small room to finish his studies. A message from the Queen called Dame

Elizabeth away. When she returned, so one story goes, the boy was slumped dead over his desk. Another version of the story is that Dame Elizabeth beat the boy to death because he blotted his books. In 1840, workmen altering the abbey found children's books between some floor joists. One book was blotted with long-dried tears.

When the body of schoolboy John Daniel was found 200 yards from his home at Beaminster, Dorset, in 1728, death was assumed to have been from natural causes. His mother swore he suffered from fits. But seven weeks later, 12 fellow pupils saw his ghost sitting at a desk in their classroom, his coffin nearby. After local magistrate Colonel Broadrep had closely questioned each boy and found that their stories tallied, he ordered the body to be exhumed. An inquest revealed that John had been strangled. The murderer was never caught. John's pathetic figure has since been seen in nearby St Mary's Church.

A ghost in Australia helped to solve a disappearance riddle in 1826. Frederick Fisher, a farmer, was jailed for debt. To stop creditors seizing his land at Campbelltown, New South Wales, he transferred his assets to ex-convict George Worrall. Six months later Fisher was freed. One night he left a local inn after a heavy drinking session and was never seen again. Police investigated, but could find no evidence of foul play, though they suspected Worrall had killed his one-time friend.

Then one dark night Fisher's neighbour James Farley saw an eerie figure sitting on a fence and pointing to a spot in Fisher's paddock. Farley fled in fear but next day returned with a constable. When they dug up the spot indicated by the ghost, they found the badly beaten body of the farmer. Worrall was arrested, confessed and was hanged.

Burton Agnes Hall is not the name of a woman, but of a beautiful Jacobean house in a village between Bridlington and Driffield, Yorkshire. It was built by three spinster sisters with money left them by their father, Sir Henry Griffith, early in the 17th century. Soon after the hall was completed, the youngest sister, Anne, was waylaid by robbers at nearby Harpham. Her screams brought villagers to the rescue, but she had been badly beaten and, although she was carried home and cared for, it was obvious she would not recover.

Just before she died, she made the extraordinary demand that her sisters cut off her head before burying her body and preserve it in the walls of the home she loved. She warned vaguely of dire consequences if her wishes were disobeyed. Horrified at the idea, the sisters reluctantly promised they would do as she bid, although they had no intention of doing so. When Anne died, she was buried intact.

A week later the trouble started. First there was a crash in one of the upstairs rooms. Seven days later the household was awakened by doors slamming in every part of the building. On the third week after Anne's death, the house shook with the clatter of people running along corridors and up and down the stairs. Then came an awful groan. The sounds continued all night, and next morning the servants packed and left. The two sisters called in the vicar. When they mentioned Anne's dying wish, he agreed to open her grave. A shock awaited them. Anne's head had been cut from her body, and the flesh on it had shrivelled away to leave a bare skull.

The sisters took the head to the Hall, and the haunting ceased. Over the years, several subsequent owners of the hall have removed the skull, known as Awd Nance. Each time, mysterious shufflings and clatterings in the corridors, accompanied by slamming doors and terrifying groans, have forced them to restore the gruesome relic to its rightful place.

Disturbed bones gave an American family a harrowing time. The incidents were described by the *San Francisco Examiner* in 1891. A Mr Walsingham, a farmer, discovered the bones shortly after moving into his new house at Oakville, Georgia. He threw them into a lime kiln. He was not a superstitious man, and when curious things started happening in the middle of the night (doors banged, bells rang and chairs were overturned), he put it down to mischief by the family or neighbours. But he began to worry when his dog began barking furiously at a wall, lunged forward, then fell back yelping, its neck broken.

Hideous laughter, shouts and wails began to come from all over the house. A daughter saw a disembodied hand grip her shoulder. And Walsingham saw the prints of a man's naked feet form beside his as he walked in the rain.

But what finally persuaded the family to leave was a horrific dinner party. During the party, guests bravely shrugged off the strange groans coming from upstairs, but then a deep red stain started forming on the white tablecloth – what looked like blood was dripping from above . . . The men in the party raced upstairs and ripped up the floorboards. But all they found was dry dust – and the red liquid continued to drip below. Chemists who later examined the tablecloth confirmed that the stain was human blood. But by that time the Walsinghams had moved out.

Ghosts are often claimed to have avenged wrongs done to innocent people. In the 16th century, Kraster and Dorothy Cook owned a small farm overlooking Lake Windermere, in Westmorland. Wealthy Myles Phillipson, who owned the land around it, wanted the Cooks' site in order to build a magnificent new house. When the farmer refused to sell, Phillipson resorted to trickery. He invited the Cooks to share his Christmas dinner, and impressed them with a beautiful golden bowl. Next day, soldiers arrested the couple. For a week they were held in separate cells without explanation. Then they arrived in court to find that Phillipson had accused them of stealing the bowl. The outcome of the trial was never in doubt, for it was heard by the local magistrate – Phillipson. When he pronounced sentence of death, Dorothy Cook cried out: 'Look out for yourself. You will never prosper. The time will come when you own no land.'

Phillipson built his magnificent home, called Calgarth Hall, and held a Christmas feast to celebrate. But when Mrs Phillipson went upstairs to fetch something, she screamed in terror – for there on the banister were two grinning skulls. Her screams brought the rest of the party racing upstairs, swords drawn. The sight sobered the merrymakers, and though the skulls were thrown into the courtyard and denounced as a tasteless practical joke, the guests were uneasy when they went early to bed.

At 2 am more screams brought them running from their rooms. The skulls were back, grinning from a step on the staircase. Over the next few days, the Phillipsons tried every way they could think of to get rid of the skulls. But every day they returned. And gradually Dorothy Cook's curse came true. Phillipson's business declined, his wealth dwindled, and when he died the skulls screamed all night.

His heirs also suffered from the skulls, which took to appearing each Christmas Day and on the anniversary of the Cooks' hanging. Only when the family became too poor to keep the hall, and were forced to sell it, did the skulls disappear.

Ghosts on four legs

Ghosts do not always take on human form - they often appear as animals

Almost every region of Britain has a legendary black dog, harbinger of death, with blazing eyes and snarling teeth. The Welsh call it Gwyllgi. On the Isle of Man it is the Mauthe. Yorkshire's version, Padfoot, is said to be as big as a donkey, while in Lancashire they call the black 'doom dog' Trash or Shriker. In the Hebrides, the dog is white and called the Lamper. The West Country has a pack of black dogs.

But the most terrifying is the one-eyed hound that haunts East Anglia, known as Black Shuck. He is said to roam the fens and marsh flatlands on dark nights, a fearsome brute waiting to scare lonely travellers to death. Many people claim to have heard his blood-curdling howls on stormy nights.

GHOSTS AND GHOULS

Maybe it was Black Shuck who terrified a young American airman and his wife in the early years of the last war. They were staying in a flat-topped hut on the edge of Walberswick Marsh, Suffolk. One stormy evening they heard a pounding on the door. Looking out of the window, the airman saw a huge black beast battering itself against their temporary home. The couple pushed furniture against the door and cowered in terror as the assault went on, the beast hammering against each wall in turn, then leaping on to the roof. After some hours, the noise died away, but the couple could not sleep. At first light, they ventured cautiously outside to inspect the damage. But there was no sign of the attack, and no paw or claw marks in the mud. A similar black dog – the Mauthe or Moddey Dhoo – used to haunt Peel Castle on the Isle of Man. Soldiers on guard duty refused to patrol the ramparts alone. One boastful sentry who did so was found jibbering insanely and died three days later.

Foot marks in the snow mystified the people of Devon in February 1855. They awoke to find a trail of prints zigzagging for nearly 100 miles through five parishes, over roofs and haystacks, through walls, in and out of barns. The trail, which began in a Totnes garden and ended in a field at Littleham, was blamed on many different sorts of animals. When dogs were brought in to follow the trail into dense undergrowth at Dawlish, they backed away howling dismally.

Horses, with heads and without, figure in many ghost stories. An Englishman hunting in the Transvaal in 1902 wrote from South Africa to tell journalist and 'ghost-collector' W. T. Stead that one day he was riding back to camp with a fine ostrich over his saddle when he heard someone behind him in a thick copse. Turning, he saw an eerie rider on a white horse. He galloped for camp, with the unearthly rider in hot pursuit. That night, an old Boer told him that another Englishman had once shot seven elephants in the copse, but when he returned the next day to collect the ivory he was never seen again. His white horse returned riderless to camp, but died next day. The Boer added: 'I wouldn't go into that bush for all the ivory in the land.'

A white tiger cost a railroad superintendent dearly at the turn of the century. Charles Da Silva, his wife and his son Eric were staying in Seconee, India. One day, Da Silva refused the pleas for help of an old blind leper, and watched as the helpless man was mauled to death by a white tiger. Before he died he cursed: 'May you also suffer my fate.' When Da Silva told one of his servants what had happened, the servant warned him to beware of the old leper's curse.

A year later, Da Silva saw the tiger at his railroad, and realized with horror that it was preparing to spring at his wife and son. He fired his rifle as the ghostly tiger leapt through the air, then vanished. But he was too late. A servant lay dead from fright. And Da Silva's son had a scratch on his cheek that within a month had caused his death.

Armies in the sky

Soldiers who returned to earth to re-fight historic battles

Old soldiers never die, it is said, they only fade away. But sometimes they refuse to do even that. They return to this world as phantom armies reliving their battles. Or so a host of legends has it.

The eerie footsteps of marching knights in armour have been heard at historic Glastonbury, Somerset . . . and headless war horses have been seen galloping through a Wiltshire valley near Woodmanton, site of ancient battles between the Romans and Britons. But Britain's most famous phantom battleground is at Edgehill, Warwickshire.

More than 40,000 men were involved in the fighting there on 23 October 1642, when Prince Rupert led the King's troops into action in the civil war against the Roundheads of Oliver Cromwell. At the end of the day the field was littered with dead and dying, and both sides withdrew to continue the war elsewhere. Then reports reached London that the battle was being fought all over again – by ghosts. Shepherds had seen a re-enactment of the conflict two months after the original battle.

Puzzled, Charles I sent four officers to investigate. They reported that the shepherds had been tending their flocks on Christmas Eve – a Sunday – when they had heard approaching drums. Suddenly the armies had appeared in the sky – firing muskets and cannon, their colours unfurled – and fought furiously for several hours, finally disappearing at 3 am on Christmas morning. Next night, the shepherds had kept their watch with 'all the substantial inhabitants of that and neighbouring parishes'. And all had been amazed when the armies 'appeared in the same tumultuous warlike manner, fighting with as much spite and spleen as formerly'. The following Sunday, the soldiers had returned again, fighting 'with far greater tumult' for four hours. They fought again the next day. And the following Sunday and Monday. The officers saw the fighting for themselves, and recognized some of the combatants from the original battle.

Since then there have been several reports of strange noises and Civil War phantoms in the area, but never again has the fighting been as dramatic.

In 1904, a party of schoolchildren were walking up Marlpit's Hill, near Honiton, Devon, when they saw a wild-looking man in a black wide-brimmed hat and a long, mud-spattered brown coat. Curiously, the teacher with them saw nothing. But the man's dazed, exhausted look frightened the children. Later inquiries revealed that, in 1685, a man who lived in a cottage on Marlpit's

Hill had escaped the carnage of the Battle of Sedgemoor – during the Duke of Monmouth's rebellion against James II – and had made his way home. But just as his wife and children were about to welcome him, a troop of soldiers rode up and cut him down with their swords.

In 1745, about 30 people saw a phantom army marching through the sky above Souter Fell, Cumbria, at the time of the Jacobite Rebellion. Ghostly warriors have also been seen at the site of the Battle of Culloden, which took place in 1746. And in 1932, two startled motorists saw cloaked soldiers near Marston Moor, Yorkshire, the site of a major Civil War battle in 1644.

The American Civil War also has its action-replays. The best known is that at the site of the Battle of Shiloh, where 20,000 men died. Next day, said locals, a nearby river ran red with blood. And several people have since seen and heard re-enactments of the fierce fighting.

The two World Wars also have their share of ghosts, the most famous being the Angels of Mons, who are supposed to have appeared during the First World War battle of Mons, in Belgium, on 26 August 1914. The ghosts were supposedly phantom bowmen – said to be archers from the Battle of Agincourt of 1415 – who caused consternation in the German trenches and allowed the British Expeditionary Force time to retreat and re-group after savage fighting.

In the September following the battle, author Arthur Machen wrote in the London *Evening News* about this 'band of angels' who had saved the British troops. He said later that he had invented the story – but many officers and men swore that they had seen the angels. An officer from Bristol was reported in his local parish magazine as saying that when a troop of German cavalry cut off his company, he expected certain death. Then the angels materialized between the two forces, and the German horses were terrified into flight. A brigadier-general and two of his officers told a similar story to their chaplain. And a lieutenant-colonel said that, during the retreat, his cavalry battalion was escorted for 20 minutes by phantom horsemen in the fields on either side of the road.

After the war came news that French and German soldiers had also witnessed unearthly allies on the British side. All three armies were exhausted after heavy fighting, and the men could have had hallucinations. But, real or not, the Angels of Mons certainly boosted morale in the British trenches.

On 4 August 1951, two English women on holiday in Dieppe, France, awoke to the sound of gunfire. For three hours they listened and noted what happened. And when their notes were compared with official Allied records, it was discovered that the women had described the Dieppe raid of 19 August 1942, when more than half an Anglo-Canadian force of 6,000 men were killed in a dawn attack on the German-held Normandy port. Yet on that morning in 1951, no one else had heard a thing.

Spirits that are heard but not seen

Terrifying phenomena that go bump in the night

Poltergeists are ghosts that are heard but not seen. They are the forces that make things go bump in the night. And in many ways they are more frightening than ghosts that can be seen.

The earliest reported poltergeist was at Bingen, on the German Rhine, in AD355. People were pulled out of bed, stones were thrown and strange noises beset the village. Five hundred years later, nearby Kembden was similarly affected, though this time a reason for the phenomenon was given by a disembodied voice that accused the local priest and some villagers of misdeeds.

Poltergeists have since struck all over the world. In 1890, psychiatrist Professor Cesare Lombroso saw bottles of wine smashed and shoes fly through the air while he was investigating a poltergeist in a small inn at Turin, Italy. In 1937, stones and other missiles rained for almost a week on a family living in Port Louis, Mauritius. The attacks continued even when they had every door and window closed.

In 1878, at Amherst, Nova Scotia, a haunting that started with terrible crashes under the bed of 19-year-old Esther Cox became more sinister when lighted matches fell from the ceiling, mystery fires started in the cellar and in a dress, plaster and planks of wood flew at a doctor, bedclothes were ripped off a bed, and an invisible hand wrote on a wall: 'Esther Cox, you are mine to kill.'

In 1721, the Groben home of German Oriental scholar Professor Schupart was disrupted when furniture and stones were hurled about. His wife was bitten, pinched and knocked down, and 12 witnesses saw him attacked violently by unseen hands.

Several French local dignitaries also witnessed stones being thrown and heard eerie noises at a house in Amiens in 1746 – and for 14 years afterwards.

Curious groans, knocking that shook the whole house, slamming doors and the sound of people running along corridors were heard by several people over 40 years at Syderstone Rectory, Norfolk, until 1833.

And in Cook Lane, London, in 1762, Dr Samuel Johnson, Horace Walpole and Oliver Goldsmith visited a house where they heard strange rappings and scratching.

One of the most famous historical poltergeists is that chronicled by John Wesley, founder of the Methodist Church, at his home, Epworth Parsonage, Lincolnshire, between December 1716 and January 1717. It began when a servant answered a knock on the kitchen door, but saw no one outside. Then, going to bed, he saw a corn-grinding handmill turning on its own. The next person to notice something strange was Wesley's sister, Molly. She was sitting in the library when she heard the door open, and footsteps, accompanied by the rustle of a nightdress, walked around her chair. One by one, each member of the family had a curious tale to tell – rappings on a table, mysterious footsteps on the stairs, banging in the hall and kitchen, the sound of an invisible cradle rocking in the nursery.

The devout family christened the ghost Old Jeffrey, and got used to hearing him walk down from the top north-east corner of the house at 9.45 each evening. Finally, the father, Samuel Wesley, challenged the spirit to stop frightening his children and face him in his study. He was convinced that Old Jeffrey was an agent of evil testing his family's faith. But when Wesley tried to enter the study, a strong force pushed the door back against him.

Poltergeists are still active today. Strange things happened when motor-cycle dealer Sid Mularney knocked down a partition in his workshops at Leighton Buzzard, Bedfordshire, in 1963. Next day, three bikes were found damaged on the ground. Then Mularney saw spanners fall off hooks and a tarpaulin fly off a motor-cycle into the air. Nuts and bolts were scattered over the floor, petrol tanks mysteriously moved and neighbours complained of weird noises.

In February 1958, the Herrmann family of Long Island, New York, saw bottles of medicine, shampoo and holy water uncapped and spilt. James Herrmann was brushing his teeth one day when a bottle of medicine slid 18 inches along a level shelf. Porcelain figures and a glass bowl later flew through the air and smashed.

In November 1967, in the Bavarian town of Rosenheim, a German lawyer called Adam saw light bulbs in his office explode. Lampshades fell off. One day all his four phones rang at the same time for no reason. Experts who checked on his story reported sudden inexplicable surges in the electricity current.

When Mrs Dora Monroe and her family moved into their new home in Poy Sippi, Wisconsin, in 1972, they found a quilt in a box, and put it on their spare bed. But guests seldom obtained a good night's sleep under it. Mrs Monroe's daughter, Florence, said she was awakened one night at midnight by the quilt being pulled from her and a voice saying: 'Give me back my Christmas quilt.'

One curious fact in nearly all poltergeist cases is that activity often stops when a young person – a servant, secretary or child of the family – leaves the home. The Foundation for Research into the Nature of Man, set up at Duke University, North Carolina, in 1964, says poltergeists may not be ghosts at all, but the result of psychokinesis (mind over matter) channelling powers from the budding energies of teenagers approaching puberty.

But the Foundation's theory cannot explain the strangest poltergeist of all time. On the Caribbean island of Barbados there is a stone-built tomb, recessed in the limestone rock of a headland above Oistin's Bay. It contains the wooden coffin of a Mrs Thomasina Goddard and is sealed with a marble slab. The site passed in 1808 into the hands of the Chases, slave-owning planters on the island. In the first year of their possession the Chases twice had to open the tomb to bury their young daughters, first Mary Ann, then Dorcas. Four years later, the girls' father, Thomas, died. But when the tomb was opened to receive his coffin, shocked mourners saw that the girls' lead caskets had been stood on end against one of the walls. Mrs Goddard's coffin, however, was where it had always been. There was no sign of a break-in.

Eight men carried the lead coffin of Thomas Chase into the tomb, and put the caskets containing the girls back into their original positions. Stonemasons then cemented the entrance slab in position.

But when the slab was rolled away four years later for the funeral of a boy relative, the same phenomenon as before was seen to have occurred. After order had been restored to the tomb, checks were made on the walls and ceiling, and the slab was once more cemented securely into position.

Two months later, and again in 1819, the same sights horrified onlookers when new coffins – also of lead – went into the tomb.

Finally, the governor of the island, Lord Combermere, took a hand. He supervised the orderly arrangement of the coffins – now six – and sprinkled fine sand around them. Then the slab was cemented into place and he fixed his seal to one of the joins.

On 18 April 1820, he unexpectedly asked the rector for the tomb to be opened. And when the slab was heaved aside (the seal was intact), the six coffins, which had been placed in a neat line, the smaller three on the larger ones, were again seen to be scattered over the tomb – all except that of Mrs Goddard. There were no marks in the fine sand.

The family could stand the notoriety no longer. All six coffins were buried in nearby Christ Church graveyard, and the tomb was left silent and abandoned.

Nobody knows what caused the sacrilege at Oistin's Bay. Flooding and earthquakes were ruled out because nothing apart from the tomb was affected, and Mrs Goddard's casket was untouched. The natives would have been too frightened to enter the resting place of the dead, and there were no signs of forced entry.

Author Sir Arthur Conan Doyle surmised that supernatural forces had moved the coffins because they were made of lead, which would delay the decay of the bodies inside. He also pointed out that Thomas Chase had committed suicide. Whatever the cause, the bodies rested peacefully once they were buried.

Chapter Seven

Mysteries of the Wild

Man has conquered almost every corner of the globe –
yet there are still areas beyond the boundaries of his
knowledge. Where, for example, was Lassiter's Lost
Reef? What are the magnetic-like forces exerted by
the Bermuda Triangle? Who were the 'white' Red
Indians of Carolina? Did Drake discover California?
Is there an elusive fortune buried in Nova Scotia's
Money Pit? And what is the monster they call
Bigfoot?

In the steps of Bigfoot

What is the monstrous creature that stalks the world's snowy wastes?

When the first gorilla was seen by a white man in the early part of the last century, the reaction to the news was one of natural astonishment. Native stories about such creatures were well known but had been largely written off as mythology. The actual discovery of these enormous, intelligent and sensitive animals was a fresh reminder that the wilder regions of the earth could still hold surprises for man.

The amazing coelacanth, fished out of the Indian Ocean in 1952, caused just as much of a shock, for it was believed to have become extinct 100 million years before. The pigmy hippopotamus, the white rhinoceros, the giant panda and the Komodo dragon are other recent discoveries of hitherto unknown wildlife. Yet these creatures have been no secret to the natives of the regions they inhabit. The tough, abrasive skin of the coelacanth, for instance, was used by the natives of Madagascar in place of sandpaper for mending punctures in bicycle tyres.

So how many more creatures may yet turn out not to be legendary, as always supposed, but real? Are there other living fossils – even missing links in the story of evolution – still hiding away in the remotest regions of the globe? There is certainly a wealth of folklore to suggest so. . .

From the still-mysterious mountains of the west coast of North America to the snowy slopes of the mighty Himalayas, there exist stories, and evidence, of the most intriguing creature that walks this earth. It is called variously Bigfoot, Sasquatch, Shookpa, Alma, Meti, Kang-mi, Migo and dozens of other names. It has also achieved international fame as the yeti, or Abominable Snowman.

The existence of the yeti was first reported to the West in 1832 by an adventurous Briton, B. H. Hodson, who went to live among the Nepalese high in the Himalayas. Hodson wrote about a tall, erect, ape-like creature covered in thick hair. But those who read his reports believed his sightings were simply of the large langur monkey or the Himalayan red bear. It was not until 1887 that an outsider first saw direct evidence of the existence of the yeti. Another Briton, Major Lawrence Waddell, of the Indian Army Medical Corps, told of remarkable footprints he had seen in Sikkim – 'said to be the trail of one of the hairy wild men who live in the eternal snows'.

When an international mania for mountaineering broke out in the 1920s and 30s, more details of the remarkable yeti were brought back by expeditions

Everest hidden in cloud.

seeking to conquer the unknown peaks of the Himalayas. It was at this time that a journalist coined the name 'Abominable Snowman'.

According to the stories of Nepalese villagers, Tibetan lamas and hardy Sherpas, yetis had always lived along the snow line that separates the thickly wooded lower slopes of the Himalayas from the desolate icy wastes above. Their terrain was between 12,000 and 20,000 ft and they were assumed to live in caves and to emerge mainly at night. The animals were said to be anything up to 12 ft high, yet extremely agile. They walked erect with a loping gait, their long arms swinging by their sides. Their heads were slightly conical and their pale, virtually hairless features were half ape-like, half human. Their bodies were covered in thick, coarse hair, the colour of the red fox. They were said to be shy and to approach human habitation only when driven by hunger. Their diet was mainly lichen and rodents, and they disembowelled their prey before eating it – a peculiarly human trait. They made a loud yelping sound when alarmed.

This then was the Abominable Snowman, as represented by local inhabitants. But where was the proof of its existence? Tibetan lama monasteries were said to contain scalps, skins and even mummified bodies of the creatures, but no Westerner had been able to remove one of these relics for analysis. The only evidence was the reports of the natives – until, in 1921, Colonel C. K. Howard-Bury became the first European to see the yeti. . .

Colonel Howard-Bury was leading a British expedition attempting to scale Mount Everest, when he and his men spotted a strange group of creatures at about 17,000 ft on the Lhapka-la Pass. When they reached the spot they found footprints in the snow – 'each of them about three times the size of a human print'. Colonel Howard-Bury was told by his Sherpas that the tracks were those of the yeti. But, despite his own description of the prints, the sceptical Englishman could not bring himself to believe they were caused by a yeti and instead attributed them to a wolf.

Further sightings followed. One scientific expedition reported seeing an ape-man pulling roots out of the ground. There was a report of a 13-year-old girl being kidnapped by a yeti, and of a yeti being sighted carrying a crude bow and arrows. In 1936, the expedition of Ronald Kaulback confirmed the widespread existence of mysterious footprints. And a year later, the first photograph allegedly showing a yeti's footprint was taken by Frank Smythe and published around the world.

During World War Two, five Polish prisoners being held in a Siberian labour camp escaped from their Soviet captors and made an incredible march across Mongolia and Tibet to Bhutan, where, in 1942, they crossed the Himalayas to India and safety. There, they recounted a strange episode which had occurred in the mountains.

They said they had looked down from a ledge and had seen two burly ape-men only a few feet below them. The creatures were aware that they were observed but showed no emotions whatever and, seemingly ignoring the strangers, continued to shuffle through the snow. The Poles watched the creatures for fully two hours, and their description fits those of most previous witnesses.

A pair of less friendly ape creatures were encountered by two Norwegian prospectors in Zemu Gap, Sikkim, India, in 1948. One of the men, Jah Frostis, said he was badly mauled about the shoulder by the larger of the beasts. But the Norwegians were armed, and when they opened fire the creatures fled. It was yet another story to intrigue the world, coming as it did from a largely unexplored region of the globe. But it was, after all, just a story. Apart from the inconclusive 1937 photograph, there was still no documentary evidence about the Abominable Snowman's existence.

All that changed in 1951. On 8 November of that year, veteran mountaineer Eric Shipton was climbing in the Gauri Sankar range with fellow Briton Michael Ward and Sherpa Sen Tensing when they came across a series of clear footprints on the Men-lung Glacier at an altitude of 18,000 ft. They were made by a creature with a flat foot and five toes, one much enlarged. The prints were 13 in. long and 8 in. wide, and indicated a creature about 8 ft tall. (A further run of prints was also photographed, but these were less conclusive: it was later suggested that they were made by a running mountain goat and were later grotesquely enlarged by the action of the sun.) The photographs and Shipton's impeccable credentials convinced many. New interest was aroused.

Scientists examined a mummified finger and thumb found at Pangboch, Nepal, and declared it to be from a Neanderthal man. Then, in 1952, Everest was finally conquered by Sir Edmund Hillary and Sherpa Tensing. But although Hillary found prints, he always denied the existence of an Abominable Snowman.

Two years later, the London *Daily Mail* sent an expedition to the Himalayas to try to prove or disprove the existence of the yeti once and for all. Sadly, it did neither. The team did, however, discover several 'yeti' scalps covered in coarse red hair. The lamas who were custodians of these relics allowed the expedition to remove a few hairs. These were later analyzed, and scientists were unable to identify the creature to which they had belonged. The *Daily Mail* expedition also found several footprints and droppings containing part-animal, part-vegetable material.

A further expedition, sponsored by Texas oilman Thomas Slick, took up the trail in 1957. They too found tracks and were told by Nepalese villagers that yetis had recently killed five people in the area. But of the creatures themselves they saw no sign.

In 1970 British mountaineer Don Whillans spent a day photographing mysterious but inconclusive tracks at a height of 13,000 ft in the mountains of Nepal. That night he saw by clear moonlight an ape-like creature bounding along a nearby ridge on all fours.

And in 1973 a young Sherpa girl was attacked by a yeti. She had been tending a small herd of yaks in the Koner area when the creature pounced from some undergrowth and knocked her unconscious. When she came round, five of the yaks were dead.

Further clues to the Abominable Snowman certainly exist in the remote monasteries of Tibet. If they were allowed to examine these relics, scientists could hope to identify them. But since the Communist takeover, Tibet has been out of bounds for Westerners. The mystery of the Abominable Snowman looks like remaining precisely that for some time to come.

More readily accessible – although in many ways even more mysterious – are the mountains and forests that make up the spectacular wilderness that runs along the entire west coast of the USA and Canada, from California in the south to Alaska in the north. In that wilderness lurks Bigfoot – an ape-like creature of no known species.

Bigfoot and his Canadian cousin, the Sasquatch, have been around for a long time. Early settlers in the West were told by local tribes about the wild, hairy creatures of the forests. They were described as being about 8 ft tall, walking stooped but on two legs, with a broad chest and shoulders but with virtually no neck, and covered with auburn hair. In the early 19th century, explorer David Thomas became the first European to discover evidence of this strange animal, in the shape of 14-in-long footprints near Jasper, Alberta. Since then, many giant prints have been found, and casts taken of them, to substantiate the Indian legends.

Nowadays, those who believe in the existence of Bigfoot are no longer regarded as cranks. And there is sufficient evidence to brush aside suggestions that it is all an elaborate hoax.

One of the earliest Bigfoot sightings was recounted by President Theodore Roosevelt – a keen hunter – in the story he told of two trappers in the Salmon River district of Idaho who were attacked by the mysterious creature. And the *Seattle Times* of 16 July 1918 published an account of an attack by 'mountain devils' on a prospector at Mount St Helens, Washington.

In 1924 came the remarkable case of a 'kidnapping' by one of the creatures. Lumberman Albert Ostman, of Langley, British Columbia, said he had been camping opposite Vancouver Island when he was snatched by a Sasquatch. He was carried away, still in his sleeping bag, to the animal's lair, where he was held for a week. The Sasquatch's family, which fed him and treated him well, consisted of an 8-ft male, a 6-ft female and two children. Believing himself to have been abducted as a suitable 'husband' for one of the Sasquatch children, the apprehensive Ostman escaped while the head of the household was examining the woodman's snuff box.

Another encounter was reported in 1924, from the area now known as Ape Canyon in Washington, close to the Oregon border. Over the years, dozens of Bigfoot creatures have been seen in that remote, mountainous region. But the first, and possibly the most dramatic, encounter was when prospectors shot one of a group of hairy 'ape-men'. The other creatures attacked the prospectors' cabin and caused considerable damage but no loss of life. Reporters who later visited the site saw hundreds of giant footprints.

In 1933, two men at Pitt Lake, northern British Columbia, saw a creature

President Theodore Roosevelt.

leisurely eating berries in a clearing. They described it as having a 'human-like face on a fur-clad body'.

The Chapman family, of Ruby Creek, British Columbia, fled their lonely farmhouse in 1940 when a Sasquatch approached menacingly. It overturned a barrel of salted fish but then lost interest and meandered away.

An insight into the feeding habits of the Sasquatch was obtained in 1955 by a man travelling near Mica Mountain, in the east of British Columbia. He watched, hidden from sight, as a female Sasquatch only 50 ft away from him placed branches of bushes in its mouth and stripped the leaves.

In 1958, a road construction worker near Bluff Creek, in Humboldt County, northern California, encountered a Bigfoot which, he said, he could get rid of only by offering it a candy bar. Suddenly Bluff Creek – more easily accessible than most previous Bigfoot haunts – became a popular hunting ground for Bigfoot-searchers.

Early one morning, after a night of weird noises, construction site workers sleeping in cabins at Bluff Creek emerged to find 16-in. footprints in the snow, made by a creature which took strides of up to 5 ft. Even more disconcerting was the discovery that a 50-gallon fuel drum had been manhandled across the camp. A party set out to track the creature, and eventually they picked it up in their truck headlights. They gave chase on boot but had to abandon the hunt in dense woodland. Their dogs continued the chase, however. Their

---

WHAT WAS *HOMO POINGODES*?
A considerable scientific argument blew up in 1969 over the authenticity of a creature encased in a block of ice and sent on a tour of fairgrounds in the United States. No one took claims about the beast's past too seriously - until two respected zoologists, Anglo-American Ivan Sanderson and Belgian Dr Bernard Heuvelmans, appeared to give it serious credence. Heuvelmans even described the creature as 'a previously unknown form of living hominid' and named it *Homo Poingodes*.

The creature was tall, half-man, half-ape, with enormous hands and feet. It was said to belong to an eccentric Californian millionaire, who eventually reclaimed it when the publicity became too hot. It was variously described as having been found floating in a solid block of ice in the Bering Sea and having been shot by a girl it attacked in the woods of Minnesota.

But despite the claims of the showmen and the probings of scientists, it is now thought most likely that *Homo Poingodes* was an extremely cleverly constructed foam rubber model.

shattered bodies were said to have been discovered some time later.

Oilman Slick, whose passion until then had been the Abominable Snowman, also launched a hunt for Bigfoot, but again without success. In 1963, however, the creature returned to the Bluff Creek area and attacked another construction site. According to newspaper reports at the time, it was even credited with sufficient strength to have overturned a truck.

The big breakthrough, however, came in 1967. On 20 October, Roger Patterson, an ex-rodeo cowboy and rancher who had decided to devote his life to Bigfoot-hunting, was tracking through forests near Bluff Creek with a part-Indian friend, Bob Gimlin. They emerged into a clearing by a creek – and saw, less than 400 ft away, a female Bigfoot loping along the bank. The creature glanced towards them, then strode off into the dense forest. But before it vanished from sight, Patterson aimed his movie camera and shot 29 ft of film – the first photographic evidence of the creature's existence. The film was later examined by experts and certified genuine. Patterson and Gimlin also took several footprint casts. The film, shown world-wide, renewed interest in the mysterious creatures, and Bigfoot-hunting became a national pastime.

In Oregon, in 1967, a family of 'ape-men' was reported to have been seen picking through a rock pile for hibernating rodents, then eating them 'like bananas'.

For the next few years there was a number of poorly documented sightings. But in 1969 more than 1,000 giant footprints were counted at a garbage dump near Bossburg, Washington. The following year, hunters chased a Bigfoot in Skamania County and discovered the half-eaten carcass of an elk, surrounded by footprints. Further authenticated sightings were made in 1972 and 1974 near Mount Jefferson and on the Hood River, Oregon. In both cases, the animals were described as timid, graceful creatures.

Despite Patterson's film and the hundreds of sightings by responsible and sincere witnesses, there is still no concrete evidence of Bigfoot's existence. No corpses or bones have ever been found.

A Canadian publishing group offered $100,000 to anyone who could capture a Sasquatch alive. That was in 1973, and no one has yet claimed the reward. Yet, precisely the conclusive evidence which sceptics have long been waiting for may have been produced a century ago. . . .

In 1884, the driver of a train travelling down the Fraser River valley in British Columbia spotted a hairy creature sleeping beside the track. He jammed on the brakes, waking the animal, which ran off. The driver and the rest of the train's crew gave chase and finally cornered the creature, knocking it out with a rock. They named their prisoner Jacko and took it to the next town down the line; Yale. There it was examined and described in the newspaper *Victoria Colonist* as being of human form but covered in inch-long hair except for its hands and feet. It was 4 ft 7 in tall – presumably a young Sasquatch – and weighed 127 pounds. Its diet was berries and milk.

So what happened to Jacko? The story is that he died while being crated for another rail journey – this time as an exhibit in a travelling sideshow. And where he is buried, no one now knows.

THE RUSSIANS HAVE THEIR BIGFOOT, TOO
Experts of the Soviet Academy of Sciences formed themselves in 1957 into four expeditions to areas where, for years, mysterious 'ape-men' had been reported. They journeyed to Mongolia, the Pamir Mountains, the Caucasus and the Himalayas. All four teams reported back that there was strong evidence that an early form of man still existed in remote areas of the globe.

The expeditions' findings were enthusiastically received by Professor Boris Porshnev, eminent director of the academy's modern history department, and his successor Dr Jeanne Korfman. In 1964, Dr Korfman set up a permanent study centre in the Caucasus to sift local reports of a race of wild men called Almas. She claimed to have discovered two lairs of the creatures, stocked with larders of berries and vegetables.

But the most remarkable evidence of the existence of Almas was produced back in 1925 by Major-General Mikhail Topilsky, who was pursuing a band of defeated White Army troops through the Pamir Mountains, near the Afghanistan border. They followed footsteps in the snow to the mouth of a cave, and after a warning they fired into the opening. A creature staggered out and fell at their feet.

An army doctor examined the body and pronounced it 'not human'. Yet it was the size and shape of a man, although entirely covered in hair. The forehead receded, the nose was flat and the jaws large and protruding - a perfect description of Neanderthal Man. The puzzled soldiers buried the creature and moved on.

Lasseter's lost reef

Somewhere in the hostile, scorching desert of central Australia may lie a fortune in gold. It is the gold reef of Harold Lasseter, somewhere beyond the Petermann Mountains.

Lasseter, a tough, down-to-earth prospector, stumbled on the reef in 1897.

But it was another 14 years before he could raise enough money to launch an expedition. Tragically, it was doomed to failure because of the dreadful desert conditions the men encountered. Lasseter and his group battled on gamely for as long as they could, but they eventually had to abandon the bid and were lucky to save their lives.

Lasseter still clung to his dream and immediately set about organizing a second expedition. It took him until 1930 to finance it, and once again it was defeated by the desert. Every one of Lasseter's companions died, leaving him to struggle on alone with two camels. Then he fell victim to sand blindness and eventually starved to death.

Years later, his body was found in a cave where he had sought shelter. But none of the prospectors and fortune-hunters who have since tried have ever been able to find the fortune that lured him to his death.

The lost gold of Arizona

Hunters for Lost Dutchman's Mine find only death

America's history is littered with stories of fabulous gold strikes, but there are none more intriguing than the tale of the Lost Dutchman's Mine in Arizona's unwelcoming Superstition Mountains. Nobody has successfully traced the location of Lost Dutchman's Mine since 1890. Yet adventurers still search for it in the hope of finding a fortune just waiting to be dug from the ground. About 20 men have died in this search.

Apache Indians were almost certainly the first to discover the mine. In the days before they feared the white man and became aware of his insatiable lust for gold, they showed the mine to Spanish monks from Mexico. Inevitably, stories of the rich ore which could be dug out by the sackful soon leaked out and set men talking and dreaming.

Many people made successful expeditions to the mine, until years later it passed into the ownership of a Spaniard, Don Miguel Peralta. In 1871, his grandson, also called Don Miguel, shared his secret with two German immigrants, Jacob Waltz and Jacob Weiser, when they rescued him from a fight in the town of Arizpe in the Sonora district of Mexico. Don Miguel told them that previous generations of his family had obtained fortunes in gold from the mine by taking with them a private army of guards and labourers so strong that the Apaches dared not attack, but that in 1864 his father and his work party had been overwhelmed by the Apaches in a bloody battle lasting three days. There were few survivors to return to Mexico, but one who did return carried a map which pinpointed the position of the mine.

Don Miguel himself had no money to finance a large guard of men for a full-scale march on the mine. So he asked Waltz and Weiser to go with him and a handful of men on a surprise raid to a spot where gold dug from the mine by the Apaches was hidden awaiting collection. The two Germans agreed and they and Don Miguel soon returned with their share of the gold, worth about $60,000.

Before setting off, Don Miguel had made it a condition that he was to receive a half share of what they brought back. When they returned to Mexico, Don Miguel changed his mind. He struck a deal with Waltz and Weiser whereby they gave up their share for ownership of the mine.

Before Waltz and Weiser could return to the area, however, the mine's existence was revealed to another man, Dr Abraham Thorne. The doctor had cared for some Apaches and, to repay his kindness, they said they would reward him with a gift of gold. If he was prepared to ride 20 miles, he could carry away as much gold as he could manage. Dr Thorne agreed and was led, blindfolded, to a canyon which contained a pile of rich ore. He was not shown the mine, but while he was loading up the gold into his saddle-bags he made a note of two distinguishing landmarks – the remains of a ruined rock fort and a sharp towering rock called Weaver's Needle – about a mile to the south.

As Dr Thorne came away with $6,000 worth of gold, he determined to find the spot again. So, a year later, he took some friends in search of the canyon – only to be driven away by a fearsome attack from the Apaches.

When Waltz and Weiser eventually returned to the area, they were alone. Using Don Miguel's map to guide them, they found the mine and started working the gold seams. But one day Weiser was left alone for a while, and when Waltz returned, his partner had disappeared. Only his blood-soaked shirt and tools, surrounded by Apache arrows, lay on the ground where he had been working. Waltz quickly packed all the gold he could into his bags and rode away from Superstition Mountains as fast as his horse would travel. He eventually settled in Phoenix, and lived there until 1891.

But, miraculously, his partner Weiser had not been killed in the Indian attack. Although he was gravely wounded, he escaped and reached the nearby home of a doctor, John Walker. He told Dr Walker all about the gold mine in the mountains, and gave him Don Miguel's map. But Walker did not make use of it, and when he died in 1890 it could not be found.

The last time Waltz visited the mine was in the winter of 1890. He travelled alone and returned to Phoenix two days later with a small sack of gold. He was almost certainly the last person to visit the mine, and when he died shortly afterwards the secret of its location died with him. Because people in the town thought from his accent that Waltz was from Holland, they called the mine the Lost Dutchman's Mine.

Before he died, Waltz told a friend that the mine was situated in country so wild that a man could be right in the centre of it and yet still be unaware of it. He said the ore was superbly rich and easy to dig from the rock. He and Weiser, he said, hit the rock with their heavy hammers, and nuggets of the precious metal simply fell into their hands. The mine was shaped like a funnel, but someone had cut a tunnel through the hillside and into the bottom of the mine to make it easier to drag the gold out.

Waltz also confessed that once, when he and Weiser went alone to the mine, they found two Mexican labourers from one of their expeditions helping themselves to the gold. They shot them dead.

Two young soldiers who stumbled on the mine by chance in 1880 suffered a similar fate. They arrived in the town of Pinal with their saddle bags full of fabulous gold nuggets and told their story of finding a funnel-shaped mine in the Superstition Mountains. They agreed to take a local man back to the mine, using their army training to retrace their steps. Some time later, their naked bodies were found. At first, it appeared they had fallen victim to the Apaches. But the bullets taken from their corpses were identified as the type used by the US Army.

Years later, an Indian called Apache Jack told the story of the way his people did their best to hide the mine. In this way, they hoped to stem the flood of unwelcome white men who invaded their territory in search of riches. In 1882, Apache Jack said, the squaws were given the task of filling in the mine with rocks. Then the entrance was covered over. There was also an earthquake in that area, and it may well have destroyed the landmarks.

In the years since then, many people have trekked to the area in search of the gold. None have found it, but at least 20 have lost their lives. In 1931, Adolph Ruth went off into the mountains after telling relatives and friends that he had bought a map of the route to the Lot Dutchman's Mine from a member of Don Miguel Peralta's family. When he failed to return, a rescue party went out to look for him – and were confronted by a macabre sight. Ruth had been shot twice in the head and then beheaded.

In a coat pocket was a slip of paper on which were written some directions, the words 'about 200 feet across from the cave', and then the Latin inscription *Veni, Vidi, Vici* ('I came, I saw, I conquered'). There was no trace of Ruth's map.

In 1947, another gold-hunter was found murdered in the area, but there was no sign of any gold and his killer was never traced.

Perhaps one day a prospector will succeed where so many others have failed. For there are plenty of clues in the countless stories of the mine and its massive gold seams. In 1912, two adventurers discovered gold nuggets in the tall grass at the very spot where Don Miguel Peralta's father and his men had been slaughtered in 1864. Not far from Weaver's Needle, a landmark that constantly cropped up in tales of the mine, there were indications that many men had once worked. There were deeply worn trails and a large pile of Mexican sandals hidden in a cave.

But despite all the clues, all the stories, to this day the vast store of riches under the ground lives up to its name . . . the Lost Dutchman's Mine.

The Bermuda Triangle

Despite the sceptics, losses of boats and planes defy explanation

At 2 pm on 5 December 1945, a flight of five Grumman US Navy bombers took off from Fort Lauderdale for a training flight in perfect weather. Shortly afterwards, the pilots radioed that their flight instruments were all malfunctioning. Their gyro-compasses were 'going crazy'. Two hours after take-off, all contact with the aircraft was lost.

A Martin bomber was immediately dispatched to search for the missing planes. Within 20 minutes, radio contact with it had also been lost. No trace of any of the aircraft was ever found. In all, six planes and 27 men had vanished into thin air.

The disaster introduced a new phrase to the English language – the Bermuda Triangle. For that was the area of the Atlantic where the long-held fears of airmen and sailors were at last proved well founded.

The disappearance of the six planes was far from being the first mysterious incident in the area – for years, navigational problems and strange magnetic forces had been reported. The disappearance was not even the greatest disaster within the triangle. That befell the 19,000-ton US Navy supply vessel *Cyclops*.

The *Cyclops* was sailing from Barbados to Norfolk, Virginia, in March 1918, when it vanished with its crew of 309 from the surface of the ocean without making a distress call and without the slightest scrap of wreckage ever being found.

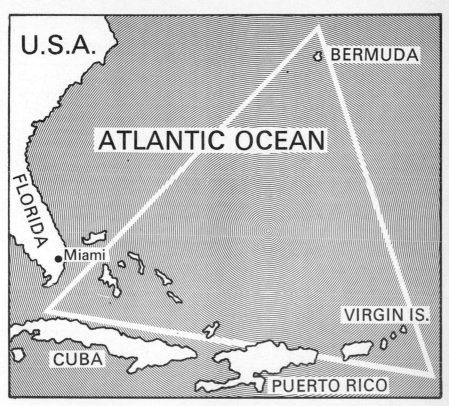

The Bermuda Triangle.

It is since 1945, however, that the Bermuda Triangle has entered legend. It has been variously labelled the Devil's Triangle, the Triangle of Death, the Hoodoo Sea and the Graveyard of the Atlantic. And it is reputed to have swallowed up 140 ships and planes and more than 1,000 people. These are some of them:

1947: Army C-45 Superfort vanishes 100 miles off Bermuda.
1948: Four-engined Tudor IV lost with 31 lives.
1948: DC-3 lost with 32 passengers and crew.
1949: Second Tudor IV vanishes.
1950: Giant US Air Force Globemaster lost.
1950: American freighter, SS *Sandra*, 350 ft long, sinks without trace.
1952: British York transport plane lost with 33 aboard.
1954: US Navy Lockheed Constellation vanishes with 42 aboard.

1956: US Navy seaplane, Martin P5M, disappears with crew of ten.
1962: US Air Force KB-50 tanker plane lost.
1963: *Marine Sulphur Queen*, 425-ft-long American freighter, vanishes with entire crew. No Mayday signals and no wreckage ever found. Two US Air Force giant stratotankers disappear on simple exercise. C-132 Cargomaster also vanishes.
1967: Military YC-122, converted to cargo plane, lost.
1970: French freighter *Milton Iatrides* disappears.
1973: German freighter *Anita*, 20,000 tons, lost with crew of 32.

US Navy seaplane, Martin P5M.

Those are just some of the major disappearing acts that have taken place within the Triangle. But in more recent years, a healthy scepticism has grown up around some of the more outlandish claims made for the area's mysterious powers.

Writing about the Bermuda Triangle became a virtual industry in the 1960s and early 1970s, and some of the theories put forward by authors have been far-fetched, to say the least. Time warps, water spouts, subterranean volcanoes, reverse gravity and black holes have all been blamed for the rash of disappearances. It has been suggested that UFOs have been collecting earthling specimens in the area, and that the people of the lost civilization of Atlantis are still exerting their powers somewhere in the deep.

One best-selling book propounded the theory that navigational instruments are thrown into confusion by a vast solar crystal that once provided the energy for Atlantis and now lies on the seabed.

Such ideas may easily be discounted. But that still leaves the mystery of those hundreds of lost lives.

The search for El Dorado

It may not have been a place after all - but a person

Adventurers have fought, killed and plundered in their search for the fabled treasure-houses of El Dorado. Often, they have given their own lives, too – chasing what may have been just a greedy dream.

It all began when the Spaniards invaded the Inca empire of Peru in 1532 and discovered incredible hoards of gold, including many beautiful works of art. They captured the city of Cuzco and could hardly believe their eyes when they saw the plunder that was there for the taking. There was gold-plating on the walls of the emperor's temple, and even the palace waterpipes were fashioned of gold.

The Spaniards overran the Inca empire and captured its emperor, Atahuallpa. Then they held him to ransom, demanding that a huge room 22 ft by 17 ft square should be filled with gold to a height of more than 8 ft. The Incas paid this enormous ransom, but then the treacherous invaders, led by the notorious Francisco Pizarro, cold-bloodedly killed their hostage. Not content with the incredible riches they had already acquired, the ruthless conquerors set about stripping the Inca empire of more of its wealth.

THE WORLD'S GREATEST MYSTERIES

Their greed knew no bounds when they heard stories of even greater treasures in the north, beyond the Inca frontiers – at a place some people called El Dorado. The stories and myths surrounding El Dorado were many and varied. Some said it was a lost city, others a treasure-filled temple hidden deep in the jungle. Some even claimed it to be a mountain of solid gold.

The most widely accepted theory, however, is that El Dorado, which is Spanish for the Gilded One, was a person – probably the chief of the Muisca people, who lived in the extreme north of the Andes, somewhere in the region which is now the Colombian city of Bogota.

El Dorado took his exotic name from a tribal ritual that marked his installation. His people would gather on the shores of the circular Lake Guatavita – which is completely ringed by high mountains – for several days of celebration. At the height of the festivities, the chief and his priests boarded a raft made of rushes and were rowed out to the centre of the lake. Incense was burned and flutes wafted their music eerily across the waters. When the raft reached the centre of the lake, the new chief was stripped naked and then his entire body was coated with gold dust. With the sun glinting on his body, he then took gold treasures and dropped them into the waters as an offering to the gods. This was the signal for the chief's people assembled on the shores of the lake to add their tribute by also throwing objects of gold into the water. In this way, the lake eventually held one of the richest collections of gold in the New World.

Strangely, El Dorado's people had no source of gold of their own. They gathered it by a combination of war and trading. They possessed the only emerald mine in the whole continent and they also had vast deposits of salt. So they traded these two valuable commodities for gold.

In June 1535, Georg Hohermuth, the German governor of Venezuela, set out to find El Dorado, having learned from the natives that 'where the salt comes from, comes gold'.

He set out with an expeditionary force of 400 men and searched for three years, encountering the most appalling conditions. When he returned, 300 of his men had perished, and, ironically, they had passed within 60 miles of the lake of gold.

The following year, Sebastian de Belelcazar, the formidable conquistador, also set out to find the lake, and a few months later a German adventurer, Nicholaus Federmann, embarked on the same mission.

At the same time, Spanish lawyer Gonzalo Jimenez de Quesada organized an expedition into the Andes. He led his men to an area rich in salt, and they captured a succession of villages. They tortured the inhabitants until they revealed the source of their emeralds. One Indian told Quesada that the village of Hunsa was the 'place of gold'. Quesada conquered it and found many

Francesco Pizarro.

gold plates in the wooden and wicker houses. He also discovered large collections of emeralds and bags of gold dust. Quesada's men took the gold rings from the ears and noses of the Indians they slaughtered. They pillaged the village chief's house – which was lined with massive sheets of gold and contained a beautiful throne of gold and emeralds.

Quesada continued in his search for El Dorado, and eventually met up with Belelcazar and Federmann in central Colombia. There they founded the city of Santa Fé de Bogota.

Ironically, even if the fortune-hunters had found the lake of gold, they would not have found El Dorado. For he no longer existed. The dynasty of Muisca chiefs who held the ceremony of the golden raft had been deposed in a power struggle a few years earlier.

In 1545, a determined attempt to rob the lake of its treasures was made by Quesada's brother, Herman. He enslaved a large number of Indians of the Muisca tribe and forced them to form a human chain from the edge of the lake to the top of the mountains. They took water from the lake in buckets and passed it along the line to be tipped away. This operation went on for three months and the level of the lake was lowered by about 9 ft. Several hundred gold objects were recovered from the receding waters on the rim of the lake before the attempt was abandoned.

A more ambitious attempt was made 40 years later. A Spanish merchant recruited 8,000 natives and attempted to cut a deep channel to drain off the water. This was more successful and the level fell by 60 ft. Many gold objects and valuable emeralds were found, but landslips eventually blocked the drainage channel and this scheme was also abandoned.

Early this century, a British company tried to drain the lake. They succeeded in drilling a tunnel which lowered the water level, but the mud on the lake was too soft and too deep to walk on. Then the fierce sun baked the mud rock-hard. By the time the company transported drilling equipment into the area it was too late to use it. The baked mud had blocked the original drainage tunnel and the rains had filled the lake again.

The Colombian government has since introduced legislation protecting the entire site from treasure-hunters. But the fabled wealth of El Dorado continues to intrigue adventurers. Modern travellers who have visited the land of the Incas say that some Indians descended from the tribes who took part in the gold ceremonies still hold secret rituals away from the prying eyes of outsiders. They journey to a secret valley high in the mountains and hold their ancient ceremonies, with the priests dancing before their people, all wearing golden masks, just as their ancestors did. So the spirit of El Dorado lives on – as well as the mystery of his treasure.

Pizarro seizing Atahuallpa (Millais).

Was Columbus the true discoverer of America?

Many nations claim they were the first to set foot on the continent

Christopher Columbus is famed as the man who opened up the New World when he sailed from Spain to the West Indies in 1492. But his voyage was far from being the first to the Americas. It is likely that before he set foot on the great land to the west, the Chinese, Vikings, Irish and even the Phoenicians had visited its shores. So who really discovered America?

Carbon-dating has established that man lived in America at least 12,000 years ago. And it is now thought that the first 'outsiders' to reach the vast continent were the Mongoloid people of eastern Russia, who crossed into Alaska some 40,000 years ago by way of a land bridge – long since vanished – across the Bering Strait. They then travelled down the Pacific coast into Central and South America.

A remarkable discovery, which dates man alongside the long-extinct giant mammoth on the American continent, was made on a farm at Tepexpan, 20 miles north-east of Mexico City, in 1950. Farmer José Cortes was digging a drainage ditch when he struck something hard. Scooping away the earth, he found the fossilized remains of a mammoth. When the fossil was examined by Mexican palaeontologists, the tip of a weapon was found in the animal's rib cage. Apparently the mammoth had become bogged in mud, making it easy prey for a band of hunters armed with spears and stone implements.

Simple tools made of stone and animal bones, seemingly belonging to the same culture, have been found in Siberia, Alaska, the Yukon and Mexico, thus adding weight to the theory that man spread down through America from Asia.

A claim that the Chinese discovered America as early as AD 458 was made recently by a Peking University professor, Chu Shien-chi. He says that a Buddhist priest, Hoei Shin, sailed across the north Pacific with four other monks and landed somewhere on the Central American coast, perhaps Mexico. Hoei Shin named the country Fusang, after a Chinese plant which he likened to vegetation growing there.

Austrian ethnologist Robert von Heine-Geldern goes further. He is convinced that the Chinese influenced the development of civilization in America around 2000 BC. Certainly, sculptures found in the ruins of some Central

American cities are similar to those used in the Buddhist religion. And China's oldest manuscript, the *Shan Hai King* of 2250 BC, contains what appears to be a description of the Grand Canyon.

A Pacific crossing even earlier than 2000 BC is suggested by pottery found on the Valdivian coast of Ecuador and dated at around 3000 BC. It is almost certainly of Japanese origin, being decorated in the same manner as pottery from the Jomon region of Japan.

On the Atlantic side, Irish monks are said to have visited North America

Columbus's first mass in America.

around the 6th century. A 10th-century Latin manuscript, the *Navigatio Sancti Brendani*, tells of the voyages of a Saint Brendan and how he set out around 540 with a party of 14 monks to find the 'Land Promised to the Saints'. The manuscript is so full of marvellous achievements and devout thinking that for years it was considered to be just a collection of tales. Brendan is said to have been helped on his way by a whale and guided from time to time by angels disguised as birds. But modern scholars think the voyages actually did take place, although they may not all have been led by Brendan.

According to the *Navigatio*, Brendan, an experienced seaman and navigator, is supposed to have set sail for the Promised Land from Kerry in a 36-ft wooden-framed boat covered with oxhide and greased with butter to make it waterproof. The party took a northerly course and eventually came across a floating tower of crystal, which suggests that they had encountered a giant iceberg and had passed around Greenland and into Davis Strait, well known

INDIANS WITH BLOND HAIR
American Indians with blond hair and blue eyes, and others who become white-haired in old age - are they mistakes of nature or the descendants of white people who landed in America centuries ago, perhaps even before Christopher Columbus set foot in the New World?

According to a plaque set up in 1953 at Fort Morgan, Alabama, by the Daughters of the American Revolution, a group of Welsh explorers led by the great Prince Madog ap Owain Gwynedd allegedly 'landed on the shores of Mobile Bay in 1170 and left behind, with the Indians, the Welsh language'. The party - accounts of the numbers vary from 50 to 300 - is said to have sailed from North Wales across the Atlantic in the sweep of the North Equatorial Current and through the narrow gap separating Florida and Cuba.

Anthropologists have found striking similarities between the Welsh and the now virtually extinct Mandan Indians, who lived along the upper reaches of the Missouri River. The Mandans used boats very much like Welsh coracles, responded immediately when they heard the Welsh language, and became white-haired with age, a characteristic not shown by other Indians. An 18th-century French traveller to the area described the Mandans as 'white men with forts and permanent villages laid out in streets'. The ruins of three Welsh-style fortresses have been found near Chattanooga, in Tennessee.

The Mandans were wiped out by men who may have had the same ethnic origins as themselves - white fur traders

for its floating ice. They passed through an area of dense mist, which could be the Newfoundland Banks, where the warm Gulf Stream meets the Arctic current. The party encountered whales and 'an animal with big eyes, tusks, a spotted belly and a bearded jaw' – a walrus? – before landing in a country of autumn sunshine, possibly Labrador.

Later Brendan and his men landed on a flat, tropical island covered with exotic vegetation, surrounded by crystal clear water and inhabited by beautiful birds and naked dark-skinned pygmies. Perhaps Brendan had sailed down the coast of North America out of sight of land and arrived at an island in the Bahamas. The pygmy people could have been the Arawaks, the original inhabitants of the islands. Brendan and his party went on to discover another land – 'odorous, flower-smooth and blest' – which is now thought to have been Florida.

The whole story is hard to believe. And not having been written down until

---

who started a smallpox epidemic among the Mandans in the mid-19th century.

Eighteenth-century explorers along the Lumber River of North Carolina found a tribe of grey-eyed Indians who spoke a kind of English and claimed that their ancestors could 'talk in a book' – which was taken to mean that they could read. Their descendants, the Lumbee Indians, still live in Robeson County – and blond hair and blue eyes are not uncommon features among them.

It is thought that the Lumbee Indians could be the remnants of Sir Walter Raleigh's lost colony of English settlers who disappeared from Roanoke Island, on the coast of North Carolina, around 1590. The colony was established in 1587 under Governor John White, who then returned to England for supplies. War between England and Spain prevented him from revisiting the colony for three years. When he returned, White found the fort dismantled. The 117 settlers, including 11 children, were missing. The only clue to their fate was the word 'Croatoan' carved on a post. White took it to mean that the settlers had moved south to the island of Croatoan, known to be inhabited by the friendly Hatteras tribe. He made no attempt to find them.

If White was right and the settlers did move to Croatoan and interbred with the natives, their descendants could be the Lumbee Indians. However some historians believe that the word 'Croatoan' refers to the name of a tribe that attacked and massacred the settlers. It is a mystery that is unlikely ever to be solved.

A Viking ship.
Opposite Columbus's *Santa Maria*.

several centuries after the events it described, it is possible that it was considerably embellished. However, the ancient sagas of the Norsemen admit that the Irish were there first.

The Viking voyages to North America are now established as historical fact. The intrepid Norsemen land-hopped via Iceland and Greenland and, under Leif Ericson, reached the coast of North America in the year 1000. The stories of their heroic voyages to this land beyond the sea – referred to as Markland, Helluland and Vinland – are told in the Norse sagas, written in Iceland between 1320 and 1350. Not much attention was paid to these sagas until as recently as 1837, when they were re-examined and it was found that their descriptions of Vinland's climate, geography and native life fitted that of the coast of New England.

The recent discovery of the stone foundations of eight houses, four boat sheds, a smithy, cooking pits and implements at L'Anse aux Meadows, on the northern tip of Newfoundland – all carbon-dated to the Viking era – lends credence to the story that Leif Ericson established a settlement on his arrival in North America. 'The find,' says Norwegian Dr Helge Ingstad, who helped make the discovery, 'furnishes the first incontrovertible archaeological proof that Europeans set foot in America centuries before Columbus's voyage of 1492.' But there is still controversy over whether the Vikings penetrated inland or confined their exploration to the coast.

THE WORLD'S GREATEST MYSTERIES

A startling find was made in 1898 by a farmer clearing land at Kensington, Minnesota. Digging out the roots of a tree, he came across a square slab of rock, 2½ ft high and 6 in. thick. An inscription of 220 characters had been chiselled on its face and along one side. It allegedly relates to a 30-strong party of Norwegians and Goths on a 'journey of discovery' west from Vinland in 1362 and tells of a massacre in which ten of the party were killed. Many experts have condemned the so-called Kensington Stone as a 19th-century fake. Others say that it is genuine and that a forger would have needed an outstanding knowledge of history, geology and Norse dialect.

Some scholars have suggested that the Newport Tower, a stone structure in the centre of Newport, Rhode Island, was built by Vikings. The tower, circular and about 24 ft high, is said to have been a church. Others differ, and say that it is the work of 16th- or 17th-century settlers.

The *Vinland Map*, a map of the world said to have been drawn in 1440 by a Swiss monk, has been fiercely argued about over the years. The map, acquired in 1965 by Yale University, clearly depicts the location of Vinland as North America. Experts on both sides of the Atlantic have carbon-dated the map and pronounced it genuine. But recently, a group of American ink analysts studying particles of the map announced that they were convinced it is a 20th-century fake.

Meanwhile, a collection of megalithic ruins in New Hampshire has raised recent speculation among American archaeologists as to whether they are of British – or at least Celtic – origin. The ruins – at a place appropriately named Mystery Hill – consist of 22 stone huts, walls, passages and what appears to be a sacrificial table with a speaking tube arrangement through which voices can be projected. Huge blocks of local granite are held in position by their own weight and by corbelled vaulting – horizontally laid stones that each project a little beyond another. Thousands of artefacts from many periods and different cultures have been found at the site, including a number of stones bearing chiselled inscriptions in what is thought to be Ogham, the ancient language of the Irish and Picts. Dr Barry Fell, of Harvard University, has been studying the stones for several years and dates them tentatively from about 800 BC to the 3rd century AD.

English historian Geoffrey Ashe visited the site in 1960 and declared that it may date back to the banishment of Cronus and the adventures of Odysseus. According to Homer, Cronus was banished to a land where the sun never set, north-west of the Mediterranean. In Homer's *Odyssey*, Odysseus sails to the far frontiers of the world, to the land of the Cimmerians, an area of fog and darkness which has been taken by some to be Newfoundland.

In a serious study, science fiction writer André Norton speculated that Mystery Hill may have been a Phoenician-Carthaginian settlement: 'In 335

Newport Tower.

THE PLATE OF BRASS

Few discoveries in America have aroused more interest than the finding of an old brass plate on the north shore of San Francisco Bay in 1936. Beryle Shinn, a shop assistant, found the plate under a rock while picnicking with his companions. He put it in his car and took it home. It lay forgotten until early in 1937, when he came across it again. He cleaned the plate with soap and water and discovered some writing on it. Shinn could just decipher the word 'Drake'.

He telephoned Dr Herbert Bolton, the professor of history at the University of California, who could hardly believe his ears. Shinn's description of the plate, especially that of a hole in it, suggested that it could be the famous Plate of Brass on which Sir Francis Drake is said to have recorded the formal annexation of California - which he called New Albion - to England in 1579. According to narratives of Drake's round-the-world voyage, the plate, which was fixed to a great post, had a hole cut in it for the insertion of a sixpence, showing the image and arms of Queen Elizabeth.

Shinn sent the plate to Bolton, who cleaned and deciphered the engravings:

BEE IT KNOWNE VNTO ALL MEN BY THESE PRESENTS
JVNE 17 1579
BY THE GRACE OF GOD AND IN THE NAME OF
HERR MAJESTY QVEEN ELIZABETH OF ENGLAND
AND HERR SVCCESSORS FOREVER I TAKE POSSESSION
OF THIS KINGDOME WHOSE KING AND PEOPLE FREELY
RESIGNE THEIR RIGHT AND TITLE IN THE WHOLE
LAND VNTO HERR MAJESTIES KEEPEING NOW NAMED BY
ME AND TO BE KNOWNE VNTO ALL MEN AS NOVA ALBION.
FRANCIS DRAKE

It was found that an Elizabethan sixpence fitted perfectly in the jagged hole beneath the inscription and that the wording tallied with accounts of the setting up of the plate. Dr Bolton was convinced of its authenticity and a few weeks later announced to a stunned meeting of the California Historical Society: 'Here it is, recovered at last after a lapse of 357 years. Behold, Drake's Plate - the Plate of Brass. California's choicest archaeological treasure.'

Sceptics were quick to challenge the authenticity of the plate and pointed out that almost anyone could have studied accounts of the voyage and engraved an inscription on an ancient piece of brass.

Chemists of the University of California, which acquired the plate, subjected it to exhaustive tests for seven months and reported: 'It is our opinion that the brass plate examined by us is the genuine Drake plate referred to in the book *The World Encompassed*, by Sir Francis Drake, published in 1628.'

No one can be absolutely certain that the plate is the one set up by Drake. But it has been pointed out that no more than ten people in the world would have been expert enough in Elizabethan English to have executed such an inscription on the plate without flaws.

BC, Aristotle, in his list of 178 marvels, names as item 84 a mysterious overseas land which the Phoenicians kept a strict secret because of trade.' The Phoenicians were, without doubt, the finest sailors in the ancient world. They circumnavigated Africa and established a trading network covering such far-flung places as Africa, India, Cyprus and Spain. And, according to interpretations of texts by Plato and Diodorus, they also traded with America around 1000 BC. From measurements made at the Mystery Hill site, it is believed that the structure was not built in yards, feet and inches, but in the ancient cubit unit of measurement used by the Egyptians and the Phoenicians. Mystery Hill indeed seems destined to remain a mystery.

Scottish claims to settlement in America before the arrival of Columbus hinge on a stone known as the Sinclair Rock, at Westford, Massachusetts, which is claimed to mark a landing point by Prince Henry Sinclair, of the Orkneys. The prince is said to have sailed with a small band from his island kingdom in 1395 and to have made several distant landfalls. The rock bears the heraldic markings of the Sinclair clan.

The mystery of which race was first to 'discover' America may never be solved. It could have been just about anyone from the Orient or the Old World. Yet Christopher Columbus remains in most history books the man who opened up the New World to the Old.

The money pit
A fabulous treasure or an unfathomable mystery?

O n a lonely island off the east coast of Canada, a fortune in pirate's gold lies buried. So, at least, goes the legend. The access to this fabled treasure is a seemingly bottomless pit which fortune-hunters have sought to plumb for almost 200 years. All have failed.

The hunt was launched in 1795 when 16-year-old Daniel McGinnis, of Chester, Nova Scotia, went exploring in the canoe his parents allowed him to use on nearby Mahone Bay. But on this occasion Daniel paddled further than usual – across the bay to lonely Oak Island. Few people had ever visited the island, and, as young Daniel ventured to the heart of it, he may have thought he was walking where no man had trod before.

Suddenly he stopped in his tracks, pulled up by a most unexpected find. Hanging from a large oak at the centre of a clearing was an old ship's tackle block. Daniel walked over to take a closer look. He noted that the main branch ·

of the oak had been cut off about four feet from the trunk. He also realized that he was standing in a depression where the ground had sunk by a couple of feet. Someone, he conjectured, must have been digging there, searching for something – or burying something.

McGinnis paddled home and returned the next day with two friends, 20-year-old John Smith and 13-year-old Anthony Vaughan. Together they began to dig. It did not take them long to clear the carefully laid topsoil and uncover a shaft, perfectly rounded and 13 ft in diameter. They immediately thought of buried treasure.

The young men went off to get picks, shovels, ladders and ropes. They virtually made their home on the island, and they spent from dawn to dusk digging for the treasure.

Their first major find was at 10 ft down. They came upon a sturdy platform of oak logs, carefully embedded into the side of the pit. Certain that treasure lay beneath, they levered the logs out, only to find new depths of firmly impacted earth below. The soil was clay with flint embedded in it, and the work of digging was back-breaking. But the three laboured on until, at a depth of 20 ft, they encountered a similar platform – and more impacted earth. The same thing happened again at 30 ft.

The three abandoned their excavation while they sought backing for their venture. They realized that they would need cash and machinery if they were to dig deeper. But no one in the little town of Chester was interested in such a hare-brained scheme – particularly as Oak Island was reputed to be haunted. It was not until 1804 that the young men raised the interest of a doctor, Simeon Lynd, who managed to persuade local business folk to back the project. The great dig continued. But after their nine-year wait the hopes of the three adventurers were quickly dashed once again. At every 10-ft interval they found yet another oak platform – even more firmly cemented in place with putty and fibre.

At a depth of 90 ft the explorers became almost feverish with excitement. They broke through the most strongly constructed platform they had yet encountered. It was bonded by charcoal, ship's putty and coconut fibre. Once they had hacked their way through this barrier, they discovered a flat stone on which were undecipherable markings. The stone was sent to the mainland for expert examination, and although it was later mysteriously lost, the Oak Island treasure-hunters were told that the message on it meant: 'Ten (or possibly 40) feet below, two million pounds are buried.'

Daniel McGinnis and his partners felt sure they were near to final success, fame and fortune. They gouged out another 10 ft of soft earth and struck something solid. It sounded like metal. But it was now long past dusk on a Saturday night and the men decided to rest until Monday.

Early on Monday the expectant partners returned to their diggings, by now labelled the Money Pit. They peered over the rim, and found the pit two-thirds filled with water . . .

Bitterly disappointed, they tried to bale out the pit, but made little headway. For several months, they abandoned their efforts. But in 1805, they returned for a brave new attempt.

They dug a fresh pit nearby to an incredible depth of 110 ft, then ran a shaft at right-angles to join the Money Pit at the point they believed the treasure to be. But they were lucky to escape with their lives when an underground channel suddenly flooded their workings. Penniless, they gave up their ten-year dream.

The next attempt at unplugging the Money Pit was in 1849. McGinnis had died a bitterly disappointed man. Of Smith there is no record. But Vaughan was still alive, and he was recruited by a newly formed syndicate to help them dig out the old workings.

The team, led by James Pittbaldo, of Truro, Nova Scotia, found it impossible to drain the old pit, so they decided to drill it instead. The drill churned easily through the first 98 ft, the depth reached by the original miners. But the new excavators found no sign of metal at that level – only a further oak platform. They pushed their way through it. By raising and examining the drill-bit at short intervals, they deduced that the drill next passed through the top of an oak chest, through some loose metal, through the bottom of the chest and then through a second similar chest. Two metal-filled chests. . . . It just had to be the treasure.

There were reports, but no confirmation, that tiny links of gold were brought to the surface on the drill-bit. What is known is that Pittbaldo removed an object from the bit – then removed himself from the mine camp. His workers believed that he had found a precious stone. It is not too unlikely a theory, because a few days later he returned to the camp with a wealthy backer and tried to buy sole rights to the venture. But by now, no one was in a selling mood. The treasure-seekers scented success at last.

It was not to be, however. The over-eager miners drilled still deeper, probing for further signs of the elusive fortune. They pushed through another wooden platform – of spruce, not oak, this time – and caused the base of the pit to collapse into what seemed to be a muddy cavern. Down into the depths, along with the wreckage of the final platform, went the 'treasure chests'.

But the excavation had not been completely futile. For the first time, it was realized that the water filling the pit was sea water, which rose and fell with the tides. The ground being of clay, the only explanation for the movement of the water was that the shaft was linked by a further channel to the open sea. A search of the shoreline soon revealed at Smith's Cove, almost 500 ft away, an elaborate, concealed system which flooded and drained the Money Pit.

The syndicate built a dam across the cove, then began to pump the water from the pit. Before they had completed their task, however, a high tide swept away the dam wall, and all work stopped. The syndicate were bankrupt.

Twenty years later another syndicate took up the search. With the optimistic title of The Oak Island Eldorado Company, they built another dam, which kept out the sea for a short time. They then pumped out the Money Pit and uncovered the flood and drainage system. It was at a depth of 110 ft and formed of stone. But before further work could be carried out the Eldorado Company's dam was breached and the pit filled yet again.

In 1894, a local businessman, Frederick Blair, formed the Oak Island Treasure Company and set about the most extensive search attempt so far to solve the exasperating mystery. Blair drilled down to the subterranean flood tunnel and dynamited it. The outlet to Smith's Cove was sealed for ever. But, amazingly, the water in the pit still rose and fell with the tide.

Blair poured dye into the pit and watched for its reappearance. It emerged not at Smith's Cove, but on South Shore – the opposite coastline. The members of the Oak Island Treasure Company were utterly baffled. They were not to know the secret that would be revealed only after many more excavations: below the level of the Smith's Cove inlet were two further channels, one, man-made, at a depth of 160 ft, also leading to Smith's Cove, and the other, at about 180 ft, seemingly a natural watercourse leading to South Shore. It was through this lower channel that the dye had run.

Frederick Blair made dozens of exploratory drillings to determine what lay beneath the original stone drainage systems 110 ft down. For a further 40 ft below this mark he encountered little but soft clay, presumably the clay into which the 'treasure chests' had sunk and broken up. But at a depth approaching 150 ft, Blair's drill hit some material which he sent for chemical analysis. The astonishing answer came back: 'man-made cement.'

Immediately beneath this thin layer was some rotten wood. Then came what Blair could only describe from the reaction of the drill as soft metal objects in the form of bars. Below this was a layer of small pieces of metal, then further bars, then a solid iron obstruction.

To the treasure-seekers, the soft metal bars could mean only one thing – gold bars. And small pieces of metal just had to be coins. This interpretation must have been an irresistible lure to Blair, who remained in the area for many years, every now and again making new tests at the site. But there was insufficient backing to launch a new and concerted attempt to recover any treasure.

In 1935, a wealthy mining expert, Gilbert Heddon, went into partnership with Blair and his son. Electric pumps were set up, powered by cable from the mainland five miles away, but the sea water continued to flow in. Three years later, Edwin Hamilton, a New York professor of mechanical engineering, launched the first scientifically based investigation of the site. Over the next four years he sank several shafts and uncovered the two lower channels which had caused Blair such trouble. But of treasure, there was no sign.

So far, the Money Pit had claimed more cash than was ever likely to be recovered from it. But in 1965, it also claimed human lives. Four men who were excavating for the Smith's Cove tunnels were poisoned by carbon-monoxide fumes from their water-pump.

But even they may not have been the first lives claimed by the Money Pit. For, five years later, a Montreal consortium calling itself the Triton Alliance lowered a television camera with powerful lighting about 200 ft into the labyrinth of pits and shafts . . . and picked up the faint outline of a human hand. Other shadowy shapes appeared to be three chests and an axe. But the team was unable to recover anything of value.

The Money Pit continues to be a magic lure to treasure-seekers. But the area has now been so heavily mined, and so many shafts have collapsed upon one another, that the precise location of the pit found by Daniel McGinnis is uncertain. Perhaps it will never be accurately located again and the questions that surround it will remain unanswered forever: who built the Money Pit, how – and why?

There are several theories, most of them put forward and investigated by author Rupert Furneaux, whose book *The Money Pit Mystery* is the classic work on this intriguing mystery. The first clue is that at the time young McGinnis first visited Oak Island in 1795 the place was thought to be haunted. Locals on the mainland spoke of midnight fires on the tiny island and the disappearance of some of the menfolk of Chester who went to investigate. No one has been able to put an accurate date to these events, but the likelihood is that the stories originated around 1700.

A rather better-known event occurred at around that time 3,000 miles away in England, where Captain William Kidd was hanged for piracy in 1701. As he went to the gallows in Wapping, London, he mouthed a curse on anyone who sought his 'treasure', the legend of which grew after his death. Could Kidd and his men have dug the Money Pit?

In the 1930s, a retired English lawyer, Hubert Palmer, found three charts hidden in a secret drawer of a desk at his home in Eastbourne, Sussex. The desk had once belonged to Captain Kidd, and, having heard of the Oak Island search, Palmer compared the charts with a map of the island. There were strong similarities but no proof of treasure – and no indication where it might have been buried.

At about the same time, Blair's partner Heddon also came across a map, this one in a book about Captain Kidd. The map was of an island resembling

Oak Island. Heddon travelled to England to trace the author, who told him that he had copied the map from one shown him by a Dutchman. Where had the Dutchman obtained it? As far as the author could remember, it had come from under a cairn of stones on an island off Nova Scotia.

Heddon examined directions marked on the map: 18 W by 7 E Rock 30 SW 14 N Tree 7 by 8 by 4. Back on Oak Island, he found two granite boulders with drill holes in them, and plotted his course from them, using the old English measure of rods. The directions led him to an overgrown thicket. On clearing the undergrowth, Heddon found a triangle of half-buried stones – pointing directly to the Money Pit. Add to this remarkable discovery the scientific reports of the Triton Alliance – that relics found in the pit were wood and iron from British ships – and the case for accepting the Captain Kidd theory becomes even more convincing.

Yet there is a flaw. The block and tackle which McGinnis found hanging from the sawn-off branch of the oak tree in 1795 could not have survived for nearly 100 years. Even the tree itself may not have existed at the time of Kidd's death. And how could a ship's crew carry out such a remarkable feat of engineering unseen and unaided on an inhospitable island?

For, whatever the purpose of the Money Pit, it was, if nothing else, a miracle of mining. From the evidence, it appears that, in total secrecy, a skilled team of engineers and a small army of labourers dug a perfectly formed pit 180 ft into the ground. On a platform at the bottom, directly over a subterranean stream, they placed their treasure – which, to have warranted so much effort, must have been of great value.

These engineers then ran a 4-ft-high shaft a distance of 500 ft to a point below high tide in Smith's Cove – without, at that stage, allowing any water to enter. They then cemented over the top of the treasure chamber, covered it with 50 ft of clay, and topped it with a platform of spruce. The next step in this remarkable enterprise was to tunnel yet another shaft to Smith's Cove, running directly above the first. To enable them to dig like moles along this narrow shaft, a further pit was sunk to act as an air vent half-way between the Money Pit and the sea. We know of this vent because in 1878 a farmer's wife was ploughing with two oxen when the ground collapsed and she fell into it.

Again somehow managing to keep the sea out of the tunnel, the miners stacked two or three 'treasure chests' on the spruce platform. They topped this with an oak platform and the mysterious cipher stone. Then came more platforms at 10-ft intervals. Finally, the ground was covered with topsoil and all evidence removed, except, strangely, for the block and tackle.

No pirate could have managed such a feat. It would have taken the resources of an army. And that conclusion led author Rupert Furneaux to his own remarkable theory . . .

THE WORLD'S GREATEST MYSTERIES

In 1778 the American War of Independence was being fought. The British garrison in New York felt threatened by Washington and British commander Sir Henry Clinton feared that the army's pay-chest might fall into enemy hands. Did he then order the Royal Engineers to conceal the money – perhaps somewhere near their outpost in Halifax, Nova Scotia?

It is an ingenious theory and, if true, raises another question. Since no great sum of money was ever reported lost by the British, did the Royal Engineers later return to Oak Island and recover the treasure through one of the side-shafts? Has the Money Pit been empty for more than 200 years?

PDO 83-1082